THE COMPLETE GUIDE TO WORKING FROM HOME

Sue Read, a former staff writer for *The Sunday Times* and the *Daily Mail*, is a freelance journalist and television producer. Her previous books include *Sexual Harassment at Work*, *The Poser's Guide* and *Hello Campers: Fifty Years of Butlins*. She has worked from her home in Putney, London, on and off for thirteen years.

Also by Sue Read

Sexual Harassment at Work
The Poser's Guide
Hello Campers: Fifty Years of Butlins

The Complete Guide to Working from Home

Sue Read

HEADLINE

Copyright © 1992 Sue Read

The right of Sue Read to be identified as the Author of the Work has been asserted by her in accordance with the Copyright, Designs and Patents Act 1988

First published in 1992
by HEADLINE BOOK PUBLISHING PLC

10 9 8 7 6 5 4 3 2 1

All rights reserved. No part of this publication may be reproduced, stored in a retrieval system, or transmitted, in any form or by any means without the prior written permission of the publisher, nor be otherwise circulated in any form of binding or cover other than that in which it is published and without a similar condition being imposed on the subsequent purchaser.

ISBN 0 7472 3651 8

Phototypeset by Intype, London
Printed and bound in Great Britain by
HarperCollins Manufacturing, Glasgow

HEADLINE BOOK PUBLISHING PLC
Headline House
79 Great Titchfield Street
London W1P 7FN

A special dedication to my Sony Word-Processor OA–S3400 No. 0115, with thanks for many years of working from home and, of course, to Jim

CONTENTS

CHAPTER 1	So you want to Work from Home	1
CHAPTER 2	Starting Your own Business	21
CHAPTER 3	You, Your Company and the Law	69
CHAPTER 4	You and Your Money	107
CHAPTER 5	Tax, Insurance and Pensions	139
CHAPTER 6	Teleworkers and Outworkers	169
CHAPTER 7	Selling and Marketing	189
CHAPTER 8	Your Home as Your Workplace	207
CHAPTER 9	Health and Fitness at Home	243
CHAPTER 10	Coping with Working by Yourself	261
CHAPTER 11	Coping with Family and Friends	275

ACKNOWLEDGEMENTS

I would like to thank the following for their information, expertise, knowledge and professional help: Citizens Advice Bureau, Merton; Lynne Davies, Davies & Chapman Financial Advisers; Allan Butnick, Accountant; British Telecom, The Quentin Bell Organisation; Alan Lacey, Wandsworth Environmental Services; Simon Peck, Wandsworth County Court; Jim Goulding; Chris Oliver, OwnBase; Brian Haynes; John Rhodes, National Westminster Bank; LiveWire UK; Prince's Trust; Health Education Council; Thomson Directories; Dr Joe Davies; Maureen Walker; British Heart Foundation; *Working At Home: The Dream that's Becoming a Trend* by Lindsey O'Connor, Harvest House; *Tomorrow's Workplace* by Francis Kinsman, British Telecom; *Ageless Ageing – The Natural Way To Stay Young* by Leslie Kenton, Century; Truck Stops of America; Leicester Low Pay Unit; Manchester Low Pay Unit; Department of Employment Small Firms Service; Henley Centre for Forecasting; Shân Morley Jones; Ruth Ampiah-Kwofi, Wandsworth Enterprise Agency; Department of Social Security; Department of Health; The Lord Chancellor's press office; and especially to all the people who work from home who allowed me to interview them and whose names have been changed to protect their businesses.

CHAPTER 1

So You Want to Work from Home

TAKING THE PLUNGE OR COME ON IN, WORKING AT HOME IS LOVELY

'The beauty of being your own boss and working from home is flexibility. But you do have to be everything; personnel, admin, accounts, marketing and the expert. I think there are some people who work in offices who look down on you if you work from home. They think you're less professional than they are, but of course it isn't true. My clients comment on my professional layout here.' Gerry runs his own successful insurance business from home, after being made redundant for the third time.

If you're about to take the plunge and join Gerry working from home, drop your shoulders and relax, even though you may feel that way, you are not alone. In fact you are just one of the two million people who have turned their backs on the hip-hugging, thigh-groping, armpit-pressing fun of daily commuting, and on the friendly back-biting, touch-you-up, put-you-down workplace. The desperate morning massacre of the coffee machine when it's empty. The comfort of the calorie-packed cream buns on the afternoon tea trolley. The hard loo paper, the jammed sanitary towel machine, the dangling wet end of the roller towel, the unpleasant yellowish glare of the strip lighting, the open-plan office where he who dares to open a window doesn't get a bourbon biscuit at tea time. Adults fighting over a space in the company car park, over the last biro in the stationery cupboard, the final fig roll in the secretary's bottom drawer. Sneaking into another department's kitchenette to steal (although if you're caught you'll say you were just borrowing) jars of Marmite or instant coffee. Watching your windowsill pot plant die. Spending time listening to colleagues' divorces, affairs, sick dogs, unruly children. Spending even more time answering other people's phones, taking other people's messages. Having to lie in order to get time off when the children are sick, need their teeth seeing to, or because they're playing the lead role as the giant cactus in the school play. Finally when you've worked late, made your way out, dragging with you the carrier bags of food that you had to rush out and buy in your lunch hour, you discover that the over-zealous security officer has locked you in. No more, you yell! Oh to work from home!

But beware of moments like these, when you go home, throw your briefcase at the dog, sling the shopping at the cat, hurl your travel and security pass to the floor and reach for a drink announcing, 'That's it, I've had enough, from now on I'm working from home.'

Life-changing decisions like these shouldn't be made in moments of frustration and despair. You have to approach it sensibly and calmly, weighing up the pros and the cons. Before you throw the luncheon vouchers and the company pension scheme out of the window, stop and read the following pages, because, one way or another, working from home changes people's lives. For some it is the great life-enhancing decision that brings an inner strength where creativity is released and resources discovered. But it is not the correct choice for everyone. Even if you are convinced it is for you, you will have trepidations that are not just to do with the technical aspects of working from home – finance, tax, selling etc., but more personal fears: will I be able to motivate myself or will I be in a dressing-gown all day? How will my partner react? Will I lose my friends? This book deals with both aspects, through direct information and advice and also by following through the case studies of people who have made the decision to work from home. Their stories carry some warnings but also provide some unexpected solutions to problems that you may now see as insurmountable.

HOW TO MAKE THE BEST USE OF THIS BOOK

This book will guide you through the maze of financial, employment, legal and personal requirements that you will need to be familiar with if you are going to work successfully from home.

Because the subject of working from home is so diverse and has psychological as well as technical and legal aspects, each chapter is divided into two parts which you can either read from beginning to end, as you would in any book, discovering and learning as you go, or you can simply flick through, guided by the relevant headings that are of interest to you, your business and your needs. If you are still making up your mind about whether to become a homeworker or not, you may find it useful to read the Case Studies in this chapter and then turn to the Help Section on **page 19**. There are 11 chapters in all:

Chapter 1   So you want to Work from Home.
Chapter 2   Starting Your own Business.
Chapter 3   You, Your Company and the Law.
Chapter 4   You and Your Money.
Chapter 5   Tax, Insurance and Pensions.
Chapter 6   Teleworkers and Outworkers.
Chapter 7   Selling and Marketing.
Chapter 8   Your Home as Your Workplace.
Chapter 9   Health and Fitness at Home.
Chapter 10   Coping with Working by Yourself.
Chapter 11   Coping with Family and Friends.

Within each of these chapters there are sub-sections which are relevant to the main section headings. For example under the main chapter heading, You and Your Money, you will find these sub-section headings: Finding Financial Advice, Finding an Accountant, Banks and Building Societies, Borrowing Money, Separate Accounts, Your Financial Analysis, Keeping the Books, Keeping a Record, Petty Cash, Getting Paid, Invoices, Methods of Payment, Payment for your Time Per Item You Produce, Payment by Royalties from a Manufacturer, Jam-Jar Budgeting.

The financial and technical sections of this book are specifically aimed at people who are going to work from home either as telecommuters, outworkers or someone who is self-employed running his or her own business. But **Chapter 5 Tax, Insurance and Pensions; Chapter 9 Health and Fitness at Home; Chapter 10 Coping With Working By Yourself; Chapter 11 Coping With Family and Friends**, cover a wide area and apply to everyone who is considering working from home. **Chapter 6 Teleworkers and Outworkers** has information that runs across the broad range of working from home, plus additional taxation and health regulations.

Some subjects overlap into others and information is relevant to more than one section. For example in the sub-section, It's a Great Idea, you will find cross-referencing to the section on Copyright and Patents. In the section on Copyright and Patents you will find cross-referencing to Solicitors. In this way the book guides you through the linked chain of events that build to working from home.

Because the book is designed to be there for you to dip into when you require different information or guidance, perhaps at different stages of your personal situation, you may be aware of some repetition; this is to allow for people who are not reading every section still to gain all the information which otherwise they might miss. Information sources for each chapter can be found at the end of the Help Section for that chapter.

At the back of each section you will find lists of the relevant organisations, plus their contact addresses or telephone numbers. There may be some organisations that are not mentioned in the section but are listed with information about their activity and purpose at the back of the section: this is because there is no additional information to give. In these lists you will find some cross-referencing to other sections, where organisations overlap more than one aspect of working from home.

Some aspects of working from home are so detailed that a book this size is unable to give you all the relevant information in depth, without it filling the whole book! In these cases you will find the name of the organisation that can help you.

The book does not always give specific figures because they are subject to constant changes and fluctuations; therefore all figures, i.e. taxation, grants, VAT, national insurance payments, benefits and trade union subscriptions, should be checked with the relevant organisations and government departments for current fees and cost.

Some rules, regulations, laws and schemes, i.e. the Health and Hygiene laws, Enterprise Allowance Scheme, Small Claims and Wages Councils are all tremendously detailed and change frequently, having also to fall in line with EEC requirements. You should therefore check with the relevant organisations for current information.

Do you have the right personality to work from home?
According to Francis Kinsman, author of *The Telecommuter*, a good homeworker must have great self-discipline. 'Working on your own, the motivation to get the job done has to come from within – there is no boss behind you telling you to get on with your work.' The characteristics of a good homeworker include: dedication, ability to work alone, confidence and communication skills. There are a lot of homeworkers who do jobs that require the technical know-how of working with communications equipment and computers, plus an ability to be flexible, adaptable and

trustworthy, because there isn't anyone to check you are doing your work. You also have to have skills in dealing with people, as well as a quick mind. All these attributes are important to the success of being a homeworker.

Home is certainly not the work-place of the macho man who revels in office politics and empire building. But entrepreneurial types who like to do their own thing will enjoy it, especially when they see how much they can get done. The main disadvantage to working from home is isolation. If work is your main source of social activity, then working from home isn't right for you. For success it is imperative, according to Kinsman, that you have a full social life outside your work and you should never let the week deteriorate into seven Mondays.

Check your personality rating for working from home
Complete the quick quiz guide and discover if you are the right personality type to work from home. Answer 'yes' if you are receptive to the idea, 'no' if it does not appeal to you.

                                                           YES   NO
1. What's more important to you:
   (a) A regular pay cheque?
   (b) Job satisfaction?
   (c) Job success?

2. Do you work better with direction from:
   (a) boss or supervisor?

3. Do you prefer to work to set hours?

4. Does the job you do have to be performed in a certain place?

5. Are you a social butterfly?

6. Is your social life based around your work?

7. Do you hate silence?

8. Do you feel lonely when you're by yourself?

9. Do you solve work problems by throwing them around with colleagues?

10. Do you prefer your work environment to your home environment?

11. Do you go to work to escape from home?
12. Do you have space to work from home?
13. Do you need/enjoy the cut and thrust of office politics?
14. Do you enjoy canteen food?
15. Do you love office gossip?
16. Do you need the creative stimulation of work colleagues?
17. Do you work better surrounded by noise and general hubbub?
18. Do you like having direct competition?
19. Do you hate working in the office when everyone else has gone home?
20. Do you hate commuting?
21. Do you need to commute as a way of switching off between work and home?
22. Are you happier working in a team?
23. Do you discuss personal problems with work colleagues?
24. Is your work your main source of friendship?
25. Do you want to be part of a corporate structure?
26. Do you think people who work from home are:
    (a) crazy?
    (b) introverted?
    (c) happy?
    (d) lonely?
27. Do you prefer to get on with your work without interference from anyone?
28. Do you think you know more than your boss?

RESULTS

YES: Over 22
You really aren't the right personality to work from home and will probably be highly successful in a structured workplace environment.

YES: Between 15–5
You could be someone who works from home successfully, but you should weigh up the pros and cons seriously before you start.

YES: Fewer than 5
You are a true homeworker and will probably be highly successful running your own business.

WHAT WORK ARE YOU GOING TO DO?
A lot of people who work from home are either telecommuters or outworkers (**See Chapter 6 Teleworkers and Outworkers**). In either case they are working for an employer, but in both cases they may find themselves being classified as self-employed, which means they have all the advantages plus the disadvantages of that employment status. (It is very important that you are aware of your employment status, **See Chapter 2 Starting your own Business** and **Chapter 6 Teleworkers and Outworkers**.) Other people are self-employed and work from home running their own business, and selling the end product. If any of these self-employed statuses appeal to you, but you aren't sure what type of work you want to do, there are some crucial questions you should ask yourself before you make a decision which will affect your whole career and life style.

Don't decide to work from home simply because you want to give up the rat race. It's better to have a more positive reason, for the more positive the reason, the more likely you are to stick to your decision when the going gets rough. Some people are forced by circumstances to stop being indecisive about what work they want to do. Rachael, for example, thought she knew what she wanted to do, but she wouldn't commit to it. She went on a free business course run by her local authority, 'You had to have an idea of what you wanted to do because the class would discuss it, so in a way that pushed me into making the decision about producing ice-cream.' If you are in Rachael's position, where you have a rough idea, but just can't decide exactly what work you want to do, then job research will help. You must also be realistic about your qualifications, skills and interests, although there is no reason why you shouldn't consider re-training, taking into account your age, family, financial commitments and previous educational qualifications.

Even so one of the simplest and most positive reasons for working from home is because the job that you do can be performed in a home environment. For Brian, who is a potter, running his own business just evolved. It happened when he and his family moved to Wiltshire ten years ago. Before moving to the country he taught pottery. When they moved he answered an advertisement and got a job as a modeller for a large local china firm, but they didn't pay very well. 'Then I discovered a porcelain factory just a few miles away and I started working for them, from home. Five years ago I decided to branch out on my own.'

In the decision-making process remember it's important that you do a job you enjoy and gives you some sort of job satisfaction. There is no point, if you can help it, in being unhappy or miserable at a job which takes up the majority of your waking life. Job satisfaction equals happiness, feelings of achievement and challenges. That usually comes when you are doing a job which utilises all or some of your skills. It may be something you do at the moment, perhaps a hobby, which you could develop into a full-time job. When Rachael's father was ill her mother needed support, so she decided to stay at home and go self-employed. 'But I didn't have any idea what I wanted to do. I enjoyed cooking and I like making ice-cream, but a lot of people go into catering so I knew I had to specialise.'

Sasha didn't know what she wanted to do either. But she knew what she didn't want to do, which was just as positive: 'Although I had worked in the wardrobe department in the theatre I knew I didn't want to make clothes. People are so fussy and there's all the measurements and choice of colour and I didn't want that much stress. Then I hit on the idea of cushions because they're easy to carry around. I started taking them to craft fairs and I always sold out because I was so cheap.'

If you are lacking in ideas, a trip to your local library or job centre can be very helpful. Another source of ideas are the small advertisements in your local newspaper. Jane didn't have to do either; she just looked at the slurry from her father's cows and had a business idea. The slurry goes through a process where it's put into a machine that separates it and it comes out as two substances, one a dirty liquid, the other a solid substance which is like fresh green horse manure, although you can't put it on grass land because it will destroy it. 'I asked my father why he didn't sell it to nursery men, but he wanted to sell it in bulk and no one was interested, so it was all building up in the yard. When I suggested he compost it and sell it to garden centres, he turned round and said, "Well, why don't you do it?" And that's basically how it started.'

If you are lacking in inspiration, it may help to look at the services on offer in your area. You may notice a gap which you could fill. Try and find out if anyone has tried before to set up the type of business you have in mind and how successful they were or if they failed and why. Talk to your neighbours and in the local shops to try and get a feel for what services are needed, what people ask for. It may be that you hit on something that stems from a personal experience. When Mandy had her first baby by Caesarean section she was grounded for three months and her relatives kept her supplied with nappies. When she did go out, she noticed all the fed-up Mums: 'They were dragging their kids around, one in the push chair, one in tow, pulling things off the supermarket shelves. I thought, I know what it's like and I've only got one. That was when I decided there was a market for a nappy delivery service.'

Check around to find out if anyone is already running the type of business you have in mind (**See Chapter 7 Selling and Marketing**). If they are, try and find out if they have more customers than they can handle, or if they are finding surviving a struggle.

You might think of starting up a small-scale manufacturing business, based, again, on a hobby or a previous job that you did. Before you do anything, ask yourself how knowledgeable you are about the type of business you want to set up. If you aren't, then go to your local library or Adult Education Centre and check out the courses available in all types of management, business skills and specific trades. You'll find that there are Open University courses, evening classes, adult education courses and colleges all for further education (**See Help Section, this Chapter**).

WHY WORK FROM HOME?

The Henley Centre for forecasting suggests that by 1995 the number of home-based workers will have risen to 4.5 million, that's between 15 and 20 per cent of the workforce. In 1921 only 250,000 workers (one in every hundred) were recorded by the census as home-based. In 1971 there were 1.5 million, in 1981 there were 2.2. million and the increase is expected to continue.

Up until the Industrial Revolution most people worked at or very close to their homes. But the economic and technological changes of the nineteenth century meant that many slow, hand processes were replaced by machine-based operations. This meant building factories to house newly developed equipment, which were located close to cities or near to the necessary raw materials. But this quickly created overcrowding, which reached a peak by the turn of the century. In order to help alleviate the situation, slums were cleared and better public transport systems were developed so that people could move away from industrial centres to what became known as commuter towns.

Today the average commuter spends 190 minutes a week travelling to and from work. For London-based commuters the time spent is 295 minutes. The average commuter spends £3.17p travelling to work each week, possibly more with continual fare increases. For the economy as a whole the annual expenditure is almost £3.6 billion, or 1.4 per cent of the consumer's expenditure.

But there are numerous reasons apart from commuting that cause people to choose to work from home. Recent research reveals that 52 per cent of executives have expressed enthusiasm for the idea of spending a proportion of their very valuable time in a home-based office and according to an industrial conference organised by the CBI and British Telecom in 1988, home-based workers are likely to be four times more productive than on-site employees, with the additional advantage of less commuting, freedom to live where they want and flexible working hours that can be fitted round the needs of the family. Of course there are other reasons for working from home. For some people it fulfils their desire to have creative freedom, to pursue their own interests, be their own boss, to realise their own ambitions, or just to opt out of the conventional rat race and workplace.

There are as many different reasons for people wanting to work from home as there are people who do it. But it shouldn't be forgotten that for many people choice is taken away when they are made redundant. Factory and company closures can force many workers with no alternatives to investigate working from home, perhaps even taking up a new skill or trade to do so. But still working from home doesn't suit everyone's personality (**See Chapter 10 Coping with Working by Yourself**), and this – along with the many other advantages and disadvantages – should be carefully considered before you even move into the planning stage of working from home.

BEFORE YOU START

If you want to make working from home a success – and obviously you do – then you have to make plans, do research and gather all relevant information before you take the plunge. It's really no different from going on a holiday. You wouldn't dream of setting off without your tickets, money, sun hat and tummy pills, so don't start working from home, which is a life-changing decision, without having some business knowledge. It's surprising, for example, how many people go to job agencies wanting advice on starting their own business when they don't even know what marketing is. When Rachael was considering starting up her ice-cream making business, she went on a free business course where they talked about selling, marketing and advertising. 'The course was good, but it would have been better if I had had some experience of running a business. Once I had been out and started making a mess of things I could relate to it. I mean, I didn't know what they meant by cold-calling and I hadn't heard of market research.'

Before you start exploring the possibility of working from home it's a good idea to make yourself a list. It can be for your eyes only, nobody else need be involved. Ask yourself some of the following basic questions:

Relevant to anyone working from home	Relevant to anyone running their own business from home
The advantages and disadvantages that you know about being self-employed and working from home (it doesn't matter how much of this is guesswork).	The advantages and disadvantages that you know about being self-employed and working from home (it doesn't matter how much of this is guesswork).

Relevant to anyone working from home

Do you need any training? If so how do you think you might go about getting it? (**See page 9 Chapter 1 So you want to Work from Home?**)

The type of business you want to set up.

How much do you understand about taxation and national insurance? (**See Chapter 5 Tax, Insurance and Pensions.**)

How good are you at handling isolation? (**See Chapter 10 Coping with Working by Yourself.**)

Have you already got an accountant? If not, do you think you should have one? (**See page 109 Chapter 5 Tax, Insurance and Pensions and page 141 Chapter 4 You and Your Money.**)

Relevant to anyone running their own business from home

Do you need any training? If so how do you think you might go about getting it? (**See page 9 Chapter 1 So you want to Work from Home?**)

To run the type of business you have in mind do you require any licences, permissions (**See page 209 Chapter 8 Your Home as Your Workplace**), or insurances? (**See page 155 Chapter 5 Tax, Insurance and Pensions.**)

How much do you understand about taxation and national insurance? (**See Chapter 5, Tax, Insurance and Pensions and Chapter 4 You and Your Money.**)

How good are you at handling isolation? (**See Chapter 10 Coping with Working By Yourself.**)

Have you already got an accountant? If not, do you think you should have one? (**See page 109 Chapter 4 You and Your Money and page 141 Chapter 5 Tax, Insurance and Pensions.**)

Relevant to anyone working from home

Relevant to anyone running their own business from home

Do you want to be a Limited Company, sole trader or go into a partnership? Is there someone for you to go into partnership with, or do you think it's a mistake to work closely with friends? **(See page 71 Chapter 3 You, Your Company and the Law.)**

How are your family going to react to having you at home all the time? Do you have the space to work in? Do you know what equipment you will need? **(See Chapter 8 Your Home as Your Workplace, Chapter 10 Coping with Working by Yourself and Chapter 11 Coping with Family and Friends.)**

How are your family going to react to having you at home all the time? Do you have the space to work in? Do you know what equipment you will need? **(See Chapter 8 Your Home as Your Workplace, Chapter 10 Coping by Yourself and Chapter 11 Coping with Family and Friends.)**

Do you have any idea how much money you will need to set up your business and where to go if you require more funding? **(See Chapter 2 Starting your own Business and Chapter 3 You, Your Company and the Law.)**

Trade Unions
Wages Councils **(See section in Chapter 6 Teleworkers and Outworkers.)**

Do you know how to contact small firms services, banks and local enterprise schemes? **(See Chapter 2 Starting your own Business.)**

Relevant to anyone working from home

What would happen if you died or were physically or mentally incapacitated? **(See page 119 Chapter 4 You and Your Money.)**

Relevant to anyone running their own business from home

What would happen if you died or were physically or mentally incapacitated? **(See page 119 Chapter 4 You and Your Money and page 157 Chapter 5 Tax, Insurance and Pensions.)**

How good are you at selling? Cold calling? **(See page 197 Chapter 7 Selling and Marketing.)**

IT'S A GREAT IDEA

If you think you are going to work from home by thinking up a Great Idea, then be aware that ideas are like cats; they don't just come when you want them to. They are a rare, treasured commodity dreamed up in the most unlikely places, such as lying soaking in the bath or sitting in a traffic jam, although don't rush to lie in the bath expecting to have a Great Idea! There is no guarantee that a Great Idea will come when you need one, or even come to you at all; there is no hard and fast formula. If Great Ideas were two a penny we would all be having them!

From a lot of muddled thinking, something suddenly clicks into place as your mind connects several disparate thoughts to create The Great Idea! Of course, what you may think is a Great Idea and what actually turns out to be a marketable, profitable and successful one can be totally different. How do you know if your idea is so great and that it's time to turn in your job, or alter your career to stay at home and develop it? This is where thorough market research is critical **(See page 193 Chapter 7 Selling and Marketing)**. The Great Idea is only just the beginning, you have to follow it through with planning, organisation and probably financial backing if it is ever to be successfully mass produced and financially viable.

To give you inspiration, here are some examples of Great Ideas through the ages, all of which could have been dreamed up at home (maybe some of them were) and have gone on to make millions. They have all been protected by patents or registration **(See page 82 Chapter 3 You, Your Company and the Law)**, so there is no chance of stealing!

*1770 Ahead of their time. Wooden slats connected with flexible links, patented for carts, later became tracks for tanks and bulldozers.

*1874 The patent that created a game. The modern game of lawn tennis grew out of a patent for erecting a net so that the ancient game of tennis, which had been played indoors, could be played outdoors.

*1930 A patent for a process. The formula for milling to preserve the wheat germ that resulted in Hovis bread. The registration name Hovis comes from the latin *hominis* meaning man and *vis* meaning strength. Together they mean staff of life.

*1946 Patenting a formula. Discoveries cannot be patented but the methods to manufacture them can, including chemical formulae. The first all-British synthetic fibre, Terylene (R) was patented as a formula.

*1969 The ingenuity of the individual. Patented invention of the Workmate (R) bench for DIY enthusiasts and registration of its name as a trade mark.

If you are fortunate enough to have the Great Idea and you have researched the market thoroughly and studied your competitors **(See Chapter 7 Selling and Marketing)**, organised business plans **(See page 39 Chapter 2 Starting your own Business)**, development, manufacturing and overhead costs and investigated financial backing **(See Chapter 4 You and Your Money and Chapter 2 Starting your own Business)**, you may be on your way to starting your own business.

And finally, working from home can change you! It hasn't all been easy for Jane, who runs her now successful fertiliser business from home. 'I got ripped off by a couple of men and lost about £500 worth of stock. Plus I had to pay the lawyer who did absolutely no good. Then I ordered non-slip bags for bagging the fertiliser and they slipped, which meant I was left with a load of useless bags, so I had to go to someone else for different ones. No one really realises just what you have to go through.'

But, as Jane found out, 'I think I'm now unemployable. I used to be really quiet and nice, now I think I put the fear of God into most men because I'm forthright and strong.' Janes lives on her own. She enjoys running her own business and being 'top dog'. 'If the business goes wrong it's my fault. I do the shovelling, bagging, selling, delivery, accounting, advertising, marketing and the buck finally stops with me, hopefully in my bank account!'

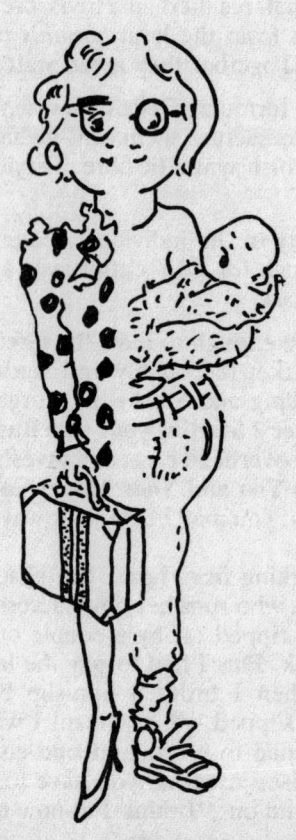

CHAPTER 1
HELP SECTION

Technical Assistance
Inventors usually have sufficient technical knowledge to manufacture the product, but they may need technical assistance to improve the design, the manufacturing process or the use of new materials. This type of information can be obtained from: CHAMBERS OF COMMERCE which can provide a wide range of information on local businesses including those which offer manufacturing and production services. For a national list of CHAMBERS OF COMMERCE contact:

THE ASSOCIATION OF BRITISH CHAMBERS OF COMMERCE 212a Shaftesbury Avenue, London WC2H 8EW. Tel: 071 240 5381/6.

BIRMINGHAM CHAMBER OF COMMERCE AND INDUSTRY PO Box 360, 75 Harborne Road, Edgbaston, Birmingham, B15 3DH. Tel: 021 454 6171.

BURTON-UPON-TRENT AND DISTRICT CHAMBER OF COMMERCE AND INDUSTRY 158 Derby Street, Burton-upon-Trent, Staffordshire, DE14 2NZ. Tel: 0283 63761.

COVENTRY CHAMBER OF COMMERCE AND INDUSTRY INCORPORATED 123 St Nicholas Street, Coventry, CV1 4FD. Tel: 0203 633000.

DUDLEY CHAMBER OF INDUSTRY AND COMMERCE Falcon House, The Minories, Dudley, West Midlands, DY2 8PG. Tel: 0384 237653/ 455558.

HEREFORD AND DISTRICT CHAMBER OF COMMERCE LTD 13 Commercial Street, Hereford, HR1 2DE. Tel: 0432 268795.

KIDDERMINSTER AND DISTRICT CHAMBER OF COMMERCE Duke Place, Kidderminster, Hereford and Worcester, DY10 2JW. Tel: 0562 515515.

NORTH STAFFORDSHIRE CHAMBER OF COMMERCE AND INDUSTRY Commerce House, Festival Park, Stoke-on-Trent, Staffordshire, ST1 5BE. Tel: 0782 202222.

RUGBY AND DISTRICT CHAMBER OF COMMERCE 9 Railway Terrace, Rugby, Warwickshire, CV21 3EN. Tel: 0788 544951.

WALSALL CHAMBER OF COMMERCE AND INDUSTRY Chamber of Commerce House, Ward Street, Walsall, West Midlands, WS1 2AG. Tel: 0922 721777.

WEST MIDLANDS INDUSTRIAL DEVELOPMENT BOARD Department of

Trade and Industry, Ladywood House, Stephenson Street, Birmingham, B2 4DT Tel: 021 631 6181.

WOLVERHAMPTON CHAMBER OF COMMERCE AND INDUSTRY Tettenhall Road, Wolverhampton, West Midlands, WV3 9PE. Tel: 0902 26726.

WORCESTER AND HEREFORD AREA CHAMBER OF COMMERCE AND INDUSTRY Severn House, 10 The Moors, Worcester, WIR 3EE. Tel: 0905 611611.

Design

THE DESIGN COUNCIL (includes The Materials Centre) 28 Haymarket, London, SW1Y 4SU. Tel: 071 839 8000 (same number for the Materials Centre).

THE DESIGN COUNCIL Norwich Union House, 31 Waterloo Road, Wolverhampton, West Midlands, WV1 4BP. Tel: 0902 773631.

Chapter information sources

British Telecom, Quinton Bell Organisation; Henley Centre for Forecasting.

CHAPTER 2

Starting Your Own Business

STARTING OUT
In this chapter we look at two areas of starting your own business from home. First, there is the tax and trading status of being self-employed and all that it entails. Secondly, there are the legal and local authority requirements of starting your own business which have to be followed, and the problem areas to be aware of.

ARE YOU ELIGIBLE TO BE SELF-EMPLOYED?
A large majority of people who work from home are self-employed. This can be defined in a number of ways:

* That either you have a say in how the business is run, or you risk your own money or you are responsible for meeting the losses as well as taking the profits.
* You provide the major items of equipment required to do the job, not just the small tools.
* You are free to hire people of your own choice to do the work that you've taken on and to pay them out of your own pocket.
* When work is unsatisfactory you have to correct it in your own time and at your own expense.

Some people choose to be both self-employed and employed. This means that they work for someone on a part-time basis and work for themselves the rest of the time, running their own business from home.

It's generally fairly clear cut as to whether someone is employed or self-employed but there are a few cases where you may be uncertain: if you are, go to your local Tax Office or Social Security office where you'll find someone who is responsible for all enquiries and decisions about employment status. Or write to the Inland Revenue or Department of Social Security for advice. (**See Chapter 5 Tax, Insurance and Pensions**.)

BEING SELF-EMPLOYED – YOUR TAX

If you've made the decision to work from home running your own business, the first thing you should do is inform your local Tax Office. It's important that it's your local Tax Office because you may find that the one that deals with your business is not necessarily the one that handles your Pay As You Earn (PAYE) or other personal tax. If you work from home, you are taxed by the Tax Office local to where you live; your PAYE papers may be at the Tax Office local to where you previously worked (**See page 142 Chapter 5 Tax, Insurance and Pensions**).

If you've just stopped working for an employer, you'll be given a P45 form which you then give to your Tax Office so that the tax that you've paid in the year up to then can be taken into account.

You'll also need to get in touch with your local Department of Social Security who'll be able to advise you about the National Insurance Contributions you'll have to pay as a self-employed person, even if you decide to continue to work for an employer (**See page 149, Chapter 5 Tax, Insurance and Pensions**).

BASIC FACTS ABOUT BEING SELF-EMPLOYED AND RUNNING YOUR OWN BUSINESS

There are advantages and disadvantages to being self-employed, but don't be starry-eyed about it. Here are some of the disadvantages that you should be aware of before you start (**See Chapter 5 Tax, Insurance and Pensions, for more detailed information**).

Questions	Answers
Will my entitlement to some state benefits be limited?	Yes, your entitlement to some benefits, such as pensions and health will be limited.
What will happen to my sick pay and occupational pension?	You cannot any longer rely on the state or on an employer. You will have to arrange your own sick pay and occupational pension.

Questions	Answers
Will I lose employment protection?	Yes. If you lose your job when you are employed earning a salary, you can collect unemployment benefit. When you are self-employed you can't. The only protection a self-employed out-of-work person has is when their savings have dropped below a certain limit and they are then able to claim income support (**See also page 177 Chapter 6 Teleworkers and Outworkers**).
Will I get paid holidays?	No. Not only will you not get paid holidays, but you will also have to pay for the cost of going away, plus you will have to bear the cost of keeping everything ticking over whilst you have no money coming in.
If I have no regular income how do I manage my cash flow?	Because you have no assured regular income, your cash flow will probably be erratic and you will therefore find it difficult to make long-term financial predictions, let alone the difficulty of monthly budgeting (**See page 132 Chapter 4 You and Your Money**).

Questions	Answers
Will it be easy to get financial backing?	Although many organisations advertise that they offer money to small businesses starting up, in practice it can be difficult to raise finance. Your business idea may not appeal to everyone, especially bankers who prefer a safe-bet business and the security that they will get their investment back.
Can I be sure of success?	No. You have no guarantee that you will be successful. A lot of small businesses run into financial difficulties. If that should happen, it can leave you in serious financial debt. Think about how you would recover. Think about any savings or any way you may have of recouping your losses.

Once you have dealt with these questions and answers (perhaps by reading the appropriate sections in Chapter 4) you should now be armed with enough basic information to move on to the next section and the idea of **setting up a business**.

START-UP CHECK-LIST
Before you start, it is very important that you consider all the aspects of the kind of business you want to set up. Here are some of the key points you should consider and be prepared to answer – in doing so try to be as objective as possible.

Questions	Answers
What do I do if I think I have a good business idea?	You should do some in-depth research into your idea, the competition, the market and the demand (**See page 192 Chapter 7 Selling and Marketing**).

Questions	Answers
Should I get some business training?	It is no good going into business with half-baked information and knowledge. You need to understand about your business idea and running a business. The state of the art in business technology, techniques, selling and marketing has progressed rapidly in the last few years. You should consider business training courses. It will not be time wasted (**See Help Section this Chapter**).
Will I require any licences before I am able to trade?	You may be surprised to discover just how many licences you need, both for legal requirements to cover your ability to trade and to protect yourself in case of liability (**See pages 156 Chapter 5 Tax, Insurance and Pensions and page 93 and Help Section Chapter 3**).
How do I know if I should be a sole trader or a limited company, or go into partnership?	Firstly try to analyse your personality type (**see questionnaire Chapter 1**) as objectively and honestly as possible. Combine this with the type of business you want to set up, and how you are going to be funded, before you decide if you should be a sole trader, partnership, limited company, co-operative, franchise or to buy an already existing business (**See page 71 Chapter 3**

Questions	Answers
	You, Your Company and The Law). You should explore all aspects of this with either your accountant, bank manager or financial adviser (**See Chapter 4 You and Your Money**).
How much money do you need to get a business started?	You can't work this out on the back of an envelope, you have to do a business plan (**See page 39 this chapter**) and investigate what the initial outlay is for starting a business similar to yours, taking into account running costs and allowing for money to buy equipment and supplies while still being able to pay the household bills. Remember there is usually a delay between doing the work and being paid for it. A lot of small businesses run into financial difficulties because of lack of capital and are forced to close (**See page 32 this Chapter.**)
Where are the best places to go for funding?	With the help of either your accountant, your financial adviser or your bank manager you will be able to discover which are the best deals for funding a small business. The secret is in shopping around.

Questions	Answers
I can't decide if I need an accountant or a book-keeper? Or if I know enough about income tax.	It depends on the size of your business, the financial complications and your knowledge of income tax, book-keeping, tax, VAT and the various tax allowances as to whether you need an accountant (**See Chapter 5 Tax, Insurance and Pensions**). Accountants are also people with whom you can discuss your future business ideas and involve in your financial planning (**See page 109 Chapter 4 You and Your Money**).
Will I have to register for VAT?	It depends on your predicted profit. You should contact your local Customs and Excise office who will advise you (**See page 145 Chapter 5 Tax, Insurance and Pensions**).
Should I get any pensions?	When you are self-employed you lose some state benefits and employment protection (**See the table in this Chapter, Basic Facts about Being Self-Employed and Running your own Business and page 160 Chapter 5 Tax, Insurance and Pensions**).

THE COMPLETE GUIDE TO WORKING FROM HOME

Questions	Answers
Will I need to employ other people?	This isn't just a matter of thinking it would be nice to have a helping hand around **(See page 74 Chapter 3 You, Your Company and the Law)**. You also have to look at your cash flow, budgeting and business plan **(See page 153 Chapter 5 Tax, Insurance and Pensions)** to see if you can afford to take on the financial responsibility of staff. For example, you have to weigh up the cost of employing someone which would allow you to go out selling **(See Chapter 7 Selling and Marketing)**.
Will my business be profitable?	Remember there are always cheap suppliers of goods and services, but what you get from selling your goods and services has to be enough to pay the cost of producing the goods or services, pay all your overheads and leave you with a profit **(See Chapter 4 You and Your Money)**.

POTENTIAL PROBLEM AREAS
National Insurance **(See page 149 Chapter 5 Tax, Insurance and Pensions)**.
Public Health problems **(See page 93 Chapter 3 You, Your Company and the Law)**.
Various Insurances – consulting an insurance broker is free **(See page 155 Chapter 5 Tax, Insurance and Pensions)**.
Licences – get professional advice.

Local bye-law restrictions – get professional advice for your area from your Town Hall.

VAT (**See page 145 Chapter 5 Tax, Insurance and Pensions**).

Keeping records and accounts (**See page 119 Chapter 4 You and Your Money**).

Income tax (**See page 141 Chapter 5 Tax, Insurance and Pensions**).

Bad debts (**See page 88 Chapter 3 You, Your Company and the Law**).

Correct pricing – do research relevant to your product. Up to a point the market will dictate the price (**See page 39 this Chapter**).

PAYE (**See page 142 Chapter 5 Tax, Insurance and Pensions**).

Over-reliance on one supplier – get professional advice relevant to your product.

Large stocks and changes in fashion – do research relevant to your product.

Contracts of employment (**See page 74 Chapter 3 You, Your Company and the Law**).

RULES AND REGULATIONS – WHERE TO GO

Now that you have identified the potential problem areas of starting up a small business, your next move is to be aware of the rules and regulations that you have to comply with and where to get help in relationship to them. The purpose of this book is to give you some of these answers, or – if it arises – to advise you that it is better to seek professional advice.

Here is a quick spot check-list of various rules and regulations that affect trading and running a business and, alongside, where to go for help. Run down it and see if any of them are relevant to you.

WHERE	WHO
Trading standards	The Local Authority
Advertising signs and planning permission	The Local Authority
Licences	The Local Authority
Trading or manufacturing prospects in the town	Chamber of Commerce or Trade and Industrial Development Officer

THE COMPLETE GUIDE TO WORKING FROM HOME

WHERE	**HOW**
Taxation	Accountant and local Tax Office
VAT and its effects on business	Customs and Excise
Changes to your Social Security	Department of Social Security
Business expertise	Further education; Trade Associations
Rating of premises	The Local Authority
Insurance	An Insurance Broker
Security	The local Police Security Officer
Public Health Regulations	The Local Authority
Fire Precautions	The local Fire Advisory Officer
Protecting your business interests	Chamber of Commerce and Trade; Trade Associations
Business statistics and information	Local reference library
Training	Training Board, local college; Department of Employment
Technical management and financial help	Management Consultant; Industrial Liaison Officer; local library

[Chart from the Small Firms Information Centre]

THE INITIAL OUTLAY TO START A BUSINESS

Capital Equipment
* Stock – also a *running cost* as you will continually have to buy it.
* Installation costs; such as having separate telephones installed with extra extensions (**See page 226 Chapter 8 Your**

STARTING YOUR OWN BUSINESS

Home as Your Workplace).
* Furniture (**See page 238 Help Section Chapter 8 Your Home as Your Workplace**) fixtures, fittings and any alterations or decorations.
* Tools, equipment, vehicles.
* Legal costs and accountants' fees – also a *running cost* (**See Chapter 3 You, Your Company and the Law and Chapter 4 You and Your Money**).
* Advertising and publicity – also a *running cost* as you should always have an advertising and publicity budget (**See Chapter 7 Selling and Marketing**).
* Licences.
* Odds and ends, such as: extra tea-, coffee-making equipment, cleaning, light bulbs, etc.
* Deposits for fuel, telephone supplies and insurances.
* Contingency.

Running costs
* Bank charges.
* Income tax, Corporation tax, VAT (**See Chapter 5 Tax, Insurance and Pensions**).
* National Insurance (**See Chapter 5 Tax, Insurance and Pensions**).
* Loan repayments.
* Insurance premiums (**See Chapter 5 Tax, Insurance and Pensions**).
* Stock (**See later in this Chapter**).
* Travelling expenses.
* Solicitors' fees (**See Help Section Chapter 3 You, Your Company and the Law**).
* Accountants' fees (**See page 111 Chapter 4 You and Your Money**).
* Advertising and publicity (**See Chapter 7 Selling and Marketing**).
* Employees' wages and National Insurance (**See Help Section Chapter 5 Tax, Insurance and Pensions**).
* Fuel.
* Lighting and heating (**See Chapter 8 Your Home as Your Workplace**).
* Telephone and postage (**See Chapter 8 Your Home as Your Workplace**).

* Office stationery **(See page 195 Chapter 7 Selling and Marketing).**
* Contingency.

WILL YOU MAKE A PROFIT?
Profits come from good commercial ideas, plus your skill, your product, the market and your income. Add these up and you should have the formula for a profit. When you are trying to work out what your profit will be (because without one your business won't exist) you should allow for the following *deductions*.

The cost of borrowing
On the financial side you must allow for the cost of borrowing the money which you will need to set up and run the business. Some of it may be to pay for your capital equipment, such as tools or a freezer, and remember when you are budgeting you need to allow for their replacement when they wear out. The rest may go towards the cost of starting up your business.

Write down the current rate of interest that you will be paying the bank if you are borrowing money (this is likely to be 3 per cent over their base lending rate but check). If there is a recession forecast, then add about another 3 per cent for safety. Add around 30 per cent for risk, or around 10 per cent if you are trying something that has been tried and tested already. What you have at the end is the capital that you will need for the year.

For example:

Capital employment say:	£50,000
Current rate of interest:	15 per cent
Provision for risk:	20 per cent
Target return on capital employed:	35 per cent

Therefore a satisfactory return will be:

£50,000 × 35 per cent = £17,500

Other business costs
The cost of your overheads:
  Heat, light, phone, postage, stationery, repairs and delivery. Plus you may need to advertise.

= £. . . . .

The cost of your materials
= £. . . . .

The cost of wages
You need to pay yourself or any helpers for the hours they work.
= £. . . . .

TOTAL MANUFACTURING COST = £. . . . .

A lot of people running small businesses, like Rachael who makes ice-cream, have made a rule that they don't borrow money, 'I will not borrow money and make the bank rich. If I can't afford it then the business goes without it until I can.'

GETTING THE FINANCE
However artistic, creative or enthusiastic you are, it cannot be emphasised enough how important it is that you calculate at the beginning how much money you are going to need. To do this you have to ask yourself a number of questions.

* Can you work successfully off the kitchen or dining-room table, or will you need to build a workshop at the end of the garden?
* How much capital equipment will you need to buy? Capital equipment being such things as a fax machine, photocopier, word-processor, a potter's wheel, industrial sewing machine, van for deliveries and other large items that are the basis of conducting your business. (**See page 32 Initial Outlay to Start a Business and Chapter 8 Your Home as Your Workplace**.) Plus the amount of money you will need to buy initial materials.

Having established how much it is going to cost to get your business started, the next move is to investigate where you are going to get the funding from (**See Chapter 3 You, Your Company and the Law and Chapter 4 You and Your Money and their Help Sections**). If you don't concern yourself with both these aspects you are very likely to find yourself and your business heading for financial disaster.

A key fact to remember is that it doesn't matter if you are running a small business from home as a one-man band outfit, if you have a partner, or if you are employing someone to help. The amount of money you need will depend on how elaborate your business idea is.

How much money you will need

If your business is something relatively simple, such as running a word-processing service, knitting sweaters or making jam, you will need to make a list of the cost of:

Your capital equipment
Your materials
Your running costs

If your business is more complicated, such as manufacturing in a small workshop, desk-top publishing or operating a photographic studio, you will need to make a longer list of the costs of:

Your capital equipment
Your materials
Your running costs

If you are managing a business involving other people or outside manufacturers, such as co-ordinating accounts, import and export, or dealing in antiques, you will need to make an even longer list of the cost of:

Your capital equipment
Your materials
Your running costs

Your cash flow forecast

At this stage you have to do a cash flow forecast (see example) which is an indication of what money is coming in and going out.

Sales
I.e. selling price multiplied by number of sales – you will need to make basic sales forecasts for the year ahead on a monthly basis. It's easy to write in make-believe figures, but you must be realistic. Show income in the month in which it is received.

Will you make it to the end of the year?

CASHFLOW FORECAST

J F M A M J J A S O N D

Totals:

Income:

    Capital:
    VAT refunds:
    Cash sales:
    Credit sales:

Outgoings:

    Opening stock:
    Stock:
    Rent:
    Business rates:
    Telephone:
    Gas and electricity:
    Insurance:
    Vehicle lease:
    Petrol:
    Promotion:
    Accountant/Solicitor:
    Materials/other:
    Wages:
    NI/PAYE:
    Capital Expenses:
    Overdraft Interest:
    VAT payments:
    Personal:

Total cash out:

Monthly balance:

Opening balance:
Closing Balance: (cum)

Grants/loans
This is income from loans. It will be the last thing to calculate after seeing how things add up. Show any grant income, e.g. money from the Enterprise Allowance Scheme.

Costs
Some of these will be fixed, some will be variable and so will depend on your monthly forecast. Show costs in the month in which you pay them, e.g. you may have to pay rent three months in advance or insurance a year in advance. Realistically estimate how long it will take you to do the work. Keep a note of all your realistic assumptions. Add in the cost of all the materials used, plus a guesstimate of your overhead costs which are heating, lighting, post, phone, etc. Then add the amount of time it will take before you are paid – probably a couple of months or the period of credit you give to your customers or take from your suppliers. This will give you some idea of the timing of cash receipts and payments. If you are a new business without a track record and if you are dealing with suppliers, you may well find that you have to pay them immediately. This will obviously have an effect on your projected cash flow, as Mandy discovered when she was trying to get her home delivery nappy service off the ground: 'I imagined that somewhere like Proctor and Gamble would let me have the nappies cheaper than the shops if I bought them direct from a main supplier. I contacted them but they didn't want to know, they wanted trade references and a regular order, but I couldn't do that because I didn't know what my turnover was going to be. To them you're just a little person.'

The reason for investigating such costs is so that you can:

* Identify potential cash short-falls before they occur.
* Allow potential cash short-falls to be identified and dealt with efficiently.
* Ensure that enough cash is available for any necessary capital expenditure.
* Encourage more efficient use of resources and reduce costs.

All of this will lead to more soundly based decisions.
If you are registering for VAT (**See page 146 Chapter 5 Tax, Insurance and Pensions**) you have to include it.

Exclude your bank overdraft, but include all other loans.

If you have any partners (**See page 71 Chapter 3 You, Your Company and the Law**) show any money they are putting in.

Your cash flow forecast will be based mainly on assumptions and not concerned with profit and loss.

Price

Once you have met your basic costs, you will have a certain amount of profit margin to play with. Rachael, who makes ice-cream, underpriced her product when she first started. 'I didn't allow for overheads like heating, lighting and stationery, and didn't know how much profit to add. My pricing still is fairly random, especially with the individual desserts.'

In order to get a foothold in the market-place you have to decide if you will vary your price by any of the following practices.

* Have a programme of introductory offers, which will allow customers to sample your product or service.
* Offer discount pricing for bulk buys.
* Decide on a high price from the beginning because you think your product/service is in the quality market and can stand it.

Fixing a price can be a juggling act between strategy, costing calculations and cash flow as Valerie discovered when pricing her sandwiches. 'A quarter of the price of my sandwiches goes in petrol, food, heating, car insurance, business insurance, tax, phone calls, heating, water, public liability insurance and on top of all that, food goes bad. Nearly all my profit that's left goes on household bills.'

Whatever you do it's very important that you don't undersell yourself just to get started, it won't pay off in the long term and it's one of the reasons why many small businesses go bust.

If, after doing your cash flow and pricing, your business idea still looks financially viable, then it's time to start converting this business structure into a full-scale business plan.

BUSINESS PLANS

Your business plan should basically be a précis of the previous cash flow forecast (**See page 37 this Chapter**) that you did for yourself. Even if you are running a small business from home, which may be just a one-person operation, you will still realise the importance of having a business plan, not only for you but also for your bank, or anyone else you are going to involve in the financial running and funding of your business. Your business plan should contain:

* Summary.
* Market analysis: meeting your objectives and strategy (**See Chapter 7 Selling and Marketing**).
* What the product or service is.
* The people: who you are, your relevant skills, qualifications and experience (**See page 42 this Section**).
* Costing and pricing.
* Cash flow forecast.
* Profit and loss account.

All of this should be brief, a maximum of ten A4 pages, preferably typed and easy to read, with short, properly defined paragraphs, numberings and definite headings, so that potential funders can quickly find the information they need. If possible put it all into a loose-leaf binder so that pages can be removed for photocopying. Back everything up with figures and the source of those figures – because no one will believe in you if they think you just grabbed them out of the thin air – and imaginative and thorough market research (**See pages 192 and 193 Chapter 7 Selling and Marketing**). You need to impress the people who you hope will support you.

Banks prefer figures to strategies, so make sure that your figures fit your plans, rather than the other way round. Substantiate your estimates, write down what you have based your costings on and what you have based your income projections on. Give them information about any experts' advice that you have used. Banks in particular like to know how you have substantiated the basis of your start-up and running costs (**See page 32 this Chapter**) and they like to see cash flow charts (**See page 37 this Chapter**).

Those assessing your plan are likely also to be looking at others, so a clear simple outline which is easy to read and stands out can help them to make a positive decision about your idea. Remember you are selling yourself as well as your business, so don't forget to highlight your personal strengths and emphasise why you should be supported. You can find below what your business plan should contain, following this order:

Summary
Although this is the first section it should be written last, as it is basically a summary of what your idea is, what service or product you are offering, how it is designed to work and how it will work in relation to the market and why you can make it succeed. Briefly outline your qualifications. What you require in order to perform your service or produce your product. Your set-up costs, any help that you may require and what assets you already have in the business. Outline future developments. ('Within ten years I intend to have . . .') Time spans, income and expenditure forecasts. Mary doubled her turnover the first and second year her business was running, but not this year, so she knows that she has to expand: 'I have to buy new equipment and be able to increase my capacity.'

Market analysis – meeting objectives and strategy
How you intend to provide the service you will offer and how to maintain it. If you have done any market research set it out in this section. You should show that you have detailed knowledge of the market, of how to approach new customers, the number of staff needed, the resources you already have, how the project will be managed and the help you require. Give details of numbers of staff and about publicity if any. Give as much detail as possible, including the source of your information.

The product or service
Say what your product or service provides and its benefits to the user, i.e. a heated rear car window has the benefit of keeping the window clear.

It may be that it also has social status, personal interest, or that it will make people's lives easier.

Give a complete description of your product or service. Go into detail about exactly what you propose to do and show in detail how you will meet the various problems as they arise.

Say what the competition is, how it operates and how your service of product differs. Where there are gaps in the market and how you could go about filling them. A unique business idea may mean you have little competition, but it may also mean that you have uncertain demand.

Outline what opportunities there might be for future expansion. Mention that there may be some technical issues that need to be explained, e.g. copyright, special legal matters etc. Don't go into too much detail on this; remember you are just giving an overview.

People
State your own skills and those of any partners. It's the individual experience, knowledge and ability that people are putting their money behind. You should focus on the following key points:

* What skills are required to make the idea work, e.g. technical skills such as selling or screen printing. But don't just deal with the technical skills – add in personal qualities such as enthusiasm, energy, etc.
* Who the people are who are going to cover these requirements. List everyone involved and any skills you may need to buy in, such as accountants or casual labour.
* Why these people will be able to meet these responsibilities. Give actual qualifications and experience, including hobbies and outside work activities if relevant.
* Training required, because you know there are gaps, e.g. a book-keeping course. You should also list any training courses the people involved have been on.
* Organisation of the people within the business and if there is any legal organisation to set up, e.g. sole trader, partnership, limited company (**See Chapter 3, You, Your Company and the Law**).

Cash flow forecast (See also page 37 this Chapter and Chapter 4 You and Your Money)
This is probably the section that any potential funder most wants to see, and it is vitally important that you know how much money you will need. Remember a lot of businesses go bust, not because they aren't making a profit, but because they haven't analysed when they will need an injection of cash. For example, you can have the orders but not have the money to buy the raw materials.

At the start-up stage you will need to phase in a lot of initial spending in order to get started, so you have to know when you will need the money (**See page 36 this Chapter**). For example, your customers may expect credit. Include information on Sales, Grants/Loans and Costs.

Profit and loss account
This is a summary of how successful you think you will be at the end of one year's trading. It is, in effect, the sum of the figures in your cash flow for the year. You should also include:

* Sales Forecast – the total expected sales for the coming year in both quantity and value.
* Direct Costs – the variable costs that relate directly to sales and volume. When deducted from sales this gives what is known as 'gross profit'.
* Fixed Costs – costs you have to pay regardless of how much you sell. When deducted from gross profit this gives what is known as the 'net profit'. Depreciation falls into this section.
* Tax – the net profit is what you are taxed on. If you are on the Enterprise Allowance Scheme this is added to your net profit, and you are taxed on the total. The money that you take out of the business, your drawings, are deducted from the profit. Anything left can be reinvested in the business to help it to grow. (Additional information here from LiveWire. **See Help Section this Chapter.**)

It's a good idea to do a business plan every year anyway as a way of monitoring your progress, giving yourself a boost and feeling in control.

PLACES TO GO TO FOR INFORMATION TO HELP WITH BUSINESS PLAN RESEARCH

* Yellow Pages.
* Thomson's Local Directory.
* Telephone books (reference libraries stock these for the whole of the UK).
* British Rate and Data (BRAD), which lists all newspapers and periodicals.
* Reports Index – 3,000 consumer and industrial research reports each year.
* Research Index – newspaper articles by industry and company.
* Market Survey Index – updated monthly.
* The Retail Directory – all UK outlets with maps.
* Directory of British Trade Associations.
* CSO Guide to official statistics.
* Mort, D. and Siddall, L. – Sources of unofficial UK statistics.

* Periodicals/newspaper articles (see BRAD).
* Trade Associations (see directory).
* Market Reports, e.g. Jordan's Surveys, Keynote, Mintel.
* Company reports, e.g. Extel and McCarthy cards.
* Business Monitor series (HMSO).
* Overseas Trade Statistics (HMSO).
* Family Expenditure Survey.
* General Household Survey.
* National Food Survey.
* National Income and Expenditure Blue Book.
* Census of Population.
* OPCS Monitors.
* Annual Abstract of Statistics.
* Regional Trends.

All these should be available from your local reference library and Local Authority.

ENTERPRISE ALLOWANCE SCHEME GRANTS

A lot of unemployed people want to start their own business but are put off by the fact that by doing so they risk losing their unemployment benefit or income support. The Enterprise Allowance Scheme is specifically aimed at helping unemployed people start their own business.

The Scheme pays you £40 a week, fortnightly, for the first year, on top of what you earn from your business. This helps to make up for the loss of benefit whilst your business is getting started. It also offers access to free business counselling, advice and training. Before Mary started her sandwich-making business she went on the Enterprise Allowance Scheme. 'It gave me a lot of confidence to deal with the health and hygiene people, the council, banks and learning about book-keeping. I felt they held my hand.'

Many banks provide free banking services and business advice for people on the Enterprise Allowance Scheme and you may be eligible to receive Housing Benefit, rent, rate or community charge rebates or Family Credit as well. You can find out more about this on an Enterprise Allowance Scheme Awareness Day. The Scheme also offers a range of practically based training courses which will help you both before and after you have started your business. Most of them will take only a few days and will give you basic business skills such as book-keeping, tax and promoting your business.

David is a professional magician and hypnotist who was accepted on the Enterprise Allowance Scheme. 'The £40 a week saw me through the slack period after Christmas.' Through the scheme he went on a one-day taxation course, as well as courses on selling and marketing.

In order to join the Enterprise Allowance Scheme you have to be over eighteen and under sixty-five years of age. Before applying you have to have been unemployed for eight weeks and receiving Unemployment Benefit or Income Support. It also counts towards the eight-week period if you fulfil any of the following conditions:

* Have had formal notice of redundancy.
* Were in employment training.
* Completed an Employment Department training course.
* Were on Employment Rehabilitation Courses.
* Were in Sheltered Employment.
* Were on a Youth Training Scheme.

If you are thinking of joining the Enterprise Allowance Scheme, you must continue to make yourself available for work to make sure you still receive Unemployment Benefit or Income Support. You local Unemployment Benefit or Social Security office will help you if you have any questions. You may be able to join the scheme without making a further claim for benefit if you are presently in any of the situations listed below and received benefit immediately before starting:

* Employment Training.
* Employment Department funded training courses (including courses at Employment Rehabilitation Centres).
* Sheltered Employment.
* Community Industry.

You must be able to show that you have at least £1,000 available to invest in your business in the first twelve months. This can be a loan or an overdraft. If you think this may be a problem for you, talk to your local Enterprise Allowance Scheme staff who will be able to recommend someone who can advise you on how to raise the money.

You must not be an undischarged bankrupt.

You must agree to work full time in the business – that's at least thirty-six hours a week.

You will not be asked to prove that your business will be a success, but in order for your business to be approved by the Scheme:

It must be legal
In other words you must be sure that you have complied with any legal obligations or requirements that apply to your business before you join the Scheme. For example, if you wish to set up an employment agency then you must have a licence from the Department of Employment. The Scheme will fund an author to write a book, but not to write pornography.

It must be new
You should not have started to run your business before you apply to join the Scheme, and you cannot take over the running of a business that's already operating. Your business will be considered to have started if you do any of the following before applying:

* Manufacture products for sale.
* Buy stock for use in the business.
* Advertise for staff.
* Advertise the products or services of your business.

If you do any of these you will be considered to have started your business and you will not qualify for the Scheme. You should also not sell the products or services of your business before being accepted on to the Scheme.

There are some things you can do towards your business which will not affect your application such as:

* Get planning permission to run your business.
* Get any necessary licences.
* Contact suppliers to check on the price and availability of materials.
* Approach potential customers to find out the demand for your proposed product or service.
* Prepare a business plan.

If you want either to take over a business that has stopped trading, or if you are thinking of starting a business which is the same or similar to one which you previously owned or part owned, ask the advice of the staff at the Enterprise Allowance Scheme.

It must not bring the scheme into disrepute
Your business will not be supported if it will bring the Scheme into disrepute. For example a business that involves gambling, promoting particular political or religious views, or involving nude modelling, sex or pornography. This is not a complete list and you should check with the Enterprise Allowance Scheme staff.

It must be based in Great Britain
If you are a partnership or co-operative special conditions apply:

* At least half of the members must be accepted on to the Scheme.
* Each member must have £1,000 to invest in the business (except for a limited company where only those receiving the allowance need to have £1,000).
* For limited companies, the applicants for the Scheme must hold at least 50 per cent of the shares.

If you have been on the Scheme once before, you may be able to go on it again as long as it's a year since you received the allowance. Ask the Enterprise Allowance staff for further advice.

You can find out more about the Enterprise Allowance Scheme at their Awareness Day – your local Job Centre will give you details.

Training in business skills is available free from the Employment Department whilst you are on the Enterprise Allowance Scheme. Your local Enterprise Allowance Scheme or Job Centre will be able to give you details of all the Employment Department and other business training courses available in your area.

Other Grants
Each local authority and some private companies and charities offer different grant-aided schemes for people who want to start their own businesses. Contact your local Town Hall for further information (**See page 133 Chapter 4 You and Your Money**).

Small firms services
Small Firms Services specialise in helping people who are either setting up a business, or have any problems later on. They will

give information, advice and counselling on such things as: trading status, expanding or diversifying once your business is established, training, preparing a business plan to present to a bank, identifying sources of money and giving advice on whether it's time to close your business down.

They have access to local and national information and if your problem is something they are unable to deal with they will arrange for you to meet a business counsellor who will have business experience and will, if necessary, visit you on your premises.

After the first three meetings you will be charged a fee of about £30.

In England the Small Firms Service is run by the Department of Employment, in Wales by the Welsh Office and the Welsh Development Agency, in Scotland by the Scottish Development Agency, and in Northern Ireland by the Northern Ireland Department of Economic Development **(See page 51 Help Section for phone numbers)**.

Enterprise agencies

Enterprise Agencies give small businesses free advice and support on such things as: trading status, sources of finance, preparing a business plan, whether your business idea is viable, dealing with problems whilst you are trading and when to stop.

The advisers are seconded from businesses, companies and banks and will therefore have particular expertise and experience. The range of topics that advisers have experience of will vary from agency to agency.

They also run training courses which are either free or cost only a small fee.

There is a local umbrella organisation of Enterprise Agencies which produces a directory of local agencies and gives details of advisers' backgrounds and what activities particular agencies specialise in **(See Help Section this Chapter for addresses and phone numbers)**.

Local authority economic units (EDU)

Some local authorities, mostly in inner city areas, have set up units which give advice and help to existing and newly set up businesses in their area. Some have bilingual advisers and are particularly intended to help ethnic minorities and small businesses.

The advisers will have a business background, such as banking and accountancy, and will often have a good knowledge of the local area and what is available, e.g. potential investors, local authority concessions for small businesses, relaxed planning controls etc. Some local authority units may be able to provide grants or loans. Contact your local Town Hall for further information.

National Federation of the self-employed and small businesses
This is a pressure group which promotes the interests of all self-employed people. There is no subscription fee and the organisation provides a free magazine, runs a twenty-four-hour legal advisory service and various insurance schemes. There are a number of regional offices and local branches **(See Help Section this Chapter for addresses and phone numbers)**.

LiveWire
This is a national scheme, sponsored by Shell, which helps young people aged between 16 and 25 to set up their own business. There is an award scheme for encouraging and publicising the self-employment option. There is a closing date for a scheme each year and entrants are paired with an adviser who will help them on an individual basis to plan and develop their business idea **(See Help Section this Chapter for address and phone number)**.

Instant muscle
This organisation gives training and advice to young people who want to set up a business. It has a nationwide network of advisers who are mostly business people who retired early or who have been made redundant and therefore have immediate hands-on business experience **(See Help Section this Chapter for addresses and phone numbers)**.

Ethnic minority small business centre
Will give advice to people who are setting up a business as well as businesses that are established. They cover such things as: business plans, marketing services and finance. They run courses **(See Help Section this Chapter for address and phone number)**.

City of London polytechnic ethnic minority business development unit

They provide short courses, information and counselling for people from ethnic minority backgrounds (mainly Afro-Caribbean and Asian people) who either own, are managing or are thinking of setting up their own business. Courses include such topics as: raising money, taxation and business plans. No qualifications are necessary. The courses are followed up by a counselling service.

There is a small fee for courses and counselling sessions (**See Help Section this Chapter for address and phone number**).

Government business shops

'One stop' centres where representatives of the relevant government departments offer advice and counselling to people running small businesses. They cover such things as: Income tax, PAYE, VAT, National Insurance, health and safety and employment law (**See Help Section this Chapter for address and phone number**).

A FOOTNOTE

If your small business fails, as many do, for financial reasons, discuss it with your accountant, bank manager or any relevant organisation that may have been assisting you. It may be that your business is suffering from an identity problem, such as poor marketing or lack of publicity, not enough investment, or simply the wrong business idea. Once you have identified the cause of your problem you can discuss solutions, such as re-thinking the basic idea or improving publicity. Many businesses are just slow to get off the ground, or it may be that you have unrealistic expectations of your profit. But do talk to the experts before giving up – there may be a simple solution that you have overlooked.

CHAPTER 2
HELP SECTION

Local enterprise development agencies

DIAL FREEFONE 100 and ASK FOR FREEFONE ENTERPRISE Contact your local ENTERPRISE AGENCY for free impartial advice about starting and developing your own business.
To find the address and phone number of your nearest ENTERPRISE AGENCY call:
BUSINESS IN THE COMMUNITY 071 253 3716.
SCOTTISH BUSINESS IN THE COMMUNITY 031 334 9876.
Number of grants available through EEC central government and local authorities call FREEFONE 0800 222999.
NORTHERN IRELAND LOCAL ENTERPRISE DEVELOPMENT UNIT (LEDU) provides comprehensive information and advisory services plus financial help to small firms: Contact 0232 491031.
SCOTTISH DEVELOPMENT AGENCY 041 248 2700.
THE HIGHLANDS AND ISLANDS DEVELOPMENT BOARD 0463 234171.
THE RURAL DEVELOPMENT COMMISSION 0722 336255.
WELSH DEVELOPMENT AGENCY 0222 222666.
In mid-Wales the DEVELOPMENT BOARD FOR RURAL WALES 0686 626965.
GOVERNMENT BUSINESS SHOPS FREEFONE 0800 222999.
Address for local shop from your local Small Firms Service.

Training

BUSINESS ENTERPRISE PROGRAMME offers both short and long courses and an open learning package for basic training for people starting a business.
Colleges, polytechnics and universities are increasingly able to meet the professional, industrial and commercial training needs (PICKUP) of small- and medium-sized firms as well as offering advice and consultancy. Contact:
CITY AND GUILDS OF LONDON INSTITUTE 46 Britannia Street, London, WC1X 9RG. Tel: 071 278 2468. Covers over 300 different areas of industry and public service. Three different levels of certificate.

THE COMPLETE GUIDE TO WORKING FROM HOME

DEPARTMENT OF EDUCATION AND SCIENCE 071 934 0888. BUSINESS and OPEN LEARNING courses enable people to study at their own pace when business permits. They cover a wide variety of short and long courses covering a full range of business skills. Contact:

TRAINING AGENCY AREA OFFICES SCOTTISH VOCATIONAL EDUCATIONAL COUNCIL (SCOTVEC) Hanover House, 24 Douglas Street, Glasgow, GT2 7NQ. Tel: 041 248 7900.

BUSINESS AND TECHNICIAN EDUCATIONAL COUNCIL (BTEC), Central House, Upper Woburn Place, London, WC1H 0HH. Tel: 071 413 8400.

Further education and training – a new career

The following books are available from libraries and may be useful for further education and re-training:

Career Change – New Working Directions by CRAC.

Commonwealth Universities Year Book by Association of Commonwealth Universities.

Directory of Further and Many Higher Education Courses in the UK by CRAC.

Opportunities by the Careers and Occupational Information Centre.

Occupations (produced annually) by the Careers and Occupational Information Centre.

Polytechnics Courses Handbook by the Committee of Directors of Polytechnics.

Second Chance: A Guide to Adult Education and Training.

UCCA Guide: How to Apply For Admission to a University by Universities. (N. Ireland) by Association of Commonwealth Universities.

Further education

NORTHERN IRELAND TRAINING AND EMPLOYMENT AGENCY Clarendon House, 9–21 Adelaide Street, Belfast 2. Tel: 0232 244300.

NATIONAL INSTITUTE OF ADULT CONTINUING EDUCATION 19b De Montfort Street, Leicester, LE1 7GE. Tel: 0533 551451.

NATIONAL INSTITUTE OF ADULT CONTINUING EDUCATION Cymru, 245 Western Avenue, Cardiff, CF5 2YX. Tel: 0222 571201.

NORTHERN IRELAND COUNCIL FOR CONTINUING EDUCATION Rathcael House, Balloo Road, Bangor, BT19 2PR. Tel: 0247 466311.

OPEN COLLEGE 101 Wigmore Street, London, W1H 9AA. Tel: 071 935 8088.

OPEN UNIVERSITY Walton Hall, Milton Keynes, MK7 6AA. Tel: 0908 274066.

SCOTTISH VOCATIONAL AND EDUCATIONAL COUNCIL (SCOTVEC) Hanover House, 24 Douglas Street, Glasgow, GT2 7NQ. Tel: 041 248 7900.

THE POLYTECHNIC ASSOCIATION FOR CONTINUING EDUCATION Polytechnic of Wales, Pontypridd, Mid Glamorgan, CF37 1DL. Tel: 0443 480480.

THE UNIVERSITIES COUNCIL FOR ADULT EDUCATION Institute of Education, Westwood Site, University of Warwick, Coventry, CV4 7AL. Tel: 0203 523835.

THE WORKERS EDUCATIONAL ASSOCIATION Temple House, 9 Upper Berkeley Street, London, W1H 8BY. Tel: 071 402 5608.

What job?

If you are thinking of re-training or starting a new career working from home, these organisations can be helpful to you. The job types are suitable for working from home.

ACCOUNTANCY

Institute of Chartered Accountants in England and Wales, PO Box 433, Chartered Accountants' Hall, Moorgate Place, London, EC2P 2BJ. Tel: 071 628 7060.

Institute of Chartered Accountants of Scotland, 27 Queen Street, Edinburgh, EH2 1LA. Tel: 031 225 5673.

Institute of Chartered Accountants in Northern Ireland, 11 Donegall Square South, Belfast, BT1 5JE. Tel: 0232 321600.

Chartered Institute of Management Accountants, 63 Portland Place, London, W1N 4AB. Tel: 071 637 2311.

AGRICULTURE

Agriculture and Horticulture:

Northern Ireland Education and Training Officer, Department of Agriculture, Room 549, Dundonald House, Upper New Townards Road, Belfast, BT4 3SB. Tel: 0232 650111.

THE COMPLETE GUIDE TO WORKING FROM HOME

ARCHITECTURE

Royal Institute of British Architects, 66 Portland Place, London, W1N 4AD. Tel: 071 580 5533.

Royal Corporation of Architects in Scotland, 15 Rutland Square, Edinburgh, EH1 2BE. Tel: 031 229 7205.

British Institute of Architectural Technicians, 397 City Road, London, EC1 V1N. Tel: 071 278 2206.

Royal Society of Ulster Architects, 2 Mount Charles, Belfast, BT7 1NZ. Tel: 0232 323760.

ART AND DESIGN

The Design Council, 28 Haymarket, London, SW1Y 4SU. Tel: 071 839 8000.

CHIROPODY

Society of Chiropodists, 53 Welbeck Street, London, W1M 7HE. Tel: 071 486 3381.

COMPUTING

British Computer Society, PO Box 1454, Station Road, Swindon, Wilts, SN1 1TG. Tel: 0793 4802.

British Computer Society (Northern Ireland), c/o Dr R. Millar, Department of Computer Science, University of Ulster, Newtonabbey, Co. Antrim, BT37 0QB: Tel: 0860 726799 (office), 0232 365099 (home).

CONVEYANCING

Society of Licensed Conveyancers, 55 Church Road, Croydon, CR9 1PB. Tel: 081 681 1000.

DANCE

Council for Dance Education and Training, 5 Tavistock Place, London, WC1H 9SN. Tel: 071 388 5770.

Scottish Council for Dance, Moray House College of Physical Education, Cramond Campus, Cramond Road North, Edinburgh, EH4 6JD. Tel: 031 336 5836.

STARTING YOUR OWN BUSINESS

DESIGN

Chartered Society of Designers, 29 Bedford Square, London, WC1B 3EG. Tel: 071 631 1510.

DIETETICS

British Dietetic Association, 103 Daimler House, Paradise Circus, Queensway, Birmingham, B1 2BJ. Tel: 021 643 5483.

EDUCATION

Business and Technician Education Council (BTEC), Central House, Upper Woburn Place, London, WC1H 0HH. Tel: 071 388 3288.

ENGINEERING

Engineering Council, 10 Maltravers Street, London, WC2R 3ER. Tel: 071 240 7891.

Women in Engineering, Women's Engineering Society, c/o Department of Civil Engineering, Imperial College of Science and Technology, Imperial College Road, London, SW7 2AZ. Tel: 071 589 5111, ext. 4731.

GRAPHICS

Northern Ireland Graphical Society, 29 Malone Road, Belfast, BT9 6RU. Tel: 0232 665284.

HORTICULTURE

Royal Horticultural Society, Vincent Square, London, SW1P 2PE. Tel: 071 834 4333.

HOTEL AND CATERING

Hotel and Catering Industry Training Board, Capital House, 9 Logie Mill, Edinburgh, EH7 4HG. Tel: 031 337 2339.

INSURANCE

Chartered Insurance Institute, 20 Aldermanbury, London, EC2V 7HY Tel: 071 606 3835.

INTERIOR DESIGN

Interior Decorators and Designers Association Ltd, 102–104 Church Road, Teddington, Middlesex, TW11 8PY. Tel: 081 977 1105.

LANGUAGES

Institute of Linguists, 24A Highbury Grove, London, N5 2EA. Tel: 071 359 7445.

Association for Language Learning, Marton, Rugby, Warwicks. CV23 9RY. Tel: 0926 632335.

MARKET RESEARCH

Market Research Society, 15 Northburgh Street, London, EC1V OAH. Tel: 071 490 4911.

MUSIC

Incorporated Society of Musicians, 10 Stratford Place, London, W1N 9AE. Tel: 071 629 4413.

Northern Ireland Musicians Association, 525 Antrim Road, Belfast, BT15 3BS. Tel: 0232 370037.

PRINTING

British Printing Industries Federation, 11 Bedford Row, London, WC1R 4DX. Tel: 071 242 6904.

PHOTOGRAPHY

British Institute of Professional Photography, 2 Amwell End, Ware, Herts. SG12 9HN. Tel: 0920 464011.

SURVEYING LAND AND PROPERTY SERVICES

Incorporated Association of Architects and Surveyors, Jubilee House, Billing Brook Road, Weston Favell, Northampton, NN3 4NW. Tel: 0604 404121.

STARTING YOUR OWN BUSINESS

TELEVISION AND VIDEO – BROADCAST AND NON-BROADCAST

Royal Television Society, Tavistock House East, Tavistock Square, London, WC1H 9HR. Tel: 071 387 1332.

Film and Television Training – A Guide to Film and Video Courses by the British Film Institute.

(BFI) British Film Institute, 21 Stephen Street, London, W1P 1PL, Tel: 071 255 1444.

West Surrey College of Art and Design, Falkner Road, The Hart, Farnham, Surrey, GU9 7DS. Tel: 0252 722441. BA Hons. Degree in art and design, film and video, animation studies, photographic.

Independent Media Training Federation, 26 Noel Street, London, W1V 3RD. Tel: 071 434 2651.

TOURISM

England: Regional Tourist Boards, the Small Firms Service (Freephone Enterprise)

The Rural Development Commission. Tel: 0722 336255.

The Scottish Tourist Board. Tel: 031 332 2433.

The Highlands and Islands Development Board. Tel: 0463 234171.

The Welsh Tourist Board. Tel: 0222 499909.

The British Tourist Board. Tel: 081 846 9000.

VALUATION AND AUCTIONEERING

Incorporated Society of Valuers and Auctioneers, 3 Cadogan Gate, London, SW1X 0AS. Tel: 071 235 2282.

Organisations that give grants, loans, advice and support for people working from home and running their own businesses
BRITISH TECHNOLOGY GROUP 101 Newington Causeway, London, SE1 6BU. Tel: 071 403 6666. Will give help to inventors, joint venture and project finance.

CITY ACTION TEAMS co-ordinate Government Programmes in the

Inner Cities and can offer extra support to individual projects which are not eligible for main programme funding. Contact: ACTION FOR CITIES UNIT, DEPARTMENT OF THE ENVIRONMENT Tel: 071 276 3053.

THE LEAGUE OF PROFESSIONAL CRAFTSMEN LTD 9 Felden Close, Hatch End, Pinner, Middx, HA5 4PU. Tel: 081 421 0594. Annual subscription ranging from £150 to £260 plus VAT, depending on the number of staff you employ. All members must be professional craftsmen and to join you must be prepared to give references plus a sample of your work. The league offers 24-hour legal advice, nationwide credit enquiry service, disputes advice, mediation and arbitration, £50,000 legal fees, debt recovery service, accountancy, taxation, VAT, sales and marketing advice, financial consultation, etc.

CITY OF LONDON POLYTECHNIC ETHNIC MINORITY BUSINESS DEVELOPMENT UNIT Room 125, City of London Polytechnic, 100 Minories, Tower Hill, EC3N 1JY. Tel: 071 283 1030, ext. 456. Provides short courses, counselling and information for people from ethnic minorities, mainly designed for Afro-Caribbean and Asian people who are thinking of setting up their own business.

RURAL DEVELOPMENT COMMISSION 141 Castle Street, Salisbury, Wilts, SP1 3TP. Tel: 0722 336255. Offers advice and consultancy to small firms in rural areas.

Co-operative development agencies
LOCAL CO-OPERATIVE DEVELOPMENT AGENCIES BUSINESS SERVICES. For details of business advice scheme offering a free initial consultation with a solicitor through:
INDUSTRIAL COMMON OWNERSHIP MOVEMENT 0532 461737.
SCOTTISH CO-OPERATIVE DEVELOPMENT COMMITTEE 041 554 3797.
WALES CO-OPERATIVE DEVELOPMENT TRAINING CENTRE LTD. 0222 225141.
NORTHERN IRELAND CO-OPERATIVE DEVELOPMENT AGENCY 0232 232755.

Department of trade and industry (DTI)
The DEPARTMENT OF TRADE AND INDUSTRY's Regional Offices promote and administer DTI and European schemes of assistance.

STARTING YOUR OWN BUSINESS

The regional offices also assist in promoting exports. Information concerning REGIONAL TECHNOLOGY CENTRES is also available from the regional offices. The services for small independent firms come under the umbrella of the ENTERPRISE INITIATIVE. The DTI can arrange for a period of free business consultancy and, if appropriate, this can be followed by financial support for consultancy in key areas such as business planning, financial information, marketing, design, quality and manufacturing systems. You can get a booklet giving details of the ENTERPRISE INITIATIVE. Tel: 0800 500200. You can get full details from the regional offices of the DTI:

East Midlands consultancy: 0602 596475,
  other initiatives: 0602 506181.
North East consultancy: 091 235 7292,
  other initiatives: 091 232 4722.
North West (Manchester) consultancy and other initiatives: 061 838 5000.
North West (Liverpool) consultancy and other initiatives: 051 224 6300.
West Midlands consultancy and other initiatives: 021 631 6181.
South East (London) consultancy: 071 627 7800,
  other initiatives: 071 215 0572.
South East (Cambridge) consultancy and other initiatives 0223 461939.
South East (Reading) consultancy and other initiatives 0734 395600
South West consultancy: 0272 308400,
  other initiatives: 0272 272666.
Yorks and Humberside consultancy: 0532 338300,
  other initiatives: 0532 443171.

Similar services are provided by:

SCOTTISH OFFICE consultancy and other initiatives: 041 248 4774.
WELSH OFFICE: consultancy: 0443 841777,
  other initiatives: 0222 823185.

DEPARTMENT OF EMPLOYMENT SMALL FIRMS SERVICE: call free on 0800 222999.

ENTERPRISE ALLOWANCE SCHEME helps unemployed people who

want to set up their own business and have £1,000 available to invest. It pays £40 a week for the first year. Contact your local JOB CENTRE for further information.

ENTERPRISE AGENCIES Give free advice and support to small businesses. Umbrella organisation which provides a directory of local Enterprise Agencies: BUSINESS IN THE COMMUNITY, 277a City Road, London, EC1V 1LX. Tel: 071 253 3716.

ENTERPRISE TRAINING AGENCY Broadway House, The Broadway, London, SW19. Tel: 081 543 6293.

ETHNIC MINORITY SMALL BUSINESS CENTRE Queen's College, 1 Park Drive, Glasgow, G3 6LP. Tel: 041 337 4000. Gives advice and runs courses for people setting up in business and for those who are established.

BRITISH FRANCHISE ASSOCIATION LTD (BFA) Thames View, Newton Road, Henley-on-Thames, Oxon, RG9 1HG. Tel: 0491 578049. Will provide an information pack currently costing £17.50, plus a booklet called 'Franchising'.

INNER CITY TASK FORCE Operates within certain urban areas, helping small businesses with grants and loans through their TASK FORCE DEVELOPMENT FUNDS. Contact: INNER CITIES UNIT DTI 071 215 6704.

INDUSTRIAL DEVELOPMENT BOARD NORTHERN IRELAND: 0232 233233. Gives advice and counselling only in Northern Ireland.

INSTANT MUSCLE LTD. (Head Office) 84 North End Road, London W14 9ES. Tel: 071 603 2604.
INSTANT MUSCLE SCOTLAND 107 McDonald Road, Edinburgh, EH7 4NW. Tel: 031 557 3796.
INSTANT MUSCLE provides training, money and advice to unemployed people to create their own business. Gives individual counselling and help with cash flow forecasts, business plans, presenting your plan to a bank, local authority and joining the ENTERPRISE ALLOWANCE SCHEME.

JOB CENTRES For information on training. Look under JOB CENTRE in your local phone book.

LIVEWIRE (UK OFFICE) 60 Grainger Street, Newcastle-upon-Tyne, NE1 5JG. Tel: 091 261 5584. Sponsored by Shell (UK) Ltd. Offers information, advice and assistance to young entrepreneurs on how to set up and manage a co-operative.

LOCAL AUTHORITIES ECONOMIC UNIT (EDU) Gives advice and help in setting up a business. Some units have bilingual advisers and are intended to help ethnic minorities. Contact your local JOB CENTRE, TOWN HALL. Look in your local Yellow Pages for your unit.

LOCAL ENTERPRISE DEVELOPMENT UNIT (LEDU) Upper Galwally, Belfast 8, Northern Ireland. Tel: 0232 491031. Only gives general advice and support to small businesses. Grants may be available.

OWNBASE 57 Glebe Road, Egham, Surrey, TW20 8BU (no phone). Yearly membership fee £17.50. Nationwide organisation run by homeworkers for homeworkers. Offers moral support and an exchange of skills and resources. In some areas members groups meet regularly. Currently looking at homeworkers' needs, it will shortly be publishing information booklets and leaflets. Newsletter monthly.

PORTOBELLO BUSINESS DEVELOPMENT AGENCY (PBDA) Portobello Business Centre, 149–251 Kensal Road, London, W10 5DB. Tel: 081 968 6656. Offers, free, a complete business planning service, advice on developing a business, marketing, raising money, Enterprise Allowance Scheme, book-keeping, tax, National Insurance, etc.

PRINCE'S YOUTH BUSINESS TRUST (PYBT) Tel: 071 498 3939 for your local PYBT co-ordinator. The trust gives grants of up to £1,500 per person. The grant is for tools, transport, insurance, fees and training, but not for working capital, rent, rates, raw materials or stock. It also provides low-interest loans of up to £5,000. Anyone aged 18 to 25 is eligible. It is not necessary to be unemployed. Loan can be for start-up or expansion. You do not have to be a sole trader – companies, partnerships and co-operatives are eligible. The people involved will have to show a sound business idea and commitment, which may well be in the form of money. The trust has 34 regional boards throughout the country.

PRINCE'S SCOTTISH YOUTH BUSINESS TRUST. Tel: 041 248 4999. Provides both grants and low-interest loans to disadvantaged young people wanting to start a business.

SCOTTISH BUSINESS SHOP 120 Bothwell Street, Glasgow G2 7JP. Tel: 041 248 6014. Runs small-firms service for Scotland giving advice and counselling.

SCOTTISH BUSINESS IN THE COMMUNITY Romano House, 43 Station Road, Corstorphine, Edinburgh, EH12 7AF. Tel: 031 334 9876.

SHELL ENTERPRISE LOAN FUND Six enterprise agencies around the country operate this loan fund. There is no age restriction although funds are primarily to help those aged up to 25. Applicants will be expected to provide some money if possible themselves. No restriction on how the money may be used, but the applicant will have to demonstrate commitment and a viable business. Low-interest loans of up to £5,000 are available. Contact:

BELFAST YOUNG BUSINESS CENTRE ARC House, 103–107 York Street, Belfast, BT15 1AB. Tel: 0232 328000.
BOLTON BUSINESS VENTURES LTD 46 Lower Bridgeman Street, Bolton, BL2 1DG. Tel: 0204 391400.
CARDIFF AND VALE ENTERPRISE AGENCY Enterprise House, 127 Bute Street, Cardiff, CF1 5LE. Tel: 0222 494411.
FALKIRK ENTERPRISE ACTION TRUST Newhouse Road, Falkirk, FK3 8NH. Tel: 0324 665500.
LONDON ENTERPRISE AGENCY LTD 4 Snow Hill, London, EC1A 2D1. Tel: 071 236 3000.
PROJECT NORTH EAST 60 Granger Street, Newcastle-upon-Tyne, NE1 5JG. Tel: 091 261 7856.

SMALL FIRMS CENTRES Birmingham, Bristol, Cardiff, Glasgow, Leeds, Liverpool, London, Manchester, Newcastle, Nottingham, Reading. Information and counselling services operated by the Department of Employment. Dial 100 and ask for FREEFONE ENTERPRISE or write to: SMALL FIRMS DIVISION, DEPARTMENT OF EMPLOYMENT, 2nd Floor, 11 Belgrave Road, London, SW1V 1RB.

THE TRAINING AGENCY Moorfoot, Sheffield, S1 4PQ. Tel: 0742 753275. Runs courses and training seminars for those starting or running businesses. It has regional offices throughout the country. Details of courses and grants are available through local JOB CENTRES or from: THE TRAINING AGENCY, Moorfoot, Sheffield, S1 4PQ. If you live in a rural area contact:

RURAL DEVELOPMENT COMMISSION 11 Cowley Street, London, SW1. Tel: 071 276 6969. Gives help, advice and sources of money to small businesses in rural areas with population of less than 10,000. Normally only helps manufacturing or service industries employing less than twenty.

WELSH DEVELOPMENT AGENCY (WDA) Small Business Unit, Treforest Industrial Estate, Pontypridd, Mid Glamorgan, CF37 5UT. Tel: 0443 841777/0222 222666. Runs small-firms service in Wales, gives advice, counselling; financial services may be available.

YOUTH BUSINESS INITIATIVE (YBI). Tel: 081 969 4562. Run by the Portobello Trust. It gives pupils who are either bored with the school system or feel they haven't achieved anything from it a chance to experience the challenge of running a small business for a few weeks or months. Of the eleven enterprises set up, six have made a small profit.

Consumer credit
The Office of Fair Trading (Consumer Credit Licensing Branch), Government Building, Bromyard Avenue, Acton, London, W3 7BB. Tel: 071 242 2858.

Advisory conciliation and arbitration service (ACAS)
27 Wilton Street, London, SW1X 7AZ. Tel: 071 210 3000. Booklets: *This is ACAS. Conciliation between individuals and employers.*

Industrial Tribunal Offices
Look under ACAS in your local phone directory. They offer free advice on planning and employment needs, communication with employees, controlling labour costs, employee representation, contracts for employment; hiring employees, rules and procedures, consultation procedures.

THE COMPLETE GUIDE TO WORKING FROM HOME

LONDON
Industrial Tribunal offices:
London Regional Office of the Industrial Tribunals, 93 Ebury Bridge Road, London, SW1W 8RE. Tel: 071 730 9161.

NORTH LONDON
Regional Office of the Industrial Tribunals, 19–29 Woburn Place, London, WC1H 0LU. Tel: 071 239 9244.

ASHFORD, KENT
Regional Office of the Industrial Tribunals, Tufton House, Tufton Street, Ashford, Kent, TN23 1RJ. Tel: 0233 621346.

BIRMINGHAM
Regional Office of the Industrial Tribunals, Phoenix House, 1–3 Newhall Street, Birmingham, B3 3NH. Tel: 021 236 6051.

BRISTOL
Regional Office of the Industrial Tribunals, Prince House, 43–51 Prince Street, Bristol, BS1 4PE. Tel: 0272 298261.

BURY ST EDMUNDS
Regional Office of the Industrial Tribunals, 100 Southgate Street, Bury St Edmunds, Suffolk, 1P33 2AQ. Tel: 0284 762300.

CARDIFF
Regional Office of the Industrial Tribunals, Caradog House, 1–6 St Andrews Place, Cardiff, CF1 3BE. Tel: 0222 372693.

EXETER
Regional Office of the Industrial Tribunals, Renslade House, Bonhay Road, Exeter, EX4 3BX. Tel: 0392 79665.

LEEDS
Regional Office of the Industrial Tribunals, Minerva House, East Parade, Leeds, LS1 5JZ. Tel: 0532 459741.

LIVERPOOL
Regional Office of the Industrial Tribunals, No. 1 Union Court, Cook Street, Liverpool, L2 4UJ. Tel: 051 236 9397.

MANCHESTER
Regional Office of the Industrial Tribunals, Alexandra House, 14–22 The Parsonage, Manchester, M3 2JA. Tel: 061 833 0581.

NEWCASTLE-UPON-TYNE
Regional Office of the Industrial Tribunals, Plummer House, 3rd Floor, Market Street East, Newcastle-upon-Tyne, NE1 6NF. Tel: 091 232 8865.

NOTTINGHAM
Regional Office of the Industrial Tribunals, 7th Floor, Birkbeck House, Trinity Square, Nottingham. Tel: 0602 47701.

SHEFFIELD
Regional Office of the Industrial Tribunals, 14 East Parade, Sheffield, S1 2ET. Tel: 0742 760348.

SOUTHAMPTON
Regional Office of the Industrial Tribunals, 3rd Floor, Duke's Keep, Marsh Lane, Southampton, SO1 1EX. Tel: 0703 639555.

SCOTLAND
The Central Office of Industrial Tribunals (Scotland), St Andrews House, 141 West Nile Street, Glasgow, G1 2RU. Tel: 041 331 1601.

Venture capital
If you are looking for British venture capital you should contact:

The British Venture Capital Association (BVCA), 1 Surrey Street, London, WC2R 2PS. Tel: 071 836 5702.
Branch Administration, Bank of Scotland, PO Box 12, Uberior House, 61 Grassmarket, Edinburgh, EH1 2JF. Tel: 031 243 5680.
Small Business Group, Corporate Marketing, Barclays Bank, 54 Lombard Street, London, EC3P 3AH. Tel: 071 626 1567.
Business Development Unit, Clydesdale Bank plc, 30 St Vincent Place, Glasgow, G1 2HL. Tel: 041 248 7070.
Small Business Services and Co-operatives Unit Co-operative Bank plc, 1 Balloon Street, Manchester, M60 4EP. Tel: 061 832 3456, ext. 5280.

Small Business Unit, Lloyds Bank plc, 71 Lombard Street, London, EC3P 3BS. Tel: 071 626 1500.

Small Business Unit, Midland Bank plc, 1st Floor, Block 2, Griffin House, Silver Street, Head, Sheffield, S1 3GG. Tel: 0742 29316.

Small Business Services, National Westminster Bank plc, 3rd Floor, Fenchurch Exchange, 8 Fenchurch Place, London EC3M 4PB. Tel: 071 374 3374.

Business Development Manager, The Royal Bank of Scotland, 42 St Andrew Square, Edinburgh, EH2 2YE. Tel: 031 556 8555.

Commercial Marketing Department, TSB Bank plc, Cannon House, 18 The Priory Queensway, Birmingham, B4 6BS. Tel: 021 212 4545.

Marketing Department, Yorkshire Bank plc, 20 Merrion Way, Leeds, LS2 8NZ. Tel: 0532 441244.

FINANCE FOR ENTREPRENEURS, LINC INVESTORS CLUB Have seven offices throughout the UK. Information from your local Enterprise Agency.

HMSO

HER MAJESTY'S STATIONERY OFFICE (HMSO) BOOKSHOPS:

BRISTOL: Southey House, Wine Street, Bristol, BS1 1BH. Tel: 0272 631201.

BIRMINGHAM: 258 Broad Street, Birmingham, B1 2HE. Tel: 021 643 3740.

LONDON: 49 High Holborn, London, WC1V 6HB. Tel: 071 873 9090.

MANCHESTER: 9-21 Princess Street, Manchester, M60 8AS. Tel: 061 681 1191.

NORTHERN IRELAND: 80 Chichester Street, Belfast, BT1 4JY. Tel: 0232 238451

SCOTLAND: (Agent) John Smith and Son (Glasgow) Ltd, 59 St Vincent Street, Glasgow, G2. Tel: 041 221 7472.

FAMILY EXPENDITURE SURVEYS (FES) Published by HMSO or available from your local library it will tell you who spends how much on what.

Tax

Leaflets from any Tax Office or Tax Enquiry Centre are free. Look under Inland Revenue in your local phone directory. Offices are open between 10 a.m. and 4 p.m. Social Security leaflets are

available and are free (up to 5) from your local Social Security Office, listed under Social Security or Health and Social Security in your local phone directory.
Leaflet No:

IR28	*Tax and Your Business – Starting in Business.*
IR56/N139	*Employed or Self-Employed?*
IR57	*Thinking of Working for Yourself?*
FB 30	*Self-Employed?*

Chapter information Sources
Inland Revenue; Enterprise Agencies; Citizens Advice Bureau; LiveWire; Department of Social Security; Department of Employment; Small Firms Information Centre; *You and Your Rights*, Readers' Digest.

CHAPTER 3

You, Your Company and the Law

YOUR COMPANY
You have three options regarding how you want to trade: partnership, sole trader or a limited company. Before you start you should consider which one is right for you, your business and your business circumstances. All three of them can employ other people. Listed below are the differences between them.

PARTNERSHIPS – LEGAL REQUIREMENTS
A partnership has to consist of two people or more (there is no limit to how many more). You don't have to go through any legal formalities to start up a partnership, but it would probably be wise to draw up a partnership agreement, which is legally binding and which says what will happen if the business fails or one partner wants to leave. In addition, it points out the general rights and responsibilities of each of the partners, then if disagreements should start everyone knows their position. It is better to do it right at the beginning using a solicitor. You will have to pay for this, but it's a worthwhile investment in the long term. It's perhaps even more important to have a proper agreement if your partner is a friend, for it is then easier to separate the friendship from the business relationship. To take up less of the solicitor's time and therefore lessen his bill, sort out any finances between yourselves before you start. (**See page 79 this Chapter**.)

It is a legal requirement, if you are registered schedule D, to submit audited accounts. The Inland Revenue will send you an estimated assessment if you haven't submitted accounts, and if this happens you cannot appeal or ask for estimated figures to be reduced – you will have to pay the estimated amount.

As a partnership you can trade under your own name or the name of the individual partners or under a trading name. If you decide to use a trading name the partners' names and the business address must be shown on all business stationery and displayed on the business premises.

Each partner is personally liable for any debts that the business might incur, but if one of the partners doesn't pay his or her share of the debt then the other partners will have to. In a partnership you personally can be made bankrupt.

If a partner leaves a partnership or dies
If a partner leaves the business, the parting should be done so in accordance with the partnership agreement, presuming there is one. If there is either no partnership agreement, or the partner chooses not to follow it, then the remaining partner should seek advice from a solicitor. If you are left as the sole remaining partner, the partnership will have to be dissolved, unless a new partner can be found.

The remaining partner or partners will be liable for any debts incurred by the partner who has left. If this happens you should see a solicitor for advice.

If a partner dies, the partnership may have to be dissolved, and the estate may be liable for any business debts.

SOLE TRADER
Running it on your own is the simplest way to start a business. There are no legal formalities involved in starting up or stopping. You aren't required to have accounts audited, although you must produce accurate accounts that show the true state of the business.

You can trade under your own name or use a trade name. If you decide to use a trade name then your own name as the owner of the business has to be shown on all stationery and displayed on the business premises.

Being a sole trader means that you are liable for any debts that the business might incur and you will have to use any assets that you have, such as your house, to pay off any business debts. If the business fails then you can be made bankrupt. In other words *you* carry any success and any failure. The buck stops with you. Being a sole trader means it isn't always easy to persuade banks to lend you money for your business. You can employ other people.

LIMITED COMPANY
A limited company exists independently of the people involved. It has its own accounts, can own things itself, pay its own debts and be sued in its own name.

Limited companies are seen by banks and clients as having a higher business status than sole traders or partnerships and for this reason being a limited company can make it easier when it comes to raising money for your business. But forming a limited company can be a very long and expensive procedure and you will need the help of an accountant (**See page 109 Chapter 4 you and Your Money**) and a solicitor (**See page 96 this Chapter**). To begin with you have to register details of the company and the directors with the Companies Registration Office (Registration of Companies and Friendly Societies, in Northern Ireland). Once you have started trading, the details of the company directors and a copy of the audited accounts must be sent annually to Companies House. The company's trading name will usually include the word 'limited' and the registered name of the company, place of registration and registration number must all be shown on all business stationery, along with the business address. If it shows the names of any of the directors then it must show the names of all of them.

Forming a limited company must involve at least two people. Each person buys shares and is known as a shareholder. An ordinary share represents an interest by an individual of their worth in that limited company. The cost of the shares can be quite small, but you will need a solicitor to advise you on what the cost should be. Two of the shareholders act as director and company secretary respectively and they keep the necessary legal records. An ordinary shareholder who is not involved in running the company will only be liable to pay for shares and not any debts the company may have. The shareholders can be clients, friends, your accountant or people who know about the business and are interested in its success. A director will be liable for the company's debts if the company has carried on trading when they knew, or ought to have known, that they were insolvent.

Directors and employees are taxed under PAYE and pay Class 1 National Insurance contributions.

If a director leaves a limited company
If a director or office-holder in a limited company wants to leave, the business can carry on. But if you are left as the sole remaining shareholder, you will need to replace the person who is leaving. A solicitor or an accountant may be willing to take this position or help you to find a replacement. You will have to go through certain formalities such as changing company records at

Companies House (Companies Registrar in Northern Ireland) and for this you will need to see either a solicitor or an accountant.

BECOMING AN EMPLOYER
There may be certain aspects of your business which you decided you don't have the knowledge or talent to do, or maybe as your business grows and thrives you aren't able to keep pace with demand. Either way, after considering your profit margins you may decide to employ other people, either on your premises or theirs. When you become an employer there are certain minimum legal requirements with which you must comply.

* Provide working conditions that comply with Health and Safety regulations **(See page 93 this Chapter)**.
* Not discriminate on grounds of sex or race.
* Pay statutory sick pay and maternity pay.
* Comply with dismissal and redundancy procedures. Give required notice.
* Pay employees' tax and National Insurance through PAYE **(See page 149 Chapter 5 Tax, Insurance and Pensions)**.
* Not unfairly dismiss.
* Give people time off for public duties, i.e. jury service.
* Pay wages in line with certain wages council and trades union agreements **(See page 179 Chapter 6 Teleworkers and Outworkers)**.

CONTRACTS
If you work from home as a freelance you will inevitably have to negotiate a contract between you and the company who is going to produce or buy your product. Contracts all have a similar structure, but the details will vary depending on what you do and who you sell it to. You may sell all your rights for ever, or you may decide only to assign a licence to exploit your work for a specific length of time in certain markets or territories.

What you should aim for is always to have a contract for a job, however small, which you and your employer have agreed and signed. You should not start any work until that has been done, however tight their deadline, however much they try to persuade you to start, sometimes by telling you that their contract is in the post. If they really want you they'll draw up a contract in a matter of hours and you can agree it on the phone. Using the ordinary post, if you don't have a fax, the contract can be on your doormat the following morning and you can sign it and send it back by return. If you are unsure about the wording of a contract show it to a solicitor, but a contract for a small freelance job should be fairly straightforward.

A contract basically defines an employer's and an employee's obligations to one another. For example, that the employee has agreed to carry out the work specified by the employer for an agreed sum starting and finishing on an agreed date. If it is a job that is spread out over a period of time, rather than being paid when the job is finished, your cash flow would be better if you agreed or suggested staged payments. This would mean that an agreed amount of money would be paid to you on signature of the contract, and other agreed amounts paid at significant stages in the work.

You may decide to accept a lump sum buy-out or a royalty.

Royalties
A royalty means that you would have an amount of money, generally fairly small, trickling in over the years. In some jobs where you are creating a product such as designing jewellery, ceramics, or creating a concept, it may be normal for you to receive a 2 per cent to 5 per cent 'royalty' (i.e. payment) of the manufacturer's sales invoice – not the shop price. The amount of the royalty is generally established through bartering. There are no set rules, but it can be helpful if you know someone working in the same field who is already receiving a royalty, to get some guidelines. In something like publishing a general writer (not getting into the nuances of illustrated and academic books here) usually gets about 7½ to 10 per cent of the cover price, which is the shop price.

Brian thinks that working on your own is fraught with danger, if you're like him as he describes himself – naïve and useless business-wise. He decided to take a stand at a gift show to exhibit his pieces of pottery. A man asked him to make a small range and it took off at a terrific rate; 'I was on a basic royalty. If it sold I got some money. Although I had a contract, I made the vital mistake of reading it but not understanding it. I have no business experience, and anyway this man and I were mates so I thought it was OK. You don't think anyone's trying to trick you and as it was only a draft contract, I thought things would be ironed out in the real thing. So I signed it. There never was another contract.'

Two years later Brian made a limited edition. The man and he argued about the price. 'It turned very nasty. He threatened that if I didn't hand over the piece he would stop my royalties and that if I took him to court it would take me two years and cost me £30,000. I sold it to him eventually for cash, enough to keep me happy, but not the amount the piece was worth.' Brian thinks that provincial solicitors don't seem to have any idea about business contracts: 'They're just used to doing conveyancing.'

If you have already assigned your copyright to an employer in an existing contract, you may not be able to gain further benefits. If you are self-employed with an original idea, the terms of the contract in which you assign your rights to a manufacturer or distributor are very important.

If you know that you are not very good at 'pulling deals' then you should find yourself an agent or solicitor to negotiate the terms of your contract. It is an agent's business to know the going rate in one particular field and therefore to be able to negotiate within that. They also spend their time building up contacts here and abroad and because they work on the basis of commission from the deal it is also to their advantage not only to secure a deal, but to make sure it is financially beneficial to both of you. You will need an agent only if you are working as a freelance.

Below are some examples of simplified contracts showing the basic sections they will contain on the left and negotiating points on the right. Let the company that you are going to negotiate with draw up the contract, but remember that no two contracts are alike, even if the businesses are similar.

General contract terms when you sell all your rights
(*not all clauses may apply to your business*)

NAME: *You* . . . agree to license NAME: *They* . . . to exploit your work on the following terms:	*Negotiating points*
1. You warrant that YOU own the rights.	
2. They agree to buy YOU out completely for a fixed amount, or unit price for agreed no. of copies.	HOW MUCH?

3. They may require non-competition agreement, or other conditions.   WHAT CONDITIONS?

General Contract Terms when you assign your Copyright for a royalty
(*not all clauses may apply to your business*)

Negotiating Points

NAME: *You* ... agree to license
NAME: *They* ... to exploit your work on the following terms:

1. You warrant that YOU own the right
2. You will be paid a royalty on the invoiced sales, or in the case of a book, the cover price.   HOW BIG A PERCENTAGE?
   YOU may be able to negotiate an advance of money.   HOW MUCH?
3. The licence will run for a period of time with an option to renew for a further period before reversion to you.   OVER HOW MANY YEARS?
4. The licence covers defined markets or exclusivity (if appropriate):
   e.g. Children's, adult, retail, wholesale, books, films, TV video, syndication.   WHICH?
5. The licence covers defined territories, (if appropriate):
   e.g. the World or UK, Europe, USA and its dependencies. Rest of the world.   WHICH?

6. You will be given copies of your work if it is manufactured. — HOW MANY?
7. You may be eligible for repeat fees.
   e.g. actors, musicians, producers. — HOW ARE THEY APPROPRIATE?
8. You may grant THEM exclusivity, or you may keep it for yourself if you are in a strong position. — WHICH?
9. You will withdraw your exclusivity if THEY fail to achieve sales or royalties of an agreed amount per year. — HOW MUCH?
10. Performance and delivery criteria: you agree, health permitting, to produce defined works, in requisite time period. — CRITERIA?
    They agree to promote it adequately. — DEFINITION?
11. You have the right to inspect their sales records.
12. They agree not to alter your work without your permission and consult you on items like promotion. — WHICH?

You should make a general rule that every job you do has a contract. But there are exceptions where this doesn't apply, such as small one-off jobs, or designing a poster, making someone a dress for a special occasion, or preparing a dinner for two. A contract doesn't have to be written down to be legally binding. The spoken word is enough to make most contracts enforceable in law. But whenever possible it is easier to have a contract in writing. For larger jobs, having a contract gives you something to fall back on if disagreements should arise. Even if you are being employed by a friend or someone you have worked for previously you'll still need a contract, because very often people's financial situations and priorities change when they are running a business or working for themselves. Friendships or previous working relationships (it may be a someone who was a colleague in a previous employment situation who has now branched out on their own) should be excluded in business negotiations.

FINDING THE RIGHT SOLICITOR
It is important to find a solicitor who is used to dealing with small businesses. You may find one who is willing to take you on, but does not have much experience in commercial law. Solicitors are becoming more specialised, so don't assume that they cover all areas of business. You may need to find different solicitors to work for you in different ways. To find a solicitor to suit your needs, go to one of the following:
Local Enterprise Agency.
Small Firms Service.
Local Authority or Economic Development unit.
Small Business Section.
Word of mouth recommendation.
Other small traders.
Chamber of Commerce.
Your local Public Library.

Seeing a solicitor
Before you go to see a solicitor you should work out exactly what information or help you need. Find out the cost and fee structure before you begin, for there is no fixed scale. You are entitled to ask for an estimate before giving instructions. The amount you will be charged is between you and the solicitor. A solicitor is entitled to be paid for all the work he or she does, including telephone calls and letters, based on the length of time it takes. Between £50 and £100 per hour is quite normal. You must let the solicitor know whether you are seeking help under the legal aid or legal advice scheme. If not, and you simply want advice, you may be able to be seen under the fixed fee scheme which some solicitors offer, for which the rate in 1991 was £5 for up to thirty minutes.

How a solicitor can help
A solicitor can help by:
Giving advice about trading status, i.e. the advantages and disadvantages of setting up a partnership.

Drawing up agreements to a partnership or limited company (**See pages 71 and 73 this Chapter**).
Giving advice about employing staff (**See page 153 Chapter 5 Tax, Insurance and Pensions**).
Giving advice about commercial contracts (**See page 76 this Chapter**).
Giving help in recovering money owed (**See page 127 Chapter 4 You and Your Money**).
Giving advice about stopping trading.

Lawyers scheme
The Law Society of England and Wales have set up a Lawyers for Enterprise Scheme. Solicitors who are taking part will provide a short, free, initial interview, working through a check-list of the general points to consider when you are either setting up or running a business. The solicitor will explain what further legal work may be needed and his charges for doing this. The check-list is set out in a leaflet.

Solicitors who are in the scheme are not required to show that they have experience of advising small firms. (For further information **See page 76 this Chapter**.)

Legal aid
If you are involved in either a criminal case (a criminal offence is one which harms public interests and is usually prosecuted by the state) or a civil case (a civil case is a dispute between individual parties, one of which is trying to obtain benefit for itself), you can often get financial assistance to help pay the court costs and legal fees under the Legal Aid scheme.

If you are involved in a court case and think you don't have enough money to pay the legal costs, you can apply for legal aid, either to the magistrates' court or to the Legal Aid Board legal office. The rules used for working out whether or not you will qualify are similar for both civil and criminal cases.

You will have to be means tested on two grounds – first to establish how much disposable income you have, i.e. the amount of spare cash left over after specified living costs have been paid. If that falls below a set limit, then you qualify for legal aid, subject to the second test, which is to establish the size of your disposable capital assets. If that figure falls below a certain limit then you qualify for legal aid, although you may be asked to pay part of the legal costs.

To apply for legal aid in a civil case, get a form from a solicitor's office or Citizens Advice Bureau. In a criminal case you get the form from a magistrates' court.

Neighbourhood law centres
You can go to a neighbourhood Law Centre for free legal advice. You may sometimes be asked to make a contribution towards the costs. Financed by local funds and staffed by legally qualified people, including solicitors, they usually take up cases involving immigration, housing, employment, social security problems. If they decide to take up your case it will be handled in exactly the same way as a private solicitor would do. Look in your local telephone directory or Yellow Pages for your local branch.

Legal advice centres
These give help or advice only for cases not involving court work. They are staffed by qualified lawyers who are volunteers. Because they attend on a rota basis you may find it difficult to see the same person twice.

Trade unions (See also page 183 Chapter 6 Teleworkers and Outworkers)
A number of Trade Unions provide legal services for their members, and may have either a lawyer on the staff or have the services of one on a consultation basis. Trade Unions mostly help with employment problems. Increasing casualisation has put pressure on many Unions to provide better and more services for outworkers, so it is worth contacting your Union over such problems as non-payment of invoices: they may be able and willing to represent you to the employer. Contact your local Citizens Advice Bureau for further information or contact your Trade Union direct.

CAB
Your local Citizens Advice Bureau will also give advice on all sorts of legal problems at no charge, whatever the enquirer's means. There are more than 700 CAB offices around the country, staffed mainly by trained volunteers, but with some professional full-time workers, including lawyers, in the larger cities. They will

also have detailed information on which solicitors in their area specialise.

LEGAL PROTECTION OF TRADEMARKS, REGISTERED DESIGNS, COPYRIGHTS AND PATENTS

All good ideas have to be protected against being stolen or copied. If you have a good idea which you think is marketable and original, there are various procedures which you can go through to protect it. These procedures vary according to the type of idea or product that you want to protect. Only paintings, photographs, drawings or artworks which are 'finished products' are protected commercially by copyright and can't be photocopied or reproduced for sale without your permission.

Trademarks and service marks

The registration of a trademark or trade name is intended to protect a reputation. A service mark or trademark also stops a supplier of the same type of goods from using the same registered name or emblem. Since 1 October 1986 service marks can also be registered. Service marks allow the supplier of a service to distinguish their service from others. For example if someone offering a service, who is not manufacturing a product – such as a solicitor – has a logo, it can be registered as a service mark. But neither service marks nor trademarks can prevent someone from copying the goods or providing a similar service: to do that you would have to apply for a patent or copyright. However, it can prevent someone from using your service mark and therefore pretending to be you. The design or word must be distinctive and original, it must not look similar to any other. If it includes a red cross, military badge, arms, crests, armorial bearings or a portrait of the royal family it will be rejected. Common words of praise, such as 'splendid', 'superb' or 'perfection' cannot be registered, as others may legitimately want to use them to describe their products. The registry will refuse a trademark if its use might be dangerous, for example if a poisonous disinfectant is given a trade name that makes it sound as if it is a delicious drink.

You cannot use public figures, such as pop singers or sports stars to promote your product without their permission. The same applies to titles of films, books, plays or songs and any characters involved. In most cases a film or television company will own the copyright for their films and shows and they sometimes register the names of shows or cartoon characters as trademarks.

The best way to get a trade or service mark is through a Patent Agent (**See page 84 this Chapter**). It will cost you about £300 and will last indefinitely, providing you pay the occasional renewal fees.

Registered designs
The law says that registered designs are concerned with the outward appearance of articles of manufacture which depend solely on aesthetic considerations, not on function. Objects such as wallpaper, a lamp or a deck-chair could have their designs registered. But if you have already been selling your deck-chair at the local garden centre it will have had its novelty exposed to the public and, as with patents, it can no longer be registered. You will still have the copyright in the original design drawings, but if someone looks at them, or at your deck-chair and goes away and makes their own copy of it, you cannot stop them, because it should have been a registered design before you put it on public display. To file an application you have to have clear representations or specimens of the design, including a statement of novelty which is its 'shape', 'configuration', 'pattern', or 'ornament'. Protection is renewable every five years for a maximum of twenty-five years after the drawing, or ten years after the date the article was first sold. After the first five years others may demand a licence to copy your design, provided you have reached an agreement on the amount of royalty payable. If necessary the amount is determined through a procedure controlled by the Patent Office (**See page 84 this Chapter**).

The best way to register a design is through a Patent Agent. It will cost you about £300 and the procedure will take a few months. (**See also Unregistered Designs page 86 this Chapter**).

Potential rights of protection you will have to establish
If you have invented something or want to register a design or trade name, you have to check first that nobody else has already thought of it. You should contact the Patent Office for their helpful DIY guide to patents (**See Help Section this Chapter**). If you decide your idea is worth pursuing, you should go to a patent agent (**See below**). This means paying a fee, but taking out a patent is a legal procedure involving potentially valuable property

rights which can become quite complex.

Once protection has been confirmed, if you discover that someone is pirating your idea you will have to try and negotiate with them to pay you damages. If that fails, you have the right to fight them in court, but beware: this can be both costly and lengthy. However, if you win you will be awarded costs, which means your opponent will have to pay your legal fees.

In practical terms the best thing about registering your claim is that anyone who comes along later is likely to be put off by the hassle of competition. If they are really interested they might offer you a licence to manufacture your idea and pay you royalties. This is good because it means that you go on getting paid over the commercial life of your idea, even though you spent the time creating it once only.

The advantage of registering a trade name or design is that it is protected from anyone copying or stealing it.

Patents
If you have invented a new device, such as a machine or an industrial process, you should apply for a patent because it will prevent anyone from copying it, as well as giving you the sole rights for twenty years to manufacture, use or commercially exploit. But this applies only if your invention is completely new. Modest improvements to something can be patented, but the new feature must be more than just an obvious development, or a simple combination of known parts. Your new concept must also involve an 'innovative step' which gives it clear advantage over what is already known. It must belong to you and not have been made known publicly by you or anyone else. You cannot patent something that is already in the public domain.

You do not need a patent in order to put your invention into practice, but if you decide not to apply for a patent and then someone else hits on the same invention they may be able to obtain a patent for it.

You shouldn't try to draft a patent specification on your own because it is a legal document and drafting one requires skill and experience. It is vitally important that its contents are correct because these will determine whether or not you will be granted a patent. For this reason you should employ a member of the Institute of Patent Agents (**See Help Section this Chapter for address and phone number**), not only because they have the required knowledge, but because you can also freely discuss with them, in confidence, your invention and they will give you their experienced opinion as to the feasibility and commercial exploitation of your invention, plus advice on how to go about setting it up.

To obtain a patent you have to pay a fee for filing, preliminary examination, search and substantive examination. If you are granted a patent, then you will have to pay an annual renewal fee to keep it enforced.

You may be unsure about whether your invention is going to be commercially profitable, because if it isn't, then it's not worth your time and money obtaining protection for it. Without revealing what you are working on, it may be wise to carry out some market research on similar ideas so that you know what their design and costs are. Get a copy of *The Organisation Book*, issued by the Market Research Society which lists members and their specialisations (**See Help Section this Chapter**).

If you are still unsure about continuing, you don't have to pay the official fee at the outset. You can start the process of getting a patent by giving a full description of your invention, together with the filing fee and the request for a patent, and you can then decide before the fee is due whether or not to continue. This is known as Patent Pending.

Patent Pending
Patent Pending confirms your title to your idea from the date which you filed your application, and it prevents anyone else from having the same idea protected. You will have a year to test how good your product is and to show its potential to customers. The use of Patent Pending arises when you may still not know if your idea is commercially viable and you may want to discover more about it. Or you may think that it's commercially viable but you need financial backing. Or your idea may still be in the early planning stages and you haven't yet completed its technical features, which means you may need to do more development work before you can decide on whether you want to go ahead and pay all the fees to get a full patent. In situations like these, you can use the patent system to establish fairly cheaply a priority date for your invention. The 'filing date' on which you disclose your invention for the first time in connection with a properly filed application for a patent is termed its 'priority date'. The point of

this is to give your disclosure priority in relation to any other patent for the same invention which has a later priority date.

If you abandon your first application and refile it later, you do run the risk that someone else has filed an application after your first date. By refiling you lose your date and someone else may have an application of an earlier date than you. Be aware that you are required to file claims and have a Patent Office search within twelve months of filing and the application published after eighteen months unless it is withdrawn.

If you file an application for a patent and do not keep it secret, for example you tell a potential customer without a confidentiality agreement, then you cannot refile the case. Within twelve months of the original filing date you will have to decide whether or not you are going to continue. If you don't, your own disclosure will be a bar to patenting the same idea later. The problem with having a Patent Pending is that you will not yet have done a search, so someone could have thought of your idea ahead of you. But if you have done your research properly at the beginning, then you should know if anyone else is selling your idea as a commercial product.

If you get a good response from your test marketing (**See Chapter 7 Selling and Marketing**), it should give you the confidence to have the other patents searched, and as long as your invention remains unique you will be granted one. If you are unlucky and someone else does already hold the patent, you could try to salvage the situation by offering to market their idea through your sales outlets.

Cost of obtaining a patent
You will have to pay fees to your Patent Agent and registration fees to the Patent Office as already stated. There is a further fee if you want a foreign patent. An initial British patent application will cost you a few hundred pounds, but by the time a full patent has been granted it will have cost you upwards of £1,500. Further government fees of about £3,000 over twenty years will have to be paid to keep the patent in force.

Unregistered designs
The principles are similar to copyright and are to provide protection for products which are designed to have a practical function, for example an electric plug made from a design drawing. Without

registration you automatically have the right to sue if your design is copied. There is no design right for methods of construction, or for surface decoration. The right lasts fifteen years from the date of the drawing or ten years from the date of the first sale.

Copyright

Basic copyright law is in the Copyright Act 1988.

Copyright need not be registered in the UK because by the very act of writing, composing or designing you automatically have the copyright in the manuscript, musical score or plans of an object in two dimensions. If you have designed a three-dimensional object such as a chair, you may have unregistered design rights or be best protected by a design registration. If you invent a computer game or computer program they too are covered.

No registration or other formalities are required in order to be protected by the Copyright Act, but there have been cases of dispute over originality or authorship of a piece of work. To avoid those situations, it may be helpful to have some evidence of when it was created. In order to do this you can either lodge the manuscript, tape or whatever in a safe place, either with your bank or solicitor, making sure it is dated and that you have a receipt for it. You can also post a copy of the work to yourself in a registered envelope and leave it unopened, or you can register it for a small fee with:

The Registrar, 7 Stone Buildings, Lincoln's Inn, London, WC2A 3SZ.

Copyright belongs to the author of the work. For published works copyright lasts for fifty years from the end of the year of publication, or the death of the author, whichever is later. With unpublished works the copyright lasts for ever.

If you work for someone, who owns your copyright?

A lot of people who are working from home are not working on a great invention or running their own small business, but are working for a company who are producing their creation. The question is who actually owns that creation? The answer lies in the contract. If you are being paid a salary, the company paying you generally owns the rights to your work. If you are being paid a fee per item, you can choose if you want to sell some or all of the rights of your copyright, which means you will be paid royalties on sales **(See page 75 this Chapter)**.

If you have chosen to keep your copyright, the company can only exploit your concept when you have both agreed conditions, or royalties, for the specific products in defined markets. This is one of the most contentious areas of contracts and it is vital that you understand your contract. The manufacturer is naturally hoping to pay you as little as possible so that he will get the maximum profit. For example, if you are designing something that a lot of other people are designing, you don't have a lot of leverage to negotiate because the manufacturer can simply go elsewhere. It is likely that unless you agree to a 'one off' fee you won't get any more work. But if you are a designer with a unique style which is in demand, you can name your own price. You will probably keep some of the rights for an agent to exploit in different markets at home and abroad. That is how the creators of the cartoon cat Garfield, for instance, can have it reproduced in books, films, on merchandise or as cuddly toys around the world.

BAD DEBTS AND THE LAW

When you run your own business you have to chase your own debts and you may find that there are occasions when you seem to have to spend more time and energy chasing payment than you did supplying the product or doing the job. Getting paid, or not getting paid is one of the most common problems for people who work for themselves and because of the cost, legal recourse is the last resort **(See page 128 Chapter 4 You and Your Money)**.

To try to avoid debts you have to keep a regular check on who owes you money and evolve a system for chasing them up. Perhaps you could put aside one morning a week for dealing with the debts. It's more constructive than spending nights worrying about them. The first thing you should do in credit control is to send out a statement invoice or account at the end of the month as a reminder of how much you are owed. Unfortunately it will probably go to the bottom of the pile, along with all the others, so you have to follow it up a few days later with a firm, positive phone call, visit or fax. It's more effective to be friendly than aggressive and explain that you have cash flow problems.

If you don't get any response, the next step is a letter from your solicitor or a debt-collecting agency, but you will have to pay for their services, so the decision you have to make before you set out on this path is whether or not the amount you are owed is large enough, once you have deducted any fees. You need to be owed a reasonable amount to make a visit to a solicitor worthwhile. You'll find that generally the *threat* of legal action will bring results. For instance, you might agree to payment by instalments or to making a slight reduction in the debt.

Factoring
Outstanding bills owed to a business can be sold to someone else who will collect them. This method is called factoring. If you sell your outstanding bills you will not be paid the amount that they are worth. But factoring does achieve two things; it removes the pressure from you having to collect the debt and it gives you some money instantly if you are having serious cash flow problems. But obviously it isn't really a good idea because you do not receive anywhere near the amount you are owed. If you are going to use either a debt-collecting or factoring agent, you should first consult either a solicitor or an accountant, because it can be complicated and varies with each case. There are no hard and fast rules.

The small claims court
A small claim is one settled in a County Court by arbitration. The whole idea is that it is resolved in one hearing before a registrar and if both parties are present there is no appeal. Under the new law, claims settled in this way are for £1,000 or less. You do not need a solicitor or a barrister. Either you as an individual or as a limited company can use this system when it comes to obtaining payment for:
1. Claims for payment of debt, whether for goods sold, work done or money lent.
2. Claims arising out of the sale of goods, including the repair of damaged goods, failure to supply goods ordered or supplying the wrong article or defective ones.
3. Claims against people providing consumer services, such as garages, dry-cleaners, repairs of electrical and other goods, in respect of faulty workmanship or failure to do the work that was agreed.
4. Claims for possession of property, arrears of rent, return of deposits or other disputes between landlord and tenant. (With the possible exception of claims for rent arrears, the return of deposits or for possession of furnished premises, it is advisable to obtain legal advice before starting proceedings of your own.)
5. Claims for damages caused by negligence, such as a claim

arising out of a road accident. These are usually covered by insurance, except where the amount is less than the excess on a policy, the insured has only third party cover or does not want to risk his 'no claims' bonus.

If you decide to go ahead, go to your nearest County Court, where you can collect the relevant forms. Court staff will help you through the procedure. (If you have difficulty in completing the forms the Citizen Advice Bureau or a Consumer Advice Centre will help.)

You will have to pay a fee to start your claim, the amount depending on the amount that you are claiming. Court staff will be able to tell you how much that is and it will be added to the money you are already owed.

Also be aware that a case can be brought against you for non-payment of debts in just the same way, so don't just keep a check on the money that is owed to you; make sure you have paid what you owe.

Enforcing payment

A defendant has fourteen days, from the day they receive the summons, to return the reply form. If they do not you can ask the court to send the defendant an order to pay the money you are owed. This is called 'entering a judgement by default'.

If you win a case in the small claims court you, not the court, are responsible for enforcing the order. You probably know better than the court what assets your debtor has. After all you should have thought about whether he had the means to pay the amount you claimed before you issued the summons, because no method of enforcement will succeed if the person who owes you money either hasn't got any or has no assets or goods worth selling. To help you to decide whether the debtor is worth pursuing further, it may be helpful to know if they have had any other county court judgements registered against them. All judgements where £10 or more is outstanding one month after the date of the judgement are registered at: Registry Trust Ltd, 173–175 Cleveland Street, London, W1P 5PE. Tel: 071 380 0133.

Anyone can call at the registry or write asking for a search to be done, setting out the name and address of the debtor and enclosing the fee. If the debtor fails to pay the judgement debt he owes you within a month, his name will be registered and will remain on the register for six years.

There are a number of ways without the use of a solicitor that you can enforce payment: via the County Court, a Warrant of Execution, Attachment of Earnings, Garnishee, Charging Order or, Receiver by Way of Equitable Execution. For all of these the County Court can levy a small fee.

Warrant of execution
County Court fee: 15p for every £1 or part thereof of the amount for which the warrant is issued.
Minimum fee £7.50; maximum fee £38.
This is an order directed to the bailiff to seize and sell sufficient of the debtor's goods in order to recover the money due to you under the judgement.

Attachment of earnings
County Court fee: 10p for every £1 or part thereof claimed.
Minimum fee £5; maximum fee £40.
This is an order to a debtor's employer to deduct a sum of money on each pay day from the debtor's wages.

Garnishee
County Court fee: on entering garnishee proceedings £12.
This is an order directed to anyone who owes the debtor money. The order requires them to pay the money they owe to the court. This method is most commonly used against a debtor's bank account and may be useful where previous payments passing between parties or information shows that a bank account exists. It is useful where the debtor is either in business or a self-employed person.

Charging order
County Court fee: on application for an order charging land securities £12.
This is an order preventing the debtor from selling his land or securities (bonds, stocks and shares) without paying what he owes you. Such an order may be useful where the debtor has no earnings or assets apart from his home. If the court agrees, the order can be further enforced by ordering the debtor to sell the land or securities to pay off the debt. This is a matter for the court's discretion. The court is unlikely to order the sale of valuable property or a family home to pay off a small debt, but a charging

order may be useful if it is known that the debtor's house is for sale.

Receiver by way of equitable execution
This has to be heard in the High Court or a County Court that has bankruptcy jurisdiction; not all County Courts have this so contact your local County Court for details. If the debtor is in receipt of money, for example a landlord who receives rent on property he owns, the court can appoint a receiver to collect the money on your behalf.

Once you have chosen which way you are going to enforce payment, the County Court will provide you with the relevant information and booklets (**See Help Section this Chapter**).

When your opponent becomes bankrupt
You can ask a court to make a debtor bankrupt only if the debt exceeds £750. But before you do this you must first of all decide whether or not they have the funds to repay you and if there are other creditors that have to be paid first, otherwise you are simply chasing shadows and wasting your valuable time and energy for possibly no financial return.

Secondly, making someone bankrupt can be expensive as you will probably require legal help and even then it doesn't guarantee that you'll get the money owed to you. If someone is bankrupt, creditors are paid in the following order:

* Secured creditors can be the bank or building society who have lent money against the debtor's house; they receive their security first. If the debt is not fully repaid the remainder becomes an unsecured loan.
* The costs and expenses of the official receiver, trustee and court fees.
* Pre-preferential debts. These include funeral expenses and executors' fees if the person dies before the estate is distributed.
* Preferential debts: tax on the previous year's earnings, VAT due over the previous six months, National Insurance for the previous year's contributions, wages owed to employees, occupational pensions contributions owed to employees.
* Then the payment of any other debts, which probably means you.

If you want to find out if a debtor is already bankrupt either telephone the court that is dealing with the case, if you know where it is; or employ a search agent to do it for you; or, if you have the time, you can visit the Bankruptcy Search Room, Room D9, Official Receiver's London Offices, Atlantic House, Holborn Viaduct, London EC1.

HEALTH AND SAFETY AND THE LAW

Under the 1974 Health and Safety Act, employers are responsible for the substances and any machinery that they send to their outworkers. Employers must make sure that any equipment and materials are safe and that there are instructions on how to use them safely.

Whether you are self-employed or an outworker it is important when you are working from home to be aware of health and safety. Be sure that when you're working you always have good ventilation, such as an open window, especially if you are working with chemicals or fibres. Most glues, varnishes and solvents give off fumes which can easily catch fire, so don't smoke. Be aware that fumes can cause headaches, sickness and allergies, while dust and fabric fibres can cause breathing difficulties. Keep all food covered and if possible try not to work in the kitchen or dining area, unless of course you are working with food. You should always wear an overall which has close-fitting sleeves. If you work with chemicals, your employer should have given them to you in labelled jars with tight-fitting lids and told you how to handle them safely if they're dangerous. If you're working with machinery, make sure it is properly mounted to stop vibrations and noise and keep it well out of the reach of children. Ask the company you are working for to service or replace any noisy machinery.

Food and hygiene

It's becoming more and more popular for self-employed people to start up their own catering or sandwich-making business because everyone has a family kitchen. But the scenario usually works out something like this. Someone with a catering background, or a cooking enthusiast, prepares a meal for a friend's dinner party. It is so successful that the friend asks them to cater for their wedding. But what the cook discovers is that there is a big difference in hygiene terms between catering for a dinner party for six and a wedding for two hundred. Research shows that many cases of infected food come from small self-catering businesses.

Before you consider starting a catering business or producing food of any kind, you should contact your local Environmental Services Officer, usually to be found at your local Town Hall, and ask for details about the Food and Hygiene regulations. You should also ask them to visit your kitchen or food preparation area so that you can discuss what their requirements will be and estimate the cost, e.g. necessary floor covering, separate handbasins, tiled walls etc. Judy hadn't realised that running her sandwich-making business from her own kitchen at home would mean her having to comply with such strict regulations, 'I'm having problems with the Health and Hygiene Officer. I thought he would just want to see it was all clean, but he said there mustn't be any wooden surfaces, not even a wooden chopping board. I had to get laminated or scratch-free surfaces. Then I was told I had to have a separate sink installed for hand washing, that's separate from the food, and no carpet on the floor, it has to be lino. I'm beginning to wonder if the business is worth it just for a few sandwiches, but they've implied that these things have to be done right away. I don't know if I'll bother, I mean, I don't want the place to look like a McDonald's.'

Hygiene regulations under the Food Safety Act (**See page 105 Help Section this Chapter**) are administered by the local council and cover all places where food is prepared or sold for human consumption. It is a criminal offence for a shop, stall or restaurant not to comply with the regulations. The maximum penalty in a Magistrates' Court is a fine of £2,000 and in a Crown Court a fine or two years imprisonment or both.

The Regulations

* Premises must be clean and sanitary and free from vermin and insects.
* Clean handbasins and lavatories must be available to staff. They must have adequate supplies of soap, nailbrushes and clean towels.
* Staff must not smoke or spit while handling food.
* Any open injury, e.g. a cut finger, must be covered with a waterproof dressing while staff are handling food.
* Unwrapped food, other than vegetables, must be displayed at least 18 inches from the floor.

YOU, YOUR COMPANY AND THE LAW

Because of the recent concern about food poisoning caused by Listeria and Salmonella, there has been a tightening of food safety regulations and an introduction of new food legislation. The Food Safety Act 1990 provides local authorities with increased powers to deal with food safety matters and stiffer penalties for offenders.

Food Safety Act 1990
Under the new Act all premises used for the purposes of a food business, as well as where any vehicles which are used for selling or transporting food are normally kept, must be registered with the local authority. There is no fee for registration. When it comes to the construction of a food preparation area or premises, even your own kitchen at home, all have to comply with the following:

* All floors, walls and ceilings must be smooth and impervious (so that water cannot soak through it and it can be wiped clean easily).
* Walls: Vinyl emulsion on smooth plaster or ceramic tiles. Tiles must be used behind work surfaces and equipment so that they can easily be wiped clean.
* Floors: Heavy-duty vinyl sealed to the wall at the edges so that there are no dust traps.
* Pipework, wiring, etc. should be enclosed in ducting to make cleaning easy.
* Large pieces of equipment should be on rollers so that they can be moved easily for cleaning. Metal shelving is best, wooden shelving must be gloss painted or varnished.
* You should be able to clean behind all equipment and cleaning should be carried out regularly. All equipment such as pots, pans, blenders, mixers which are used to prepare or handle food must be cleaned before use with hot water that is regularly changed.
* You should have one sink for food preparation and another for washing-up. Both sinks must provide hot and cold water.
* You must have one handbasin in the food area as well as one near the water closet. Hot and cold water, soap, nailbrush and hand-drying facilities, e.g. paper towels, must be supplied.
* A lobby with lighting and ventilation must be built between the toilet and any food room. The lobby must not be used for storing any food or drinks.

* Sinks, handbasins, toilets and surrounding areas must be kept clean at all times.
* You must provide refuse bins with tightly fitting lids and arrange for them to be emptied and cleansed regularly.

There are further regulations for lighting, ventilation, pest control and the reheating of certain foods, as reheating and frying does not destroy germs or the poison that they produce (**See below**).

New businesses will have to register at least four weeks before opening to enable enforcement officers to make inspections and ensure they are satisfactory. There is no fee for registration. Anyone engaged in the handling, preparation or serving of food must have basic training in food hygiene and have the practical skills and knowledge appropriate to their job.

Temperature control
The following foods must by law be kept cold at a temperature no higher than 8° Centigrade, or if they are already cooked and waiting to be eaten hot, they must be kept hot at a temperature of at least 63° Centigrade:

Cooked products containing

* Meat
* Fish
* Eggs
* Substitutes for meat, fish or eggs
* Soft or hard cheeses
* Cereals (rice and other grains)
* Pulses
* Vegetables
* Cooked pies and pasties containing meat, fish (or substitutes for these) or vegetables encased in pastry, unless they are intended to be sold on the day of their production or the next day and have had nothing (e.g. no gelatine) added to them after baking
* Cooked sausage rolls, unless intended to be sold on the day of their production or the next day
* Smoked or cured fish
* Slices cut from smoked or cured meats (except uncooked bacon)

* Ripened cheeses
* Prepared vegetable salads
* Uncooked or partly cooked pastry and dough products containing meat, fish or substitutes, e.g. uncooked or partly cooked pizza and fresh pasta with meat or fish filling, e.g. ravioli
* Prepared sandwiches or filled rolls containing meat, fish, eggs, or substitutes for these, or ripened soft cheese, or vegetables
* Some dairy-based desserts
* Cream cakes.

Some foods are especially prone to contamination by microorganisms which multiply at very low temperatures and have to be kept extra cold at no higher than 5° Centigrade. These foods are:

* Portions or slices of ripened soft cheeses
* Cooked products which are ready to eat without reheating and which contain:
* Meat
* Fish
* Eggs
* Substitute for meat, fish or eggs
* Soft or hard cheeses
* Cereals
* Pulses
* Vegetables
* Smoked or cured fish
* Slices from smoked or cured meats (except uncooked bacon)
* Prepared sandwiches or rolls filled with any of the foods mentioned above, unless intended to be sold within twenty-four hours of preparation.

These rules are being introduced in stages to help businesses to make sure that their refrigeration equipment can keep food at these temperatures.

When you are storing high-risk food (as listed above) remember that poor temperature control is responsible for a large number of outbreaks of food poisoning. Therefore:

* Do not leave high-risk food at room temperature.
* Cool cooked food as quickly as possible and then place it in

a refrigerator or cold display cabinet until it is required for sale.
* Do not cool and warm up stews and gravies because this will encourage germs to multiply very quickly and cause food poisoning.
* Ensure that all cooked high-risk food (as listed above) is maintained either hot (above 63° Centigrade) or cold (below 8° Centigrade).
* Check the temperature of your display cabinet, fridges and freezers regularly.

Enforcing food and hygiene regulations
Local authorities are responsible for enforcing the law in two main areas. Their Trading Standards Officers deal with the labelling of food, its composition and most cases of chemical contamination. Environmental Health Officers deal with hygiene, with cases of microbiological contamination of foods, and with food which, for any reason including chemical contamination, is unfit for human consumption. In non-metropolitan areas of England and Wales, trading standards work is carried out by the county councils, and environmental health work by the district councils. The London boroughs and the metropolitan authorities carry out both functions. In Scotland, all food law enforcement is carried out by the Environmental Health Departments of district and island councils. In Northern Ireland this work is undertaken by the Environmental Health Departments of district councils.

* Officers can enter food premises to investigate possible offences.
* Officers can inspect food to see if it's safe.
* Officers can detain suspect food or seize it and ask a Justice of the Peace (JP) or, in Scotland, a magistrate or the Sheriff to condemn it.

It is a criminal offence for a shop, stall or restaurant not to comply with the regulations. The maximum penalty in a Magistrates' Court is a fine of £2,000 and in a Crown Court a fine or two years' imprisonment or both. In Scotland equivalent penalties may be imposed by the Sheriff.

Food labelling
The Food labelling regulations apply to all food sold in this country and require that certain basic information is shown.

* Product name.
* All ingredients listed in order of amount present and weight. For example fruit juice is not sufficient – the actual fruit must be identified.

Sell-by dates
Pre-packed foods must be labelled with their 'minimum durability'. This must be done either by a sell-by date or a best-before date.

Storage
Any special conditions such as 'keep refrigerated' must be shown.

Instructions for use
Any instructions must be clear.

Name and address of manufacturer
Plus packer or seller within the EEC and the country of origin if manufactured elsewhere.

You should submit draft labels to your local authority for their approval.

[Source Information Wandsworth Environmental Services and the Department of Health.]

CHAPTER 3
HELP SECTION

Bankruptcy
BANKRUPTCY SEARCH ROOM Room D9, Official Receiver's London Offices, Atlantic House, Holborn Viaduct, London, EC1 (No telephone). If you discover that the debtor is already bankrupt, you are barred from pursuing your debt and will have to claim from either the official receiver or the trustees.

Help
CITIZENS ADVICE BUREAU (CAB) In your local phone book or contact:
NATIONAL ASSOCIATION OF CITIZENS ADVICE BUREAUX (NACAB) 115–123 Pentonville Road, London, N1 9LZ. Tel: 071 833 2181.
ONE PLUS 39 Hope Street, Glasgow, G2 6AE. Tel: 041 221 7150. Write or phone for free, confidential advice on housing, benefits, taxation, etc.
CITIZENS ADVICE SCOTLAND 26 George Square, Edinburgh, EH8 9LD. Tel: 031 667 0156.
NORTHERN IRELAND ASSOCIATION OF CITIZENS ADVICE BUREAUX (CAB) 11 Upper Crescent, Belfast, BT7 1NT. Tel: 0232 231120.

Law and law centres
LAW CENTRES FEDERATION Tel: 071 387 8570.
LEGAL AID FOR CIVIL AND CRIMINAL CASES from your local EMPLOYMENT OFFICE or JOB CENTRE.
LAWYERS FOR ENTERPRISE Tel: 071 405 9075.
THE LAW COMMISSION ENGLAND AND WALES Conquest House, 37–38 John Street, Off Theobalds Road, London, WC1N 2BQ. Tel: 071 411 1220.
SCOTTISH LAW COMMISSION 140 Causewayside, Edinburgh, EH9 1PR. Tel: 031 668 2131.
THE LAW OBSERVERS OFFICE Royal Courts of Justice, Strand, WC2A 2LL. Tel: 071 936 6000. The function of this organisation is to monitor the Solicitors Complaints Bureau's handling of complaints made to it about the conduct of solicitors or their employers.
THE LAW SOCIETY OF ENGLAND AND WALES, Law Society's Hall, 113

Chancery Lane, London, WC2A 1PL. Tel: 071 405 9522.
LAW SOCIETY OF NORTHERN IRELAND 90–106 Victoria Street, Belfast, BT1 3JZ. Tel: 0232 231614.
LEGAL AID BOARD 5th and 6th Floor, 29–37 Red Lion Street, London, WC1R 4PP. Tel: 071 831 4209.
LAW SOCIETY OF SCOTLAND 26 Drumsheugh Gardens, Edinburgh, EH3 7YR. Tel: 031 226 7411.
SCOTTISH LEGAL AID BOARD 44 Drumsheugh Gardens, Edinburgh, EH3 7SW. Tel: 031 226 7061.

Patents and registered trade marks
Telephone for general Patent
enquiries and information pack: 071 438 4700.
Copyright: 071 438 4778.
Design: 0633 814000, ext. 5162.
Trade and service marks: 0633 814706.
Search and advisory service: 071 438 4761.
REGISTRAR OF COMPANIES 21 Bothwell Street, Glasgow G2 6NL. Tel: 041 248 3315.
COMPANIES REGISTRATION OFFICE 55 City Road, London, EC1Y 1BB. Tel: 071 253 9393.
COMPANIES REGISTRATION OFFICE Companies House, Crown Way, Cardiff, CF4 3UZ. Tel: 0222 388588.
THE CHARTERED INSTITUTE OF PATENT AGENTS Staple Inn Buildings, High Holborn, London, WC1V 7PZ. Tel: 071 405 9450. They have a list of patent agents all over England which costs £2.
HOW TO GET A EUROPEAN PATENT European Patent Office, Erhardtstrasse 27, D–8000, München 2, Germany.
PATENT OFFICE 25 Southampton Buildings, Chancery Lane, London, WC2A 1AY. Tel: 071 438 4700.
THE MARKET RESEARCH SOCIETY *Organisation Handbook* 15 Northburgh Street, London, EC1V 0AH. Tel: 071 490 4911.
INSTITUTE OF PATENTEES AND INVENTORS Suite 505a, 189 Regent Street, London, WC1R 7WF. Tel: 071 242 7812.
PCT APPLICATION GUIDE World Intellectual Property Organisation, 34 Chemin Des Colombettes, 1211 Geneva 20, Switzerland.
Introducing Patents – A Guide For Inventors by the Department of Trade and Industry 1983.
SMALL FIRMS INFORMATION CENTRE Freefone 24444.
REGISTERING TRADE MARKS The Registrar, 7 Stone Buildings, Lincoln's Inn, London, WC2A 3SZ. Tel: 071 242 2535.

THE TRADE MARKS REGISTRY Newport. Tel: 0633 815696. Or you can read it up in the SCIENCE AND REFERENCE LIBRARY, 25 Southampton Buildings, London, WC2 1AX.

Leaflets and reference guides:
Notes For Guidance on Business Names and Business Ownership from Companies Registration Office (address as above).
Protecting Your Ideas and Copyright from the Association of Cinematograph Television and Allied Technicians (ACTT) 111 Wardour Street, London, W1V 4AY. Tel: 071 437 8506. Booklet free to ACTT members; £1 to non-members.
Format Rights: The Protection on Ideas For Radio and TV by Moira Burnett, EBU Review Vol. 39, No. 1, reprinted in International Media Law 6/50.
Development AIP 17 Great Pultney Street, London, W1R 3DG. Tel: 071 437 7700.
Writers' and Artists' Yearbook A & C Black Ltd.

Libraries
BIRMINGHAM REFERENCE LIBRARY also has a comprehensive patent database.
THE BRITISH LIBRARY SCIENCE, REFERENCE AND INFORMATION SERVICE 25 Southampton Buildings, London, WC2A 1AX. Tel: 071 323 7494.
BIRMINGHAM PUBLIC LIBRARIES Business Information Department, Chamberlain Square, Birmingham, B3 3HQ. Tel: 021 235 4531.
SCIENCE, REFERENCE AND INFORMATION SERVICE contains one of the largest collections of national and international patents.
WESTMINSTER CENTRAL REFERENCE LIBRARY, St Martins Street, London WC2. Tel: 071 798 2034.

Matters relating to patents in the UK are governed by the PATENTS ACT 1977 and the PATENTS RULES 1982, which are available from HMSO (**See Help Section, Chapter 2**) and libraries. Register your patent for a small fee with: The Registrar, 7 Stone Buildings, Lincoln's Inn, London, WC2A 3SZ. Tel: 071 242 2535.

Small claims
For information and booklets contact your local court or:
The LORD CHANCELLORS OFFICE, Trevelyan House, 30 Great Peter Street, London, SW1P 2DA. Tel: 071 210 8500.

LEAFLET 1 *What is a Small Claim?*
LEAFLET 2 *How Do I Make a Small Claim in the County Court?*
LEAFLET 3 *No Reply to my Summons – What Should I Do?*
All leaflets are available from your local County Court. The address and phone number of all courts is under COURTS in the telephone book. Courts are open weekdays 10 a.m.–4 p.m.

All judgements where £10 or more is outstanding one month after the date of judgement are registered at: REGISTRY TRUST LTD 173 Cleveland Street, W1P 5PE. Tel: 071 380 0133.

Solicitors
Legal advice on any matter concerning the formation or running of a business is available from solicitors. Details of the solicitors who are taking part in a free initial consultation scheme for small and new businesses are available from your local Enterprise Agency or:
LAWYERS FOR ENTERPRISE.
Details of firms taking part in the scheme from: The Law Society of England and Wales, Law Society's Hall, 113 Chancery Lane, London, WC2A 1PL. Tel: 071 405 9522 or visit your local Enterprise Agency.

Health and safety
Advice on reducing energy costs available from THE DEPARTMENT OF ENERGY'S REGIONAL OFFICES – look under ENERGY DEPARTMENT OF . . . in your local phone book. THE WELSH OFFICE INDUSTRY DEPARTMENT and THE INDUSTRY DEPARTMENT OF SCOTLAND.
Essentials of Health and Safety at Work from HMSO price £2.95.
HEALTH AND SAFETY EXECUTIVE for advice on health and safety requirements or your LOCAL AUTHORITY'S ENVIRONMENTAL HEALTH DEPARTMENT.
HEALTH AND SAFETY COMMISSION (Secretariat) Baynards House, Chepstow Place, London, W2 4TF. Tel: 071 243 6000.
HEALTH AND SAFETY EXECUTIVE (Public Enquiry Point) Baynards House, Chepstow Place, Westbourne Grove, London, W2 4TF. Tel: 071 221 0870.
WOMEN AND WORK HAZARDS GROUP (health and safety hazards for homeworkers) A Women's Place, Hungerford House, Victoria Embankment, London, WC2N 6PA. Tel: 071 836 6081.

Health and hygiene

BRITISH HOTELS, RESTAURANTS AND CATERERS ASSOCIATION (BHRCA) 40 Duke Street, London, W1M 6HR. Tel: 071 499 6641.
CONSUMERS' ASSOCIATION (CA) 2 Marylebone Road, London, NW1 4DX. Tel: 071 486 5544.
DEPARTMENT OF HEALTH AND SOCIAL SECURITY SERVICES (NI) (DHSS) Dundonald House, Upper Newtonards Road, Belfast, BT4 3SB. Tel: 0232 650111.
DEPARTMENT OF HEALTH Richmond House, 79 Whitehall, London SW1. Tel: 071 210 3000.
FOOD AND DRINK FEDERATION (FDF) 6 Catherine Street, London, WC2B 5JJ. Tel: 071 836 2460.
INSTITUTE OF ENVIRONMENTAL HEALTH OFFICERS 48 Rushworth Street, London, SE1 0RD. Tel: 071 928 6006/8.
INSTITUTE OF TRADING STANDARDS ADMINISTRATION 4/5 Hadleigh Business Centre, 351 London Road, Hadleigh, Benfleet, Essex, SS7 2BT. Tel: 0702 559922.
HOTEL, CATERING AND INSTITUTIONAL MANAGEMENT ASSOCIATION (HCIMA) 191 Trinity Road, London, SW17 7HN. Tel: 081 672 4251.
LOCAL AUTHORITIES CO-ORDINATING BODY ON TRADING STANDARDS (LACOTS) PO Box 6, 1A Robert Street, Croydon, CR9 1LG. Tel: 081 688 1996.
THE FOOD SAFETY DIRECTORATE, MINISTRY OF AGRICULTURE, FISHERIES AND FOOD (MAFF) Whitehall Place, London, SW1. Tel: 071 270 3000. Main enquiries.
THE CONSUMER PROTECTION DIVISION, MINISTRY OF AGRICULTURE, FISHERIES AND FOOD (MAFF) Egon House, 17 Smith Square, London, SW1P 3JR. Tel: 071 238 3000.
FOOD LABELLING AND FOOD LAW. Tel: 071 238 3000 ext. 6463.
FOOD SAFETY. Tel: 071 238 6550.
NATIONAL FARMERS UNION (NFU) Agriculture House, Knightsbridge, London, SW1X 7NJ. Tel: 071 235 5077.
NATIONAL CONSUMER COUNCIL (NCC) 20 Grosvenor Gardens, London, SW1W 0BD. Tel: 071 730 3469.
RETAIL CONSORTIUM 1–19 New Oxford Street, London, WC1A 1PA. Tel: 071 404 4622.
RESTAURATEURS ASSOCIATION OF GREAT BRITAIN (RAGB) 190 Queensgate, London, SW7 5EH. Tel: 071 581 2444.
SCOTTISH OFFICE AGRICULTURE AND FISHERIES DEPARTMENT

(SOAFD) Pentland House, 47 Robbs Loan, Edinburgh, EH14 1SQ. Tel: 031 556 8400.
WELSH OFFICE (WO) PHF2 Cathays Park, Cardiff, CF1 3NQ. Tel: 0222 823475.
For your local Health and Hygiene Officer contact your local Town Hall.

Booklets – health and hygiene
The Food Safety Act 1990 and *You – A Guide for the Food Industry*, available from: Food Sense, London, SE99 7TT. Tel: 081 694 8862.
Stay Safe – Keeping Food at Controlled Temperatures Makes Sense, available from: Health Publication Unit, No. 2 Site, Heywoods Stores, Manchester Road, Heywood, Lancashire, OL10 2PZ. (Mail Order enquiries only).

Chapter information sources
The Food Safety Act; Small Claims Court; Wandsworth Environmental Services; The Law Society; The Patent Office; The Small Firms Service; Citizens Advice Bureau; *Know Your Rights*, Reader's Digest.

CHAPTER 4

You and Your Money

The important relationship between chocolate sandwich gateau, and a small Business Loan ......

AN ACCOUNTANT

You will probably at some stage during the financial setting up or planning of your business, or while you are trading, need the help of a chartered accountant, one that has experience of small businesses and will be able to give you advice on your trading status – i.e. sole trader, partnership, or limited company – and set it up for you (**See page 73 Chapter 3 You, Your Company and the Law**). An accountant will also deal with the Inland Revenue, give advice about VAT registration (**See page 146 Chapter 5 Tax, Insurance and Pensions**), help you produce budgets, annual accounts, audited accounts if you are a limited company, and send them to Companies House, as well as doing book-keeping if you don't feel capable of doing it yourself.

If you feel capable, enjoy doing tax returns and have a very small business, then you probably don't need an accountant. But if you're like the majority of people who struggle with tax returns and are unfamiliar with the workings of the Inland Revenue, then the best advice is to get help. In any case, it's a good idea to get an accountant to do at least your first year-end returns because accountants have an established relationship with the Inland Revenue and know what can and cannot be claimed for expenses (**See page 141 Chapter 5 Tax, Insurance and Pensions**). They also know how to apportion the 'grey areas' of things such as car costs to private mileage, and when you can charge for the cost of extra meals while away on business. The more complex your business or the less expensive it is, the more you need an accountant to point out the tax savings.

It's an idea in some circumstances to have an accountant before you get started, because they can help you with your plans (**See Chapter 2 Starting your own Business**), assess the commercial potential of your venture and give you advice on such things as whether you should operate as a sole trader, partnership or limited company. If you run a limited company, you will *have* to employ an accountant who will audit and certify your accounts for submission to Companies House. This will provide an accurate benchmark to see what your business has achieved in the past year compared with your management accounts. You have more protection if you use a qualified accountant.

An accountant will advise you on how to keep your books and the best way to obtain financing. Some people require an accountant only to do their annual tax returns and give advice on tax efficiency, and prefer to use a book-keeper as an alternative, or do their books themselves – which is obviously the cheapest way.

If you do decide to use an accountant, be aware that the less conscientious you are about book-keeping, then the more tax and accountancy bills you will have to pay. For every pound of expenditure you forget to claim, you are giving the Inland Revenue 25p. Brian discovered this when he finally got an accountant after doing his own accounts for years. 'We hadn't ever had any trouble with the tax office and when the accountant looked at our books, he said he wasn't surprised, we had been very generous. He immediately saved us a lot of money.'

It's important that you and your accountants mutually agree on a satisfactory system. It will mean that their work and your bill will be less than if they have to plough their way through a bulging carrier bag full of your shambolic papers every year. Usually it's too expensive for an accountant to keep your books on a monthly basis. They will prepare your profit and loss accounts, a balance sheet and your accounts once a year.

An accountant will also deal with your Income Tax return, which you sign and are responsible for checking is accurate. If you're preparing a business plan for a bank loan (**See page 39 Chapter 2 Starting your own Business**), it may be a good idea to get your accountants' advice and let them prepare the financial part and run through it with you.

To sum up, an accountant can help you with: advice on trading status; taxation for both you and your business; preparing quarterly returns for Customs and Excise; dealing with PAYE and National Insurance of any employees; producing budgets, financial plans; book-keeping; annual accounts and audit accounts if you are a limited company, and sending them to Companies House.

Your choice

If you decide that you do need a chartered accountant, you should first make a list of what you think your needs are. Be clear and exact about why you are going to see one and what information you need, for there is more than just personalities involved. Think about the size of the job you want them to do, the specialist skills, if any, that you require them to have, the location of the firm's offices and, of course, their fees and fee structure. Accountants should discuss their fees with you for each particular job before they start and be able to give you a rough estimate of the time it's going to take, plus their charges. If they don't offer this information, then you must ask. Chartered accountants generally charge an hourly rate, which will relate to the number of hours involved in preparing your accounts and negotiating with the Inland Revenue, but there is no set standard fee. An efficient accountant should be able to prepare your accounts within a few weeks of receiving your business records.

Finding an accountant

The best way to find a chartered accountant is through personal recommendation, but if that isn't possible, look in your local Yellow Pages and Thomson Local Directory or contact your local District Society of Chartered Accountants, which you'll find listed in your telephone directory. The Institute also publishes a Directory of Firms which is available from any Citizens Advice Bureau or at District Society offices (**See Help Section this Chapter**). It lists the specialist services offered by various accountants, plus addresses and fees. The Institute of Chartered Accountants cannot recommend individual firms, but if you need advice, you can contact the Practitioner Bureau at the Institute (**See Help Section this Chapter**).

What to take to your accountant

* Business records.
* All your receipts.
* All your bank or building society paying-in books.
* All your bank statements.
* All your used cheque books with completed cheque stubs.
* Copies of all your invoices and statements.

* Details of amounts owed to the business by debtors at the end of the year.
* Details of amounts owed by the business to creditors at the end of the year.
* Details of all the stock at the end of the year.
* All calculations connected with VAT.
* Records of all wages paid to any employees, with amounts paid under PAYE.

BANKS AND BUILDING SOCIETIES
Banks and Building Societies offer free financial advice on a range of subjects. They will choose whether or not to offer you independent financial advice, their own products, or reduce your choice down to those of one single company. They should tell you which kind of financial advice they are giving you. But if they don't, remember to ask. These days there is increased competition between banks and building societies and you will find that they are falling over each other to give you advice and get your custom. Basically they are all offering the same facilities but the cost of those facilities will vary, which is where the competition between them is to your advantage, and you should shop around.

You can get financial advice from a solicitor (**See page 79 Chapter 3 You, Your Company and the Law**) or chartered accountant (**See previous section**), but always ask, because they usually charge a fee.

You will probably find that you will need financial advice from all the various sources at different times. The advantage of going to a bank or building society is that they do not charge a fee, but you must ask if their advice is impartial. You will have to pay an accountant, and again, you must ask if their advice is impartial. Financial advisers (**See page 114 this Chapter**) will not charge you a fee, but if they are independent their advice should be impartial and they should offer you a range of products. Check that a financial adviser is fully authorised by contacting the Securities and Investment Board (**See Help Section this Chapter**), who have a central register which is updated daily.

The bank manager
A good relationship with your bank or building society manager is very important because that is the person who will probably be your source of financial advice on a day-to-day basis. But it's

important to remember that you are the customer and you do have a say in what you need and the way you are treated. Shop around. Go to all the banks. When Jane was starting up her garden fertiliser business she found it difficult to be taken seriously, especially when she decided to call her company, 'Lady Muck'. 'It was all a gamble, and even my bank manager didn't take me seriously. He wouldn't lend me £2,000 to buy machinery and a car, so I changed banks. I didn't want to invest a lot because it could have flopped.'

Always ask for a meeting with either the bank manager or the assistant manager. Don't be in awe of them. Always ask for a list of charges for various banking services. If you don't feel the manager is sympathetic or you don't agree with their charges or services, go elsewhere. Once you have decided on a bank, don't become an anonymous account holder. Go and see the manager at regular intervals, not just when they send for you. Tell them about your business projects, progress and disappointments.

Before meeting your bank manager, apart from dropping your shoulders and breathing deeply to relax, it's very important that you know what services you want. Do you need cashing facilities? How frequently do you need bank statements and what cheque books and cheque guarantee cards do you require? Decide on the type of account that you want: for example, one bearing interest. You may also want a separate deposit account which you can use for any surplus money that you want to gain interest towards your expenses and any other bills such as tax, which will come later. Building Societies also provide interest-bearing accounts, so shop around and compare rates.

The majority of banks have a section which specialises in dealing with small business and people who are self-employed. Through this facility you will be able formally to arrange an overdraft or a loan for a fixed period. You will have to repay it with regular monthly repayments and you should be able to negotiate the interest that will be charged on the total amount. Banks have a list of their services and charges.

Take along your cash flows, business plans **(See pages 37 and 39 Chapter 2 Starting your own Business)** and any supporting documents which you feel are relevant. The more research you have done the fewer problems you will have, and your bank manager's eyes will light up if you can show some firm orders to back your project.

The interest you will have to pay on a loan is usually lower than for an unsecured overdraft and the interest on loans can be claimed against tax (not if you are trading as a company), which is not the case with an overdraft.

The bank manager will need to know how long you want a loan or overdraft facility for and at what rate you can pay it back. They may also need a guarantor, which is another person who signs a document saying that they will pay your debts if you can't. Or they may ask for security, such as a charge on your house. But do be very sure of your business idea before you do this or you could end up losing your home. If you are married or have a live-in partner discuss it with them, for it's their home as well that you are laying on the line. The best rule in gambling – and most business ventures are a gamble – is never to risk more than you can afford to lose. If you have put aside a few hundred pounds for a special holiday but decide to invest it in your business instead, if things go wrong you will only have lost your holiday. But if you lose your home, you could find yourself living on the street. It does happen. Plan to survive the worst (**See page 118 this Chapter**) and, as it's seldom that bad, so you will almost certainly come out on top!

The thing to remember is that most banks are happy to lend you money when you are OK and business is going well, but as soon as you need to borrow because things are a bit tight, then they will be more reluctant. So plan ahead and don't rely on them.

You'll find that many bank managers lead contained lives, secretly wishing they were as brave as you – starting a business and working from home, so include them in your business hopes and plans. Take along a sample of your product to show them, even if you think it's something they won't be particularly interested in; it's surprising what broad minds bank managers can have when they are involved in the initial business outlay. Make them feel involved in the whole project, not just the finances. Keep in touch, keep them up to date every couple of months, not just when they ask to see you. Try to foresee difficulties, letting them know early on, and share some of the good news with them as well.

FINDING FINANCIAL ADVICE

If you decide to set up a business, or if your business is already up and running but circumstances change, you will need some professional financial advice on things such as the most tax-efficient way of setting up a pension scheme, life assurance, pensions and unit trust contracts, managing investments, budgeting, mortgages and health insurance. If you are not going to start a business but are going to work as a self-employed person, you will also probably find that you need financial advice from time to time on things such as pensions or mortgages. There are various places where you can go for advice such as banks, building societies and independent financial advisers (**See under appropriate headings, this Chapter**).

You do not have to pay either an independent financial adviser or a company representative, because they are paid a commission for any business which results from their advice. Independent financial advisers receive payment from the investment companies who get business from their recommendations, and company representatives will offer you advice from that company's product range. An independent adviser will offer you advice from the whole market place and, added to the information you give them, this will be tailored to your requirements and is totally impartial.

The Financial Services Act stipulates that advisers cannot advise unless they know your 'vital statistics' such as your mortgage repayments, life assurance policies, pension arrangements, tax bracket, investments and philosophy, commitments, expectations and lifestyle. It is on this information that they can base their 'best advice'. Whatever products they recommend must best suit your specific requirements. The Financial Services Act also established the Securities and Investment Board (SIB) to regulate the investment industry. It operates five Self-Regulatory Bodies (SROs) and Recognised Professional Bodies (RPBs) who have the names of all authorised businesses in your area (**See Help Section this Chapter** for addresses and phone numbers).

BORROWING MONEY

However much of a financial jam you are in, or however much you want to expand your business, stop and think before you borrow money. Ask yourself if you can afford the repayments. On almost all borrowed money you will have to pay the going interest rate. Bank loans and overdrafts tend to be a cheaper way of borrowing compared with overdrafts or loans from a finance company.

If you have debts, you won't be considered credit-worthy and so will have to pay higher rates of interest on any loan. If you own a house, one way of paying off debts is to re-mortgage, which may increase your monthly mortgage payments. If you do this, you must not borrow more than between 80 and 90 per cent of the value of the property because, as we know, property prices don't always rise. The cheapest way to borrow money, if it is possible, is from friends or relatives who generally are unlikely to charge you interest and because they are aware of your circumstances may be more willing to wait a long time for repayment. But be aware that this is frequently the cause of the end of a beautiful relationship!

If the bank refuse you a loan it may be because they have the wrong information about your credit-worthiness, or perhaps you hadn't given them enough detail. Bank managers vary widely, and if you are refused a loan the best thing to do is try another branch or another bank.

If a lender or supplier asks for your personal guarantee for a loan, make sure that when you have repaid the loan your security is cancelled. If not, the lender could keep your home as security for further loans without getting agreement from you again. In this way you can limit your personal liability for any debts (**See page 88 Chapter 3 Your Company and the Law**).

SEPARATE ACCOUNTS

Open a business bank account, use it only for business transactions and keep it separate from your personal bank account to avoid financial problems. The advantage of this is that when you receive your monthly statement, either you or your accountant, if you have one, can check it without having to define which were business and which were personal transactions. This is useful for items such as the cost of the car or telephone which may be used for both personal and business purposes. The total sum can be entered in the business account and paid through your business bank account. Later on you or your accountant will agree on apportionment with the tax inspector. Services such as gas, electricity, goods supplied to your business and the telephone you should sign for in the business name that you trade under. If you use your own name as your business name make sure that the account is kept separate from your own personal account.

The disadvantage of having separate personal and business bank accounts are the banking costs, as well as the need to be organised and keep all your financial transactions separate. However, the disadvantages are minimal compared to the advantages.

YOUR FINANCIAL ANALYSIS

It's surprising how many people don't know what they are worth, or what they would do financially if one of life's disasters struck. It's important to know what you are worth for your own knowledge, plus it gives you a greater degree of control over handling your future cash flow and budgeting. It is also important when it comes to making a will, or considering inheritance tax.

Before considering business problems, it's important that you understand your own financial situation. Start by completing this chart, which you should do annually.

PERSONAL FINANCIAL ANALYSIS

Annual Income: Regular Gross: Net (after tax):
(Customer pays you
regularly at end of each
month)

Irregular Gross: Net (after tax):
(one-off payments)

(consult current
tax leaflets)

ASSETS (WHAT YOU OWN)

Cash available (deposits in the building society or bank):

INVESTMENTS In order of liquidity (shares may be sold tomorrow, but a house might take months):
Value of personal effects: car, art, wine, jewellery, antiques, etc.
Value of shares.
Value of unit trust/bonds.
Value and maturity date of savings plans, endowments, etc.
Equity in property (value less any outstanding mortgage).

PAYABLE ON DEATH
Sums payable under:

Mortgage policies.
Company death insurance benefits.
Personal Insurance:
　Term　　　　　　　　　　surrender value.
　Whole Life　　　　　　　surrender value.

DISABILITY PAYMENTS
State Benefit (consult relevant DHSS leaflets).
Duration of statutory sick pay.
Benefits under company disability/accident schemes or early retirement options.

BENEFITS UNDER PERSONAL SCHEMES
Private Health Insurance.
Accident.
Critical illness.
Life Assurance.

PAYABLE ON RETIREMENT
OAP for single person (dependent on National Insurance payments record. See relevant pension leaflets for up-to-date payment).
Company Pensions.
Personal Pensions.

LIABILITIES (WHAT YOU OWE)

Amount of mortgage and redemption date.
Amounts outstanding on credit cards.
Amounts outstanding on bank loans (and dates to be cleared).
Amounts in overdraft.
Amounts outstanding on personal loans or those other than banks (with dates when to be cleared).
Amounts outstanding on hire purchase (and dates when to be cleared).
Unpaid tax.

Contingencies and plans – the worst scenario
You should plan for the worst events that can happen to you, such as death or retirement, separation or illness. There is no point in saying it won't happen, because in reality things do happen unexpectedly to all of us. Anticipating life's crises and having a responsible attitude towards them, even though they

might not exist at the moment, means that you plan financially and legally for all eventualities. For example, if you have planned financially for your death, then your family and loved ones, apart from having to deal with grief, will not have to worry about how they can manage financially without your income. Nor will they have to tie up the messy loose ends of your business. Or if divorce should arise, you will know how to make financial arrangements for your children. You should make contingency plans for the four life crises listed below, and you may have your own that you want to add. When you've done that, you can have the pleasure of making plans for luxuries and future fantasies – not everything is doom and gloom!

What if you died?
* Have you made a will? Are you or your dependents/family/business financially distraught in the event of your own or anyone else's death?
* What needs replacing, e.g. capital debts, income, car?
* Have you got enough life cover for dependents?
* Have you any life cover to mitigate inheritance tax? (Don't forget you bequeath your debts as well as your assets.) Don't forget burial expenses.

If illness stopped you working
* Would someone be able to support you?
* What would your minimum income requirements be?
* Would you need any capital?
* Have you got adequate insurance cover? If we die people normally get by, but if we live and carry on spending we must still maintain our liabilities.

If you separated or divorced
* Can you discuss your financial concerns with your partner?
* What if you had to sell the house and/or maintain the children? Can you save enough to cover the cost?
* Could you benefit from a legal agreement on property rights?

Retirement
* Most people when they retire do not want to have to change their lifestyle, in fact you might want some extras such as a new car, more holidays, etc.

* Will your mortgage be paid off?
* Is your pension index-linked? You might live on for another twenty years or more and inflation can erode the value of a fixed pension quicker than you can imagine. Its purchasing power could easily be halved in seven years.

Other plans
What luxuries and fantasies would you like in the future or in the next five, ten or twenty years? Are you saving enough to make your dreams come true?

[Chart: Davies and Chapman, financial advisers]

DAY TO DAY FINANCIAL MANAGEMENT

When you are running your own business, it is very important that you keep accurate and up-to-date accounts. It is important not just for the Inland Revenue, Customs and Excise (if you have to register for VAT) the DSS for National Insurance Contributions, for your bank or any other lenders, but also for yourself so that you get a financial feel for your business. You know what money is coming in and how it is going out and how the business is progressing. If your business is a limited company, then your accounts have to be audited by an accountant and a copy sent to Companies House or Registry of Companies in Northern Ireland **(See page 73 Chapter 3 You, Your Company and the Law and Chapter 5 Tax, Insurance and Pensions)**.

Make sure your records are complete, with notes on all business transactions, because different financial information will be required by different organisations. For example, the Inland Revenue will require information on your earnings and outgoings, whereas your bank manager will want to see cash flow forecasts and future budgeting plans. Keep all paperwork such as receipts **(See page 122 this Chapter)**, cheque stubs, bank statements, petty cash books and your accounts all up to date.

Keeping the books
If you should want a loan to start up your business **(See page 34 Chapter 2 Starting your own Business)**, you will most probably be asked to produce a chart of projected costs. Once the business is up and running you should continue to keep records of continuous costs for tax purposes. If you ever need to borrow or take out a

further loan, you will have the information about your business and its running costs to hand for when you need to do a projected cash flow forecast. (**See page 37 Chapter 2 Starting your own Business and this Chapter**).

You can either employ a book-keeper or do your books yourself, which is obviously cheaper. If you decide to do them yourself, first buy an accounting/book-keeping book; you'll find them in any stationers. Put in it simple headings for groups of business costs such as:

COSTS:
Overhead running costs.
   Travel: buses, trains, tube trains, taxis, foreign travel.
   Hotels.
   Excess cost of meals while away.
   Professional subscriptions.
   Magazines, books and papers connected with your business.
   Printing, stationery and postage.
   Secretarial help.
   Insurances.
   Equipment repairs.
   Light and heat.
   Telephone.
   Legal fees.
   Accountants' fees.

WORKING COSTS:
   Materials.

CAPITAL COSTS
Equipment such as a typewriter, cars, tools or a freezer, should be in a separate group as they have different tax deductible rules based on a declining percentage of their value each year.

Rates of depreciation and stock can be discussed with your accountant as appropriate to your business.

Keep a separate list of your income, money that is due and debts, all with appropriate dates.

The date when you start trading can become the beginning of your tax year. For example if you start on 15 October 1991 you will submit your accounts a year later on the same date.

Around December the tax inspector will use the previous year as a guide and assess the tax he believes is due on your expected results. It is normal to 'appeal' in the sense that once the tax office have had time to accept your actual accounts they will demand the additional amount due if your business is growing, or refund you the over-payment if you aren't doing as well as last year. These overlaps can become complicated so it is vital for an accountant to keep it in order and prevent you from losing out. If you are self-employed you must keep all your bills and records for the past six years in case the Inland Revenue want to check your returns.

As your business grows it might become worthwhile investing in one of the home computer programs. Your local adult education classes will probably run a course on computing, the Open University certainly do (**See Help Section this Chapter**). This will help you to keep your accounts, project your business income and your outgoings over the next few months on to a spread sheet, which is important when you want to check if the success you predicted is really happening.

Keeping a record
Receipts and bills are very precious when you are running your own business or working for yourself. Without them you cannot claim expenses. They are proof of what you have spent, a record of your cash flow and you may be able to claim some of the cost against tax. If you are registered for VAT (**See page 146 Chapter 5 Tax, Insurance and Pensions**), you must get receipts with the seller's VAT number on them in order to claim back the VAT on your purchase. But those tiny pieces of paper can become very elusive, especially when you work at home. No sooner do you put them down than they are being used for a shopping list, to jam open a window, as a jotter for telephone messages or for doodling on. It isn't any use hoarding them in coat pockets or screwed up in the bottom of your briefcase or handbag, crammed into the loose change slot in the dashboard of your car, or folded under one of the magnets on the fridge door, because when you need them you won't be able to find them – and you'll need them when it comes to doing your accounts. It's no good then producing something that looks like a screwed-up piece of confetti or not being able to produce any receipts at all.

The safest way to keep receipts is in files, one labelled 'Business

Receipts', the other marked 'Personal Receipts'. File all receipts at the end of every month, or weekly if you find it easier. Or you can use two large envelopes taped open to the wall. Put them either near your desk or the edge of your work table and throw all your receipts into them and then file them at the end of every month. Then again, you can clip them together in a giant bulldog clip or stick them on to a spike.

Make sure you get receipts for everything, even if it means you have to ask or wait for a copy of the bill, which is something you might not bother to do when you are in a hurry. Get receipts for small items such as stamps, parcels, taxi fares or newspapers, as well as larger things. Keep an envelope in your bag, briefcase or car, marked 'receipts', and put them into it. This is especially useful for petrol and garage receipts. Empty the envelope at the end of every week or they tend to become car rubbish.

Car mileage is important for claiming travel expenses. Keep a notebook in your car and write down your mileage before and after each journey. You'll never remember it otherwise.

To keep account of all your phone calls, you can have a notebook by the phone for jotting down the time of each call, number called, person spoken to and a rough estimate of the length of time. For a more precise figure you could invest in a small machine called a Printacall which provides a printout after each phone-call which shows you the length of the call, time, date, cost per unit and cash total. It also has a memory recall facility which shows the total number of calls made, total number of units used and total cost of calls to date. Although it's more expensive than a notebook, it's probably a worthwhile investment if you make a lot of business calls or if you are claiming expenses (**See page 241 Help Section Chapter 8 Your Home As Your Workplace**).

Keep all your bank statements. Banks usually provide a folder or spiral-bound file for statement storage. All statements are numbered, so you know if any are missing and you can keep them in order. This helps you to see where your money is going, what cheques have been cashed and that standing orders have been paid. If you use a hole-in-the-wall bank machine for cash, always get a receipt and file it. File all letters or printed material from the tax, VAT, Social Security or DSS offices. File all letters from your employer, wages slips and invoices.

Petty Cash

There are some business out-goings that are too small to pay for by cheque or bank notes. But it's just as important that you keep track of their payment. For this reason it may be a good idea to have a weekly amount of petty cash, which is really the business equivalent of housekeeping money. Buy a petty cash book from any stationers and write in any money that you spend out of the weekly amount you have allocated for petty cash. You will only use this money for small things such as paying a messenger, buying stamps, registering letters, cash for telephone call-boxes and parking meters, a light bulb and small stationery items such as a box of drawing pins or a roll of tape. These things can add up and the money can disappear without you having any record of it. Always get a receipt and keep it in your petty cash book as a record of payment.

GETTING PAID
(See also page 88 Chapter 3 You, Your Company and the Law.)

Methods of Payment

Depending on the type of work you do, you can either be paid for each job or item you produce or you can be paid a royalty by a manufacturer for each item they sell.

Payment for your time per item you produce

For example, if you are typing letters, doing someone's accounts or knitting jumpers, however hard you work you can produce only so much each week, the amount usually being dictated by the number that the company who are employing you wants. Your fee or salary is also dictated by the going rate for the job and it's difficult to increase that and therefore earn more.

If you work for yourself running your own small business, then the only way you can increase your income is to take a further step in developing your business by finding outworkers, organising them and taking a mark-up percentage on each sale. In that way you will soon stop doing the work yourself and become an organiser and marketing agent for others, if that's the direction that you choose.

YOU AND YOUR MONEY

An hourly rate

Some people have a professionally accepted hourly rate, set either by a Wages Council, Trade Union or simply by market trends **(See pages 181 and 183 Chapter 6 Teleworkers and Outworkers)**. It means that for every hour you work you charge your hourly rate. You usually tell your client how many hours you think the job will take, what they will get for that time and what your hourly rate is. If you think you might have to work more hours than your estimate, you have to inform your client. Jim, a designer, says that people ask him why he doesn't just work out how many hours it takes him to do the work, multiplied by his hourly rate, and bill them like that. 'But I don't think it works like that. When things get to a certain standard, rates are no good. I made millions for one company and I don't see why I should work on an hourly rate.'

If you are unable to value your work in hours, because either you can't judge how long it's going to take, or you feel the work is more a question of your expertise and skill than the time it takes to do it, then you must agree a lump sum.

Payment by royalties from a manufacturer

A lot of homeworkers live on royalties. The principle of royalties is that you only do the job once but you get paid over and over again. In order to benefit from royalties you have to write, compose, design or invent a product that machines can reproduce for a company to sell in quantity. A lot of people working from home who are offered a royalty deal don't know how much to ask. This happened to Brian when he was offered a royalty deal by a firm he was working for. He asked the advice of another modeller who told him what the going rate was, and that was what he asked for, although eventually the company negotiated him down.

Some companies that buy creative ideas only deal by paying you once for 'all rights' **(See page 75 – Contracts, Chapter 3 You, Your Company and the Law)**. This means you get paid immediately, which can be helpful if funds are tight, but you run the risk that if your idea is successful you don't get paid again – the company that manufacture it do. Provided you can manage without a large amount of money up front, you are better trying to negotiate a royalty deal. In some royalty deals you can negotiate an advance, which is an amount of money paid to you up front while you are producing the product. A company will pay you an advance only if they like your idea and think it will sell. You then sign a contract, agreeing to give them the product once it is completed, and if it sells they pay you a royalty after the product has earned back its advance.

The gamble is that if you don't take a one-off payment and stick out for royalties and the product doesn't continue to sell, the royalties will either be very small or stop altogether. You have to try to weigh up if your product is going to have a long life. For example, once you have designed your jumper, composed a song or written a block-buster novel and found a company that will manufacture and market it and who believe that it has a long life, if they are right it will continue to sell and they will continue to pay you. If they are wrong and no one wants the product after a few months, you don't get any more money. It's a difficult one to judge, but there are times when you have to take the up front one-off payment because you need the cash. If things aren't financially too tight, you can gamble on a royalty, but only do it if both you and the manufacturers believe that they know the market (**See Chapter 7 Selling and Marketing**). One of the biggest advantages of taking a royalty deal is that you go on getting paid, which finances you while you get on with another project.

CHASING DEBTS

If you are working from home either for someone else or on a short contract, one-off commission or freelance basis, getting paid when the work is done can often take you as long as doing the actual job and it can be even more exhausting.

You may find that while you were doing the work or providing the service you were taken to lunch, made to feel a vital part of a team, invited to several meetings and telephoned at all times of the day and night. But when it comes to paying you, the pressure and the friendliness from your part-time employers suddenly disappears, rather like they do. You can't get hold of them on the phone, they always seem to be in meetings, when before they were ever available. Your invoice (**See page 132 this chapter**) has obviously gone to the bottom of the pile because you haven't heard from them since you sent it. Brian, a potter who works from home, thinks that self-employed people are treated badly until the company needs them. 'When you rise to the top you don't have so much trouble because they need you and they pay more attention to keeping you happy. But when you're small, people kick you around. I never had to go to court for money, but some people make you wait.'

You will be apprehensive about hounding the company too much, firstly because it makes you feel uncomfortable and secondly because you hope to work for them again. Finally, having paced up and down for days, you'll decide to check with their accounts department that they actually received your invoice in the first place. If it's a large company they will tell you that they have so much paper work they will call you back – and they won't. Or, they'll tell you that they did receive your invoice and they're running three months behind with their payments. You'll probably be humble and agree to wait, grateful that it's only three months. If it's a small company they'll tell you the person who deals with the invoices only comes in once every two months, and you just missed them. Or that the bottom has fallen out of their business and they're thinking of going into liquidation. You'll humbly agree to call back in a couple of months and then chew the carpet, hoping they won't go bust before you get your money. If it was a really bad company, they either won't exist when you call them about your invoice or they'll deny that they ever agreed to pay you that amount in the first place, or insist that your invoice was excessive for the type of work you did, which they can now reveal, despite their initial glee, wasn't as good as they first thought and they had to call someone else in to do the job again. All of this will send you into despair and self-doubt and instead of pursuing your money you'll try to decide if your life assurance will pay up if you walk off the end of the pier!

Chasing up

It often happens that getting paid for work or services completed can create problems. Many sales are made on credit terms, i.e. you invoice when you deliver the goods and then you have to wait for, probably, thirty days before payment is due. In order to avoid debts mounting, you have to keep an eye on who owes you money and how long they have owed it to you. (You must always keep a date of when you started and completed a job, or service.) In addition, record if anyone has only partly paid and who has paid you in full. For those who still owe you all or part of their debt, you have to try and evolve a system of invoices and statements to chase them up (**See page 132 this chapter**). It may take up your valuable working time, or be something that you hate doing, but you aren't going to be able to pay your debts and overheads if no one pays you.

Your first step in credit control is to check that the goods or services you provided arrived in good condition and that there hasn't been a clerical error in the invoice. Having done that, you then send a statement to whoever owes you money at the end of the first month. But this doesn't always guarantee payment. People who don't want to pay or who are having their own cash flow difficulties generally put statements to the bottom of the pile. Because of this, you should follow up your statement a few days later with either a firm but friendly telephone call – after all you don't want to lose the customer yet – or a fax. You may decide to do this for a couple of a months in succession, but don't do it for any longer. When Brian is owed money, he has found that continuously telephoning gets results. 'Either that or actually going to see them and embarrassing them.'

Sometimes it works, and you'll get paid. If you don't, you should check again that the goods or services arrived in good condition and that there hasn't been any clerical error in the invoice. If everything is correct, then you will have to move on to the next step, which is a letter from either a solicitor or a debt-collecting agency (**See page 88 Chapter 3, You, Your Company and the Law**), but you should be aware that you are going to have to pay for either of these services. It might also spur payments if you write to the person who owes you money telling them that you are about to seek legal advice or use the services of a debt collector. But be prepared to carry this threat through, in case they think you're bluffing and still don't pay.

However, before you move on, stop and work out how much you are owed against how much it is going to cost you to get paid. It could be that it simply isn't worth chasing the debt, because by the time you get the money, and have paid either your solicitor or a debt collector, you have lost any profit.

If you are owed a reasonable amount, then move on to the next stage. You'll find that a solicitor's letter often works magic: the threat of legal action can quickly produce a cheque! David who *is* a magician is usually paid cash on the night by most of the pubs and clubs where he performs. This means he doesn't have to do any invoicing and doesn't have to wait to be paid. 'It usually works very well. I've only been caught a couple of times. At one club where I hadn't ever worked before they said they had sent my agent a cheque – I was using two agents at the time. I went back and checked and they hadn't been paid, so I went back to the club and they had some other excuse. Then they offered me £30 less than we had agreed, and I said no. That was five months ago. Now I think I might send them a solicitor's letter. I've got a friend who's a solicitor and he won't charge me, and I bet you it'll do the trick.'

If none of these things works it could be that your customer has their own financial problems and the best thing you can do is to limit your losses. You can try using reason and hopefully agree on small regular payments over a period of time, until the debt is cleared. Although you will be losing interest, it's better than losing everything.

If matters have gone beyond reasonable agreement, then ask your solicitor to issue a writ for payment.

If you have a contract and the work is completed (**See page 74 Chapter 3 You, Your Company and the Law**) and your employers don't pay you, chasing the debt is fairly straightforward as there is a legal process which can be followed. But if you have agreed to a job without a contract and you are having difficulty getting paid you must be firm in all your correspondence. Don't get involved in arguments that sidetrack the issue of payment and don't get involved in anything that puts the blame on you; you simply want to be paid for the work you have done. Be tenacious about phoning them, but non-aggressive. If you aren't getting anywhere with their accounts department, go and see them. It's not as easy for them to put you off when you are physically there. If you are a member of a Trade Union or another professional body ask them for advice.

One of the ways to avoid this situation, apart from having a contract, is to insist on part payment up front before you start the job. Then ask for stage payments if the work is spread out over more than a couple of weeks.

If you have a new client or customer, don't extend them much credit. If you are involved in a large deal, ask for references or to see their accounts, or check with your Trade Union or the professional body for that trade to see if they can give you any background on the company. These organisations frequently know who the bad payers are. If you are unsure, ask for a deposit or issue a pro forma invoice requiring payment before delivery. In

THE COMPLETE GUIDE TO WORKING FROM HOME

EXAMPLE INVOICE

Invoices are bills you send to your customers with your goods or services. Or you may find it more convenient to take a block of time at the end of the month to work on your accounts and send all your invoices out together. But remember if you do it this way, you will have deprived yourself of the extra income over the weeks in between!

INVOICE

Date: ....

Invoice number: ....

Order number: ....

Our reference: ....

Your reference: ....

From: ....

Phone: .... VAT number: ....

To: ....

Quantity	Description	Ref	Price per item	Net Value £

Delivery/P&P: £

Total: £

VAT: £

Invoice Total: £

All goods remain the property of the supplier until paid for.
*A discount of £ . . . will be allowed if payment is received by ....

---

*You may wish to offer an incentive to encourage prompt payment. Perhaps 2% if settled within one month from the invoice date.

YOU AND YOUR MONEY

EXAMPLE STATEMENT

Statements are reminders to pay unsettled invoices and should be sent out each month. If this still has no effect, see the section on what to do if you can't get paid, and how the Small Claims Court can help (**Chapter 3**).

STATEMENT

Date: ....   Order number: ....

Our reference: ....

Your reference: ....

From: ....

Phone: ....   VAT number: ....

To: ....

Date	Type	Order no.	Description	Invoice	Amount £

*Over 120 days: Total £
 Over 90 days:
 Over 60 days:
 Over 30 days:

---

*If the bill has not been paid by the end of the first month, you may wish to add interest to the amount you are owed until it is paid.

doing this you may risk losing a new client, but at the end of the day that's something you have to weigh up – it may be better than doing a lot of work and not being paid for it.

Invoices and statements
Your invoice should be drafted professionally, **(See page 130)**. Do not send out something that has cat paw prints on it or spilt baked bean stains. You don't need expensive letter heading, and can type an invoice on plain paper **(See page 195 Chapter 7 Selling and Marketing)**. It does look more professional if it's typed, but if you don't have access to a typewriter, neat hand writing is all right. Always put your VAT number on if you are VAT registered **(See page 146 Chapter 5 Tax, Insurance and Pensions)** and a reference number so that you can keep track of your invoices. If you are dealing with goods, you should include a clause that states that they become the property of the creditor only when they are paid for. This allows you to recover them from a liquidation, provided you can identify payments – so keep details and all serial numbers.

Do not get behind with your invoicing. The later you send the invoice, the later you will be paid. As soon as the work is finished you should immediately send an invoice. Always keep a copy invoice either on paper, or if you have a computer keep it on disk. Invoicing is something you should do regularly at the end of each week.

Punish late payers by adding on a percentage if they take longer than thirty days to pay. Let them know about this right at the beginning – some people have it printed on all their invoices. Most of Jane's customers pay cash, but she has a few on account: 'I have now started to add a 5 per cent payment charge if they go over fourteen days. I discovered that big companies take a long time to pay.'

JAM-JAR BUDGETING
There are good reasons for keeping track of your expenditure, apart from keeping your accountant, bank manager and tax office happy. The drawback is that when you are working from home you will have to do your own budgeting, understand and control your own cash flow and be your own accounts department, wages clerk and financial whizz-kid. After a while you may devise your own system for keeping tabs on cash flow, but you may need some tips to start you off. For instance, you can use a very simple

system for dealing with paying bills such as labelled jam-jars which you keep cash in. You would have a jar labelled electricity bill, another telephone and so on. The advantage is that you can literally see where the money is and it's easy to get at it – you just unscrew the lid! The disadvantages are security: having money around the house, and the temptation to borrow from the jar! You could write on slips of paper the amount you are paying into each account and put that in the relevant jar. Of course, there are other more conventional ways of saving such as a post office, bank or building society account. You can have as many accounts as you like and name them after the bills that they pay.

The drawback is you will have a paying-in book for each account and, unlike the jam-jars, the paper work mounts. The way to keep tabs on outgoings is that if there are two of you, only one of you deals with paying the bills and handles the money. It's easier to know what the outgoings are if only one of you is handling them.

At the end of each week, make a list of all your outgoings, from stationery down to your daily newspaper. With a coloured highlighter underline all the things that you didn't really need, or shouldn't have bought. In that way you can see where the extra costs are going and how to cut down on them the following week.

Make a list of:
Those costs which are determined by outside forces and which have to be met if you want to maintain a roof over your head:

    Mortgage/rent.
    Community charge.
    Water-rates.
    Certain insurance policies.

Your regular costs which you have to anticipate:
These are costs determined by us and over which we have some choice:

    Light and heat.
    Telephone.
    Food.
    Household costs.
    Childcare.
    Travel.
    Repairs.

Your disposable income:
Fun money for extras:

Holidays.
Car/repairs/petrol.
Consumer goods.
Gifts.
Entertainment.
Cleaning.

Your rainy-day nest egg:
Savings.

Anything you may want in the next five years – work out approximately the cost and the monthly figure to save in a conventional building society.

Add together the four totals =£   Per month
                                  Per annum

[Chart: Davies and Chapman, financial advisers]

BUSINESS EXPANSION SCHEME (BES)

This is a government scheme designed to encourage investment in small businesses. Your business is eligible only if you are trading as a limited company.

Under the Business Expansion Scheme investors can invest up to 30 per cent of the business. The investors will get tax relief on their investment, but they must be UK tax payers and they must not be connected with the business they are investing in. They will have to invest their money for a minimum of five years. Investors can be friends or some relatives, but not parents, grandparents, children or a spouse. The minimum investment is £500 and the maximum is £40,000.

Organisations who will be able to suggest potential investors in your business are:

Banks.
Local Enterprise Agencies.
Small Firms Services.
The Rural Development Commission.
The Co-operative Development Agency.
Local Authority Development Unit.
Small Business Clubs.

Local organisations for particular ethnic groups.

(See Help Section this chapter for addresses and phone numbers.)

LOAN GUARANTEE SCHEME

This scheme is available to new and growing businesses. The government acts as a guarantor to a bank for a small business who cannot otherwise get a loan because of lack of security. The money is lent at the bank rate of interest and the government guarantees to pay 70 per cent of the loan to the bank if you are unable to. The loan is repayable over a period of between two and seven years. It may be possible for you to delay paying off the capital part of the loan for up to two years from the beginning of the agreement, but interest will still have to be paid from the beginning of the loan.

The loan can be taken up in four instalments to a maximum amount of £75,000. You will have to apply through a bank and they will want to see an up-to-date business plan. **(See page 39 Chapter 2 Starting your own Business)** The bank will recommend you to the scheme only if you have adequate security. Loans are available to all sorts of trades. Ask the bank for more information.

RURAL DEVELOPMENT COMMISSION

This organisation helps business in rural areas with a population of less than 10,000. Generally it will help only manufacturing or service industries and businesses that employ less than twenty skilled employees. It will not give help to businesses which are agricultural or horticultural. The Rural Development Commission has its own limited loan funds which can fund such things as helping businesses that are setting up to find sources of money; funding part of the cost of a project; expanding the business; technical advice; help with preparation and business plans; accountancy and book-keeping; employing staff – training on an individual basis or for a group of employees in practical skills; grants in rural development areas to convert buildings into workshops.

Initial advice will be given by a Rural Development Organiser who will usually visit your premises. If they are unable to help they will arrange for a Rural Development Commission Adviser to give specialist help on technical and professional problems, e.g. accountancy, marketing, which type of equipment to buy, etc. There is no charge for the services provided, but there is a fee for the training courses and meetings with advisory officers.

CHAPTER 4
HELP SECTION

Accountants
Booklet *Why You Need a Chartered Accountant* published by: The Institute of Chartered Accountants in England and Wales, PO Box 433, Chartered Accountants Hall, Moorgate Place, London, EC2P 2BJ. Tel: 071 628 7060.

Banking
If you have any complaints about your bank contact either THE BANK MANAGER or:
The Office of THE BANKING OMBUDSMAN Citadel House, 5–11 Fetter Lane, London, EC4A 1BR. Tel: 071 583 1395.

Bankruptcy
BANKRUPTCY SEARCH ROOM Room D9, Official Receiver's London Offices, Atlantic House, Holborn Viaduct, London, EC1. (No telephone.) If you discover that the debtor is already bankrupt, you are barred from pursuing your debt and will have to claim from either the official receiver or the trustees.

Booklets
Debt – A Survival Guide by the Office of Fair Trading. Published by HMSO.
Equal Pay – A Guide For Employees to the SEX DISCRIMINATION ACT 1975. Published by Equal Opportunities Commission. HMSO.
Equal Pay – A Guide to the Equal Pay Act, 1970 revised 1976. Published by Department of Employment.
Equal Pay For Women – What You Should Know About It. Published by the Department of Employment.

Consumer credit
CONSUMER CREDIT The Office of Fair Trading (Consumer Credit Licensing Branch), Field House, 15–25 Bream's Buildings, London, EC4A 1PR. Tel: 071 242 2858.

YOU AND YOUR MONEY

Courses
OPEN UNIVERSITY Parcifal College, 527 Finchley Road, London, NW3 7BE. Tel: 071 794 0575. They run courses in Accountancy.

Financial advice – banks
HIGH TECHNOLOGY BRANCHES, BARCLAYS BANK plc, in most areas of the UK, information through your local branch.
SMALL BUSINESS SECTION, DOMESTIC BANKING DIVISION, NATIONAL WESTMINSTER BANK plc, Fenchurch Exchange, 8 Fenchurch Place, London, EC3M 4PB. Tel: 071 374 3374.
BUSINESS ADVISORY SECTION, Domestic Banking Division, Lloyds Bank plc, 71 Lombard Street, London EC2P 3BS. Tel: 071 626 1500.
SMALL BUSINESS UNIT, Business Development Division, Midland Bank plc, Griffin House, Silver Street, Head, Sheffield, S1 3GG. Tel: 0742 29316.

Financial advisers
To check if a financial adviser is authorised contact:
THE SECURITIES and INVESTORS BOARD, 3 Royal Exchange Buildings, London, EC3V 3NL. Tel: 071 283 2474.
A GUIDE TO INDEPENDENT FINANCIAL ADVICE published by (IFA) Independent Financial Promotions 4th floor, 28 Greville Street, London, EC1N 8SU. Tel: 071 831 4027.
Hotline for list of independent advisers Tel: 0483 461461.

Leaflets: tax, social security, national insurance
Leaflets from any TAX OFFICE or TAX ENQUIRY CENTRE are free. Look under INLAND REVENUE in your phone book. Offices are open between 10 a.m. and 4 p.m. SOCIAL SECURITY leaflets are available (up to 5) free, from your local SOCIAL SECURITY OFFICE listed under SOCIAL SECURITY or HEALTH AND SOCIAL SECURITY in your phone book.
Leaflet numbers are:
Accounting For a Small Firm.
CGT 11 *Capital Gains Tax and Small Businesses.*
CGT 14 *Capital Gains Tax – An Introduction.*
IR 40 *How Your Profits are Taxed.*
IR 90 *Independent Taxation – A Guide to Tax Allowances and Reliefs.*
IR 84 *Income Tax – Have You Anything to Declare?*

IR 72 *Inland Revenue Investigations – The Examination of Business Accounts.*
IR 73 *Inland Revenue Investigations – How Settlements are Negotiated.*
IR 103 *Private Medical Insurance.*
IR 71 PAYE – *Inspection of Employers' and Contractors' Records.*
IR 78 *Personal Pensions. A New Pensions Choice – A Guide For Tax.*
IR 104 *Tax and Your Business – Simple Tax Accounts.*
IR 106 *Tax and Your Business – Capital Allowances for Vehicles and Machinery.*
FB 26 *Voluntary and Part-Time Workers.*
NP 38 *Your Future Pension – How to Check Your Right to an Additional Pension.*

Chapter information source
Institute of Chartered Accountants; Department of Employment; Davies and Chapman, Financial Advisers; Citizens Advice Bureau.

CHAPTER 5
Tax, Insurance and Pensions

TAX
You pay tax on the profits of your business. If you are a limited company you can either pay corporation tax or give the directors of the company dividends of the profits, on which they pay income tax. If you have anyone working for you, you deduct tax from their earnings and pay it to the Inland Revenue.

To make sure you are always able to pay your tax bill, you should put money aside regularly. You can either put it in an interest-bearing bank account, or the Inland Revenue run a Tax Deposit Scheme. You must keep accurate and up-to-date records of what you spend and receive, both for the tax office and for yourself, so that you will have a rough idea of what your income tax bill will be. There are considerable tax advantages in being self-employed, and in order to derive full advantage of them it is probably worth employing an accountant (**See page 109 Chapter 4 You and Your Money**) as they know what expenses are allowed, are familiar with the tax office and in some circumstances you could find that this results in a reduced tax bill.

What to take to your accountant
* Business records.
* All your receipts.
* All your paying-in books.
* All your bank statements.
* All your used cheque books.
* Copies of all invoices.
* Details of amounts owed to the business by debtors at the end of the year.
* Details of amounts owed by the business to creditors at the end of the year.
* Details of all the stock at the end of the year.
* All calculations connected with VAT.

* Records of all wages paid to any employees with amounts paid under PAYE.

Tax assessments
Tax collected from self-employed people is different from the system under PAYE (Pay As You Earn). Under PAYE, tax is deducted from earnings by the employer before the employee receives it. If you are self-employed you don't pay tax as you go along, but pay it at the end of the tax year. You have to fill in a tax return and then you will be sent a tax assessment on the profits and the tax that is payable. The Tax Inspector will base his assessment on your tax return and the accounts.

If you haven't completed and sent in a tax return and your accounts, the Inland Revenue will have to issue an assessment, usually in the autumn, which is based on an estimate of your income for the year. You will normally have to pay your tax in two instalments – one on 1 January and the other on 1 July. If the assessment is late, then both instalments may be due together. If you disagree with their assessment, you or your accountant has to write to the Tax Inspector saying that you are appealing, either because the amount estimated is excessive or the assessment is not in accordance with the information you submitted. You have thirty days in which to appeal against an assessment and apply to postpone payment of tax and class 4 National Insurance contributions.

Since 1 April 1990 small businesses (a small business is defined as one that has an annual turnover of less than £10,000) do not have to support their tax returns with detailed accounts. They have only to state their total turnover, total business purchases and expenses and net profit. If you are going to use an accountant, this will reduce your bill as they will have to do less work on your accounts. If you are going to do your accounts yourself, it means less work for you.

Taxable profit
Self-employed people pay tax on the profit their businesses make. The profit is what is left after you have deducted all your running costs (**See following Sections**) and for tax purposes is known as Taxable Profit.

Losses

You will really need an accountant (**See page 109 Chapter 4 You and Your Money**) to work out for you a tax-efficient way to use your losses. If your business losses are greater than your total trading income, your accounts will show a loss and therefore no tax will be payable. Losses can be offset against income in future years or any other income in the year of assessment and in the year in which the loss was sustained. For example, if in one year you make a loss of £7,000, maybe because you're just starting up, and in the second year of trading, because you've become established, you make a profit of £7,000, you would normally have to pay tax on the £7,000 profit. But because you made a loss the previous year, you can carry that loss forward, which means you don't have to pay any tax. Another example is that if in one year you make a loss of, say, £10,000 and in your second year of trading you make a profit of £7,000, you can carry your £3,000 loss into the third year until eventually your loss has been used up and you are into real profit and pay tax on those profits at the normal rate.

Allowable business expenses

You can offset against income tax expenses that you have incurred which are set down by the Inland Revenue as being 'wholly and exclusively' for the purpose of your business. Claims must be made each year on your income tax return. Self-employed people can claim a lot more deductions than people who are employed. Expenses that can be offset against income tax are:

* Raw Materials and the cost of goods bought for resale.
* Advertising and publicity.
* Bank charges on your business account.
* Books, journals and trade journals necessary to your business.
* Postage, stationery, telephone.
* Subscriptions to trade associations and professional bodies necessary for your business.
* The running costs of a car, van and motor bike.
* Equipment that regularly needs renewal such as paintbrushes or saw blades.
* Gifts worth less than £10 which promote your business.
* Cost of hiring any equipment.
* Interest charges on loan or HP.

* Insurance such as employer's liability insurance, building insurance, etc.
* Legal costs relevant to the business, i.e. if you need a solicitor to help you recover a debt or draw up a contract.
* Wages and National Insurance contributions paid to employees.
* Accountant's fees.
* Repairs and maintenance of any machinery or vehicles.
* Theft by customers or employees.
* Travelling expenses.
* Use of home or part-use of home for your business (if you claim this you can be liable for Capital Gains Tax on any increase in the value of the property).
* Protective clothing – boots, overalls, etc.
* Some charitable donations (*See leaflet for set limit*).
* Expenditure in preparing the business for opening incurred in the five years before trading begins.

Not allowable business expenses
* All private payments, i.e. expenses connected with family or domestic activities.
* Your withdrawals from business income, regarded as taxable profit. When you spend part privately and part on the business, only the business expenditure can be claimed.
* Capital cost such as buying equipment or vehicles.
* Depreciation of the building.
* Cost of fighting a tax appeal.
* Entertaining UK and overseas customers.
* Fines and penalties for law breaking.
* Gifts over the value of £10.
* Income tax and other taxes.
* Health and life insurance.
* Interest on business capital paid to you or your business partner.
* Interest on overdue tax.
* Legal costs for setting up your business.
* Payments to political parties.
* Travel between home and work (for own business run from separate accommodation).
* You and your business partners' wages.
* Normal everyday clothing.

TAX, INSURANCE AND PENSIONS

The expenses that can and cannot be offset against income tax are clearly defined by the tax office (**See Help Section for addresses, phone numbers and leaflets available**). You will also have to give information on your tax forms about your mortgages, life insurances and pensions.

VAT

VAT is a tax on consumer expenditure. It's collected on business transactions and imports, and as most business transactions involve supplies of goods or services, VAT is therefore payable. When you buy goods or services and you have to pay an extra percentage for VAT, you are generally the last in the chain. Each trader further back in the chain of manufacture and supply has to pay the tax when they buy, but generally recover the cost by charging the tax when they sell.

In 1991 VAT was charged at 17½ per cent (but check with your local Customs and Excise office for up-to-date changes). You have to register for VAT if you are a trader and your turnover exceeds more than £35,000 a year (as of 1991 but, again, check with your local Customs and Excise office for changes) and you have to pay your VAT every quarter. You cannot charge VAT unless you are registered. If you are a smaller trader earning below the VAT registered amount you do not have to register, unless you decide to do so voluntarily (**See section later this Chapter**).

Goods can be free of VAT by being either **zero rated** or **exempt**. If you are selling only zero rated goods you can claim back the VAT that you pay on your business expenditure; this is called input tax. If you sell only exempt goods or services, you cannot claim back input tax. This adds to your business expenses. Some of the services and goods that are zero rated for VAT include:

* Most food (but not catering, which includes meals in restaurants, cafes, etc. and hot take-away food and drink).
* Books and newspapers.
* Sales, long leases and construction of new housing and some other new buildings (but not work to existing buildings).
* Young children's clothing and footwear.
* Export of goods.
* Dispensing of prescriptions and the supply of many aids for handicapped persons.
* Mobile homes and houseboats.

Exempt supplies are business transactions on which VAT is not chargeable at either the standard or zero rate, which is nil. They are not taxable supplies and do not form part of your taxable turnover. Taxable turnover is the total value of all the taxable supplies you make in the course of your business. If you make only exempt supplies, you cannot be registered for VAT. Exempt supplies include such things as:

* Most sales, leases and lettings of land and buildings (but not lettings of garages, parking spaces or hotel and holiday accommodation).
* Insurance.
* Betting, gaming and lotteries (but not gambling machine takings, admission to premises, club subscriptions and certain participation charges).
* Provision of credit.
* Certain education and training.
* Services of doctors, dentists, opticians, etc. (but some practitioners are not exempt, eg. osteopaths).
* Certain supplies by undertakers.
* Membership benefits provided by trade unions and professional bodies.
* Entry to certain sports competitions.

You should start keeping VAT records and charging VAT to your customers immediately you know that you are required to be registered. VAT records are records of all the supplies you make and receive and a summary of VAT for each period covered by your VAT returns. If you are already in business you will probably find that your normal business records can be adapted (**See following Sections**).

Registering for VAT
By law you have to approach the Customs and Excise within thirty days with a view to registering for VAT, if at any time you believe that within the next thirty days your taxable turnover for the past twelve months will have exceeded the annual limit, which in 1991 was £35,000 a year.

Either a limited company, a partnership (including a husband and wife partnership) or a self-employed individual sole trader can register for VAT (**See pages 71 to 73 Chapter 3 You, Your Company and the Law**). Your local VAT office (Customs and

Excise address in your local telephone directory) deals with registration. They will give you a registration number and an effective date of registration. From that date you must charge VAT on your supplies.

Every three months you will receive a VAT return form. Fill it in with the details of supplies you have made and received during that period and pay the total that you owe to the Customs and Excise. You deduct the VAT you have paid on materials and services and add VAT to your prices. For example, VAT at 17½ per cent on your purchases has a 14.89 per cent VAT component which you deduct from the full price you paid. Or claim a repayment if tax is owed to you. Since tax periods end on fixed dates throughout the year, it is unlikely that your first VAT return will be for exactly three months. Your quarterly return with your payment must be sent within thirty days of the end of each accounting period.

If at any time you believe your future taxable turnover, which is the value, not just the profit, of all your taxable supplies, will exceed the above amount you must, within thirty days of the first day from which the grounds existed, fill in Form VAT 1, available from your local Customs and Excise office and return it to them. It is no excuse to say that you weren't expecting to earn that much, as the VAT office will deduct it anyway when they eventually find out.

You can apply for exemption from VAT registration if your taxable supplies are mainly zero rated. If you apply for exemption you must complete form VAT 1. If you are granted exemption you will not be able to reclaim the VAT you pay on purchases of goods or services for your business.

Voluntary VAT registration
If your taxable turnover is below the limits, you may apply for voluntary VAT registration. You should consider this if you have heavy start-up costs involving VAT. For example, £40,000 spent on equipment could carry another £6,000 or more on VAT which could be reclaimed when registered. VAT on vans, not cars, and properly valued stock can be reclaimed irrespective of when they were purchased, but they must be used for the business and you must have VAT invoices. VAT on services such as solicitors' fees, if you have incurred them less than six months prior to the date of registration, can also be claimed.

If you have a lot of purchases and a large part of your sales go to VAT-registered traders, your price will have to reflect the VAT you have paid on your inputs. However, your customers will not be able to claim back the VAT they are paying you unless you register and can issue them with a VAT invoice. For example, if you have to pay VAT on the material you buy to make a dress, if you aren't VAT registered you have no way of claiming it back. But if you are VAT registered you add it on to your selling price and can claim back the VAT on your purchases.

Registering for VAT will increase the selling price of your product so you have to consider if it can stand the VAT mark up. But if you think it can, then, as explained above, there are certain advantages to VAT registration. You will have to satisfy Customs and Excise that your activities constitute a business, for VAT purposes.

Once you have registered you will have to account for output tax on all your taxable supplies and you may only take credit for input tax that is attributable to your taxable supplies. You will also have to send in regular VAT returns and keep proper accounts for inspection by visiting VAT officers. Voluntary VAT registration has benefits only if you do your own VAT every three months. You lose the financial benefit if you employ an accountant for what amounts to a small amount of work.

If you trade in phases or seasonally, buying a lot of materials to work on, then some months you will receive more back in VAT than you have spent. Your profit will not be affected as the customer pays the VAT. On some capital expenditure, for which you may only be able to claim a small percentage from your Inland Revenue tax, you could be able to deduct the VAT, which will help considerably.

The Customs and Excise who operate VAT have a lot of power. If your VAT returns are late they can punish you with a penal rate of interest. They will make regular inspections by coming to your home to check every figure and every receipt, so it is very important that you keep accurate records. You will probably be visited eighteen months after being registered. After that the interval between visits will vary, depending on the size and complexity of your business. It's a good idea to visit your local VAT office at the beginning and ask them to show you how the system works and how to fill in the simple forms. It isn't as complicated as you may think.

TAX, INSURANCE AND PENSIONS

A VAT invoice
Only if you are VAT registered can you issue a VAT invoice, which must have on it the VAT registration number allocated to you when you apply for VAT registration. If the value of the supply including VAT is less than £50, the invoice does not have to show the amount of VAT separately, but it must show that the total price includes VAT and the date. Always get a proper VAT invoice from your suppliers, dated and with their VAT registration number. You cannot claim back VAT unless you have a purchase invoice.

If you run a retail business, i.e. you sell to the public, you do not need to give a VAT invoice unless you are asked for one, but if you are asked you must produce it. Your retail customer may be self-employed and require a VAT invoice to claim back their VAT. If you are running a retail business there are several VAT schemes which simplify accounting. Your local Customs and Excise office will have the leaflets appropriate to your business **(See Help section this Chapter for addresses and phone numbers)**.

NATIONAL INSURANCE
National Insurance contributions are paid to secure an assortment of basic benefits such as: sickness benefit, invalidity benefit, retirement pension, widow's benefit and maternity allowance. In order to be eligible for these basic benefits you, or sometimes your husband or wife, must have paid a certain amount of contributions or been awarded enough credits. The amount of contributions needed varies for different benefits. For some benefits the required total can be made up of contributions from the different National Insurance classes.

There are four different kinds of National Insurance contributions:
Class 1 is for you and your employer. This is earnings related – the amount you pay depends on the amount you earn.
Class 2 is for self-employed people and is a flat-rate contribution.
Class 3 you pay voluntarily to help you to qualify for some benefits.
Class 4 is for self-employed people whose profits are over a certain amount.

If you fail to pay the appropriate contributions, your benefit may be reduced or cancelled. For example, to qualify for unemployment benefit you must have paid, in one income tax year, a certain amount of Class 1 contributions (**See following Section**), which will vary according to your circumstances. For full benefit you will have to have paid, in addition, at least fifty times the amount payable on a weekly earnings limit. These contributions must be paid in the income tax year which ended in the calendar year before that in which you claim benefit. If you have less than fifty times the required amount, but at least twenty-five times, benefit is still payable at a reduced rate.

Class 1 National Insurance contributions
These are earnings related and based on a percentage of an employee's earnings. They are made up of a combined payment by employee and employer. The employee's contribution is deducted from his pay by his employer before he receives it. Class 1 contributions are payable only if you are over sixteen and your gross earnings are at or above the lower earnings limit (£46 a week in 1990/91; contact your local Social Security office for any changes). If your gross earnings are at or above this level, contributions are payable on all earnings up to an upper limit of £350 per week (check with your local Social Security office for any changes). Gross earnings include overtime pay, commission, bonus, etc., without deduction of any superannuation contributions. If you earn more than the upper earnings limit, you have to pay contributions on all earnings up to this amount, but not on any earnings over it. Women who marry for the first time no longer have a right to elect not to pay the full contribution rate. Married women and widows who before 12 May 1977 elected not to pay contributions at the full rate retain the right to pay reduced rate over the same earnings range, which covers industrial injuries benefits and a contribution to the National Health Service. They lose the right if, after 5 April 1978, there are two consecutive tax years in which they have no earnings on which primary Class 1 contributions are payable and in which they have not been at any time self-employed earners. No contributions are due on earnings paid for a period on or after the employee's pension age, even when retirement is deferred (**See page 153 this Chapter**).

Secondary class 1 contributions
These are payable by employees or employed earners and office holders. The upper earnings limit for employers' contributions has been abolished and secondary contributions are payable on all

employees' earnings if they reach or exceed £46 a week (as of 1990/91; check with your local Social Security office for changes).

If you are an employee but are outside the Class 1 age range, i.e. between sixteen and sixty-five (sixty for women) you can ask at your local Social Security office for an exemption certificate and give it to your employer. Men and women pay the same contributions (**See page 154 this Chapter**).

Class 2 National Insurance contributions

If you are self-employed, a sole trader or a partner and over sixteen, earning more than the small earnings limit of £2,600 in 1990/91 (check with your local Social Security office for any changes) you will have to pay Class 2 contributions (contact your local Social Security office for details) every week, including holidays. These contributions are a flat-rate payment. If you earn less than the small earnings limit or if you are over retirement age (sixty for women, sixty-five for men) you will not have to pay Class 2 contributions, but you must apply for a small earnings exemption certificate at your local Social Security office. But be aware that if you take that option you could lose out on your right to Sickness Benefit and Retirement Pension. If you are exempted you could voluntarily pay either Class 2 or Class 3 contributions. Paying either contribution will protect your pension entitlement. Self-employed people, whether or not they pay Class 2 contributions, may also be liable for Class 4 contributions based on profits or gains within certain limits (contact your local Social Security office for current information). You can make your contributions monthly either by direct debit of a bank or Giro account, or by buying Class 2 National Insurance stamps at your local post office and attaching them to a contribution card which you can get from your local Social Security office.

You must pay Class 2 contributions as you earn, either by direct debit from your bank or National Girobank account, or by stamping a contribution card obtained from your local Social Security office.

Class 3 contributions

If you are over sixteen these are voluntary flat-rate contributions for people, such as those who have taken a short break in their employment or who are considering taking early retirement, who would otherwise be unable to qualify for Retirement Pension,

Widow's Benefit and other benefits because they haven't got sufficient record of Class 1 or Class 2 contributions (**See page 154 this Chapter**). Generally, voluntary contributions have to be paid before the end of the second tax year in which they are due. Before deciding if you should pay, contact your local Social Security office for advice.

Class 4 contributions

A person who is self-employed and aged between sixteen and retirement age (sixty for a woman and sixty-five for a man) and earns more than the lower earnings limit (contact your Social Service office for up-to-date information) must pay Class 2 National Insurance contributions. You may also have to pay Class 4, which is based on profits or gains chargeable to income tax under schedule D. The current rate is 6.3 per cent of all profits between £4,750 and £18,200 or more, but check with your local Social Security office because it's subject to change. Half the cost of Class 4 contributions can be deducted as an expense for income tax purposes.

Class 4 contributions are normally calculated, assessed and collected at the same time as you pay your schedule D income tax. If you are self-employed and either under sixteen, or – at the beginning of the tax year – over pension age (even where retirement is deferred), you are not liable to pay Class 4 contributions. If you have a job for which you pay Class 1 contributions, you are still liable for Class 2 and perhaps Class 4 payments on your self-employed earnings. Although being self-employed you will contribute at a higher rate, you are still not entitled to all the benefits of employees. For example, if you lose a job but have some self-employment you cannot draw Unemployment Benefit unless you can prove that your private earnings do not exceed a prescribed maximum (contact your local Social Security office for up-to-date information) and that you are available for full-time work.

You have to supply all the necessary figures and either your accountant, if you have one, or your Tax Office, will work out what contributions you owe. If you want to check the figures, read leaflet 1R 24 which is available from your local Tax Office or tax enquiry centre, which explains how profits assessed for Class 4 contributions are related to profits assessed for income tax purposes (**See page 166 Help Section**).

Employer's contribution
If you employ other people, you are responsible for paying their National Insurance contributions. You will have to deduct these from their earnings and together with your contribution send them to the Inland Revenue.

Self-employed and employed at the same time
If you are both self-employed and employed at the same time, you will be liable for Class 1 contributions and Class 2 contributions, up to a specified amount (contact your local Social Security office for up-to-date information). There is a maximum amount of contributions which an individual has to pay in a tax year. If you have high earnings from your employment, you can apply for deferment of Class 2 and Class 4 contributions, see leaflet NP 18 **(See page 166 Help Section)**.

If your earnings are low
To be eligible for small earnings exemption you have to be self-employed and not earn very much in one particular year, then you can apply not to pay Class 2 contributions. The certificate will generally be effective from the date of your application, although sometimes it can be backdated up to thirteen weeks. But think carefully about it before you apply, because not paying Class 2 contributions may effect your entitlement to National Insurance benefits later on. The exemption limit usually changes annually, so check first.

Married women and widows
If you are a self-employed married woman or a widow, you will still have to pay Class 4 contributions if your profits are over the set limit. You can choose to pay your contributions at a reduced rate, which means you are not liable to pay Class 2. If you are unsure ask at your local Social Security office **(See Help Section this Chapter for addresses and phone numbers)**.

BENEFITS

Retirement pension
If you are on the basic retirement pension, it will not be affected by any earnings you have. You can decide not to receive your pension when you reach pensionable age (sixty for women, sixty-

five for men) and for a period of up to five years you can earn extra pension called increments.

State earnings related pension (SERPS)
Under this scheme retirement, invalidity and widows' pensions for employees are related to the earnings on which National Insurance contributions (**See pages 149 to 153 this Chapter**) have been paid. For employees of either sex with a complete insurance record the scheme provides a category A retirement pension in two parts, a basic and an additional pension. (Contact your local Social Security office for up-to-date information.)

If you are self-employed and you pay the correct National Insurance contributions, you are eligible at retirement age for a basic pension (**See National Insurance sections this Chapter**).

Other benefits
If you hit a financial problem, it's good to know what your benefits will be. Your local Social Security office will have these leaflets:

FAMILY BENEFITS
Child Benefits.
Maternity Benefits.
Maternity Allowance.

BENEFITS FOR HANDICAPPED OR DISABLED PEOPLE
Mobility Allowance.
Attendance Allowance.

BENEFITS FOR THE ILL OR UNEMPLOYED
Sickness Benefit.
Invalidity Benefit.
Severe Disablement Allowance.
Invalid Care Allowance.
Unemployment Benefit.

PENSIONS AND WIDOW'S BENEFIT
State Pension.
Widow's Allowance.
Widowed Mother's Allowance.
Widow's Pension.
Retirement Pension.

FAMILY INCOME SUPPLEMENTS AND LOANS.
SUPPLEMENTARY BENEFITS.
GRANTS FROM LOCAL AUTHORITIES.

Benefits are subject to frequent political changes so check the up-to-date situation with your local Social Security office or Job Centre (**See Help Section this Chapter for addresses and phone numbers**).

INSURANCE

It's important that you take out adequate insurances because you may find that some companies won't give you work if they find you aren't properly covered. If you aren't insured and someone makes a claim against you, it could be so costly that it could lead to you becoming bankrupt or going into liquidation. If your insurance cover isn't sufficient, you may find that your insurance company will have every right to refuse to meet your claim. Insurance premiums for any business insurance are deductible expenses which can be set off against tax (**See page 144 this Chapter**).

There are some insurances which are compulsory such as: **employer's liability insurance** and **vehicle insurance**. Public liability insurance isn't compulsory, but it is strongly recommended if members of the public are coming to your home, either to work, or, for instance, to have lessons. There are other insurances which you should investigate and seriously consider if you think they are relevant to your business:

* Product liability insurance.
* Premises insurance.
* Contents, stock and materials insurance.
* Consequential loss insurance.
* Health and accident insurance.
* Personal life assurance.
* Mortgage protection and professional indemnity insurance.

(**See following pages for further information.**)

It is better to get the advice of an insurance broker, who will be able to tell you the appropriate policies for your type of work. But do some research first, because you will find that a lot of trade associations will arrange special insurance policies which are designed for specific trades and this is generally cheaper. Your relevant trade association will be listed in the phone book.

Employer's liability insurance
If you employ someone (**See page 149 National Insurance Section**), even if it's a relative, or if you sub-contract, you have to take out this insurance. It covers claims that an employee might bring after being injured or becoming ill as a result of being employed by you. You must be insured for at least £2 million and you must display a current certificate of insurance, which it is best to take out with an authorised insurance company.

Vehicle insurance
Any vehicle used for your business must be insured, even if you already have another vehicle for your private use. If the business vehicle is going to be driven by someone other than you, you must make sure that this is specified in the insurance policy.

Public liability insurance
This insurance covers you against any claims brought by a member of the public who has been injured, or whose property has been damaged as a result of your employees' negligence at work.

Product liability insurance
This insurance covers any claims which might arise out of any faults in something that either you or someone employed by you have made or serviced.

Premises insurance
This insures the premises you are working in. If you are working at home and you already have an insurance policy, it will generally cover only residential use of the property. So either take out a new policy or amend your existing one.

Contents stock and materials insurance
This insurance is to cover the replacement of any stock or materials and other contents such as fixtures, fittings, tools, equipment, stock – which includes raw materials and any goods already allocated to customers, whether or not they have been paid for. It also covers any goods in transit, any goods which belong to a customer and are on your premises either to be serviced or

repaired and any goods that are on a sub-contractor's premises. Even if you already have a home contents insurance policy you will find it usually only covers residential use of the property. Either take out a new policy or amend your existing one.

Consequential loss insurance
This insurance covers the continuing overhead costs if your business should come to a standstill because fire destroys the premises. It should cover all overhead costs for a limited period – usually a year.

Health and accident insurance
When you are self-employed and running your own business, one of the worst things that can happen is that you suffer an illness or accident that prevents you from working. Your finances could just about hit rock bottom if this situation lasts longer than a few days, and for this reason permanent health assurance is vitally important, even though it isn't cheap. It pays out a fixed sum for every week that you are unable to work, and is the only insurance that pays a fixed sum in benefit every week that you are unable to work at your usual job as a result of illness or injury.

Permanent health insurance will pay you the maximum amount which can be paid out weekly. This will always be less than the salary that you normally earn. The usual rule for calculating what you will receive weekly is the income paid by the policy, plus state benefit, plus income from any other insurance policies which should not add up to more than a fixed percentage (which is usually 75 per cent, although the percentage can be reduced if you are on a higher income) of your average earnings over the year prior to the policy being taken out. If you return to work part-time or to another job that pays you less than your previous one, the policy will usually pay you a weekly benefit which will partly make up the difference between your previous earnings and now. Some permanent health insurance policies allow the maximum weekly amount payable to be increased to help keep pace with any increase in earnings.

If you are ever ill and you do have to make a claim on your policy, the insurers cannot increase the premium or cancel the policy. But you must inform them if you change your job or if you temporarily move abroad for more than a year. If you don't inform them they can cancel the policy, especially if you change your job to one which is unacceptably dangerous. If they decide that your new job is dangerous or that you have taken up a risky leisure activity, they may increase your insurance premiums.

Before choosing permanent health insurance, shop around. Get a number of different quotes and compare them, to see how each policy is different.

Mortgage protection insurance
This insurance covers your mortgage repayments if you die or if your business fails.

Professional indemnity insurance
If you are a professional person who gives advice, such as an accountant, architect or computer consultant, you should be covered by this insurance in case any liability arises from wrongful advice or negligence.

Life assurance
For most people the point of having a life assurance is so that they know there will be payments made after their death. If you are self-employed it is very important to have some form of life assurance policy, but before you decide which one, collect as much information as you can from different insurance companies. In other words, shop around. What you are looking for is a policy that fits your lifestyle. You can get life assurance policies that are flexible and you can choose elements of protection and savings which allow you to change the balance to suit your needs. Don't be talked into agreeing to something by some smooth, fast-talking insurance sales person. Remember that taking on a life assurance is a major financial long-term commitment which you cannot usually get out of without some financial loss – this is why you must always remember to read the small print before you sign anything.

You can get life assurance through banks, building societies, solicitors, accountants, insurance brokers, full-time insurance company representatives, consultants or directly from an insurance company. There are different types of life assurance, which are described below.

TAX, INSURANCE AND PENSIONS

Whole life, temporary or term assurance
On these types of policies payment is made only on the death of the policy holder. When that happens, the person who is named in the policy is the beneficiary to the estate of the deceased. This type of policy does not have a maturity date so no payments are made until the policy holder dies. The policy holder has to make fixed premium payments for the whole of their life or, say, until they are sixty-five.

Temporary or term assurance
This is generally the cheapest type of life assurance. It covers the policy holder in the event of the policy holder's death within a fixed period of time. For example if you die within twenty-five years, payment will be made by the insurance company. But if you are still alive at the end of that time, then the policy simply lapses and no payments are made. The most common term assurance is a mortgage protection policy which is taken out together with a repayment mortgage loan. The length of the policy is the same as the mortgage. If the policy holder dies, the outstanding loan – in this instance the mortgage – is paid off by the insurance company.

Endowment assurance
There are a wide range of policies to choose from within this basic outline. This type of policy makes payment either when the policy holder dies or on a given date when the policy matures, whichever is first. One of the advantages of this type of policy is that if you want to you can get the policy to pay out at an important family time, such as when a child reaches eighteen or twenty-one. As well as giving you life assurance cover, an endowment policy can also be a good way to save, because the money cannot be withdrawn without penalty.

Endowment and whole life assurance policies
This type of policy is generally offered on a 'without profits' basis, which means that a guaranteed fixed sum of money will be paid out either on the death of the policy holder or when the policy matures. The problem with this type of policy is that the value of it is reduced by inflation.

If the policy is 'with profits', it means that the basic sum insured remains at a fixed level and grows as bonuses are added each year. You will be sent a notice each time a bonus (called a revisionary bonus) is announced, which will tell you by how much the benefits that are payable will be increased. The premium payments will be higher for a policy 'with profits' than for a policy 'without profits' because the policy holder shares in the profits of the insurance company. There is no guarantee that a bonus will be declared every year, but once it has been declared it cannot be withdrawn. An additional terminal bonus is often paid when the policy holder dies or the policy matures. But if the policy is 'without profits' the exact amount of the payment on death or maturity cannot be known.

Unit linked policies
These are similar to a 'with profits' policy. The amount the insurance company pays out when the policy holder dies depends on the value of the insurance company's investments. The value of the benefit to be paid after that increases or falls. You will be notified of any changes in value.

Tax relief on life assurance policies
The majority of policies taken out before 13 March 1984 were eligible for tax relief on their premiums, and tax relief can still be claimed on policies taken out before 13 March 1984. However, tax relief cannot normally be claimed on policies taken out since this date, except for certain special policies which were taken out by people who are self-employed or in jobs without occupational pensions.

PENSIONS
You will get a state pension when you reach retirement age (sixty for a woman and sixty-five for a man) (**See page 154 State Earnings Related Pensions (SERPS)**). The amount depends on your National Insurance contributions (**See pages 149–153 this Chapter**).

As a self-employed person you won't be part of a company pension plan, which means that you can probably look forward only to the basic state pension when you retire, which is currently (1991/92) £52 per week if you are single or £83 per week if you are married. This could mean that when you retire you would have to take a reduction in your income. If you can afford the payments, a personal pension will certainly help to top up your state pension.

TAX, INSURANCE AND PENSIONS

The subject of pensions is far too intricate to cover in depth in this kind of book – after all we're talking about working from home – but there are two basic types of personal retirement pension; one is called **with profits** and the other is called **unit linked**.

With profits
This type of policy means that your money is largely invested by the pension company in gilts and government interest-bearing bonds. These will produce a predictable but modest pension when you retire.

Unit linked
This type of policy means that the pension company invests your money in the stock market. Over the last few years the stock market has generally out-performed interest-bearing trusts. But there is a certain amount of risk tied to the stock market, such as the crash of 1987 – it has its ups and downs. But if you're lucky a 'unit linked' policy could provide you with a higher pension than one 'with profits'. You have to choose a balance between wanting a modest return on a secure pension, which is what you will receive from a 'with profits' pension, or possibly a higher pension but with a greater risk, which is what you will receive with a 'unit linked' policy. A pension adviser will be able to explain this in more detail and help you to decide on which policy you should have.

Personal pensions are tax free up to a certain limit. The following table shows the maximum percentage of net relevant earnings which may be contributed in the 1991/92 tax years.

AGE ON 6 APRIL 1991	RETIREMENT ANNUITY	PERSONAL PENSION
35 or less	17.5 per cent	17.5 per cent
36 to 45	17.5 per cent	20.0 per cent
46 to 50	17.5 per cent	25.0 per cent
51 to 55	20.0 per cent	30.0 per cent
56 to 60	22.5 per cent	35.0 per cent
61 to 74	27.5 per cent	40.0 per cent

One of the other advantages for people running their own business is that with certain pension plans you can borrow against them.

You will have to pay the same rates as if you were borrowing from the bank, but it does save you having to go to the bank, and it could get you out of a hole if your business was in real difficulty.

Before getting a pension plan, you should shop around. Contact your bank, accountant, independent financial adviser and the various pension companies.

CHAPTER 5
HELP SECTION

Life assurances, unit trusts and pensions
Self Regulatory Organisation (SROs). There are five different SROs, each covering broadly different areas of investment and business.

FIMBRA (FINANCIAL INTERMEDIARIES, MANAGERS AND BROKERS REGULATORY ASSOCIATION)
Regulates the independent intermediaries, advising on life assurance, pensions, unit trusts and financial management. This is the most important organisation for most investors.
Hertsmere House, Marsh Wall, London, E14 9RW. Tel: 071 538 8860.

IMRO (INVESTMENT MANAGEMENT REGULATORY ORGANISATION)
Regulates investment managers. If you have a complaint about the management of your funds go to them.
Broadwalk House, 5 Appold Street, London, EC2A 2LL Tel: 071 628 6022.

LAUTRO LTD (LIFE ASSURANCE AND UNIT TRUST REGULATORY ORGANISATIONS)
Regulates the marketing of life assurance, pensions and unit trust products. If you have any query or complaint about advertising or a complaint against any of these products you can lodge it with them.
Centre Point, 103 New Oxford Street, London, WC1A 1QH. Tel: 071 379 0444.

TSA (THE SECURITIES ASSOCIATION)
Regulates the dealing in shares on the stock exchange, and they will take up any irregularities.
The Stock Exchange Building, London, EC2N 1EQ. Tel: 071 256 9000.

THE COMPLETE GUIDE TO WORKING FROM HOME

AFBD (ASSOCIATION OF FUTURES BROKERS AND DEALERS LTD)
Regulates the futures and options industry which makes them answerable to options and futures investors.
Section B, 5th Floor, Plantation House, 4–16 Mincing Lane, London, EC3M 3DX. Tel: 071 626 9763.

BRITISH INSURANCE AND INVESTMENT BROKERS' ASSOCIATION
14 Bevis Marks, London, EC3A 7NT. Tel: 071 623 9043.

INSURANCE BROKERS REGISTRATION
15 St Helens Place, London, EC3A 6DS. Tel: 071 588 4387.

THE INSTITUTE OF INSURANCE CONSULTANTS
121a Queensway, Bletchley, Milton Keynes, MK2 2DH. Tel: 0908 643364.

CORPORATION OF INSURANCE AND FINANCIAL ADVISORS
6–7 Leapale Road, Guildford, Surrey, GU1 4JX. Tel: 0483 39121/ 35786.

If you have problems settling an insurance claim contact:
The Secretary, The Policy Holders Protection Board, Aldermary House, Queen Street, London, EC4N 1TT. Tel: 071 248 4477.

Insurance brokers
INSURANCE BROKERS OMBUDSMAN BUREAU 31 Southampton Row, London, WC1B 5HJ. Tel: 071 242 8613.

Insurance booklets
It Might Never Happen – But. A guide to Household Insurance by The Office of Fair Trading. Published by HMSO.

Pensions – books and magazines
What Will My Pension Be? A Consumer Publication.
Pension Management. A *Financial Times* monthly publication.
The Daily Telegraph Pension Guide by Barry Stillerman. Published by Telegraph Publications.
Planning Your Pension by Tony Reardon. Published by Allied Dunbar Library Money Guides. Longmans.
Occupational Pension Schemes 1987. Eighth survey by the Government Actuary. Published by HMSO.

TAX, INSURANCE AND PENSIONS

The Essential Guide To Pensions – A Workers Handbook by Sue Ward. Published by Pluto Press.
Daily Mail – Personal Pensions – the Choice is Yours by Norman Toulson.
You and Your Pension. How To Find The Right Pension and Make It Grow by Which? Books. Published by Consumers Association and Hodder and Stoughton.
Pensions, monthly, United Trade Press, Bowling Green Lane, London, EC1R 0DA.
Pensions Management, monthly, FTBI, Greystoke House, Fetter Lane, London EC1.
Pensions World, monthly, Tolley's, Tolley House, Scarbrook Road, Croydon, Surrey, CR0 1SQ.

The Insurance Company, Legal and General, run a Pension News Service, which is a sheet of press cuttings. To be put on the mailing list write to: Pensions Publicity, Kingswood House, Kingswood, Tadworth, Surrey, KT20 6EU.
All books are available from your local library, book shop or the publisher.

Pensions – official and semi-official publications
New Pensions Choices A general guide to the pension changes, NP40 from your local DHSS.
Information for Employers NP41.
Information for Employees NP42.
Further fact sheets from: Leaflets Unit, PO Box 21, Stanmore, Middlesex, HA 1AY.
Pensions Advice and Management Authorisation Under the Financial Services Act Securities and Investment Board, 3 Royal Exchange Buildings, London, EC3V 3NL. Tel: 071 283 2474.

Pensions – useful addresses and material
PENSION FUNDS AND THEIR ADVISORS (annual directory) lists all major pension funds and advice firms. AP Information Services Ltd., 33 Ashbourne Avenue, London, NW11 0DU. Tel: 081 458 1607.
PENSION FUND TRUSTEES AND THE LAW (free) Bacon and Woodrow, 55 East Street, Epsom, Surrey, KT17 1BL. Tel: 0372 729600.
A General Introduction to Institutional Investment by A J Frost

and D P Hager, published for the Institute and Faculty of Actuaries, Heinemann, 1987.
DSS Benefits Division, Long Benton, Benton Park Road, Newcastle-upon-Tyne, NE9A 1YX. Tel: 091 213 5000. Contracting Out: 091 261 2341.
OCCUPATIONAL PENSIONS BOARD Lynwood Road, Thames Ditton, Surrey, KT6 0DP. Tel: 081 398 4242.
OCCUPATIONAL PENSIONS ADVISORY SERVICE (OPAS) 11 Belgrave Road, London, SW1V 1RB. Tel: 071 233 8080.

Social security – DSS
(DSS) DEPARTMENT OF SOCIAL SECURITY Your local office will be listed in the phone book.
FREELINE SOCIAL SECURITY for any questions about benefits, pensions or national insurance (FREEFONE 0800 666555).
SOCIAL SECURITY ADVICE LINE (SSALE) free telephone enquiry service 0800 393 539.
Leaflets from any TAX OFFICE or TAX ENQUIRY CENTRE are free. Look under INLAND REVENUE in your phone book. Offices are open between 10a.m. and 4p.m. SOCIAL SECURITY OFFICE listed under SOCIAL SECURITY or HEALTH AND SOCIAL SECURITY in your phone book.
Leaflet No:
IR 106 *Tax and Your Business – Capital Allowances for Vehicle and Machinery.*
CGT 11 *Capital Gains Tax and Small Businesses.*
CGT 14 *Capital Gains Tax – An Introduction.*
CA1 *Income Tax and Corporation Tax – Capital Allowances on Machinery and Plant.*
NI 255 *Class 2 and Class 3 National Insurance Contributions: Direct Debit – The Easy Way to Pay!*
NP 18 *Class 4 National Insurance Contributions.*
IR 24 *Class 4 National Insurance Contributions.*
IR 14/15 *Construction Industry: Tax Deduction Scheme* – explanatory booklet for contractors and sub-contractors.
NI 269 *Employer' Manual on National Insurance Contributions.*
FC 10 *Family Credit.*
IR 105 *Tax and Your Business – How Your Profits are Taxed.*
IR 24 *Class 4 National Insurance Contributions.*
IR 26 *Income Tax Assessments on Business Profits – Changes of Accounting Date.*

TAX, INSURANCE AND PENSIONS

IR 91 *Independent Taxation – Guide for Widows and Widowers.*
IR 92 *Income Tax – A Guide for One-Parent Families.*
IR 93 *Income Tax – A Guide to Separation, Divorce and Maintenance Payments.*
IR 37 *Income Tax and Capital Gains Tax – Appeals.*
IR 40 *Income Tax – Conditions for Getting a Sub-Contractor's Tax Certificate.*
IR 84 *Income Tax – Have You Anything to Declare?*
IR 72 *Inland Revenue Investigations – The Examination of Small Business Accounts.*
IR 73 *Inland Revenue Investigations – How Settlements are Negotiated.*
NP 27 *Looking After Someone at Home? How to Protect Your Pension.*
NP 28 *National Insurance For Employees.*
NI 27A *National Insurance For People With Small Earnings from Self-Employment.*
NI 1 *National Insurance For Married Women.*
NI 17A *Maternity Benefits – A Guide.*
NI 95 *National Insurance For Divorced Women.*
NI 51 *National Insurance For Widows.*
NP 28 *National Insurance For Employees.*
NI 41 *National Insurance For Self-Employed People (Class 2 Contributions).*
NI 42 *National Insurance Voluntary Contributions (Class 3).*
NI 48 *National Insurance – Unpaid and Late Contributions.*
NI 244 *Statutory Sick Pay – Check Your Rights.*
IR 78 *Personal Pensions. A New Pensions Choice – A Guide for Tax.*
IR 34 *Income Tax – Pay as You Earn.*
IR 71 *PAYE – Inspection of Employers' and Contributors' Records.*
IR 103 *Private Medical Insurance.*
NP 18 *Self-Employed National Insurance Contributions Class 2 and Class 4* gives information about exemption limit.
IR 28 *Tax and Your Business – Starting in Business.*
IR 53 *Thinking of Taking Someone on?*
FB 22 *Which Benefit?* (available in Bengali, Chinese, Gujerati, Hindi, Punjabi, Turkish, Urdu, Vietnamese and Welsh).
IR 52 *Your Tax Office – Why it is Where it is.*

NP 28 *Your Future Pension – How to Check Your Right to an Additional Pension.*
FB 23 *Young People's Guide to Social Security.*
NI 196 *Social Security Benefit Rates.*

THE CAPITAL TAX OFFICE ENGLAND AND WALES Minford House, Rockley Road, London, W14 0DF. Tel: 071 603 4622.
SCOTLAND 16 Picardy Place, Edinburgh, EH1 3NB. Tel: 031 556 8511.
NORTHERN IRELAND Law Courts Building, Chichester Street, Belfast, BT1 3NU. Tel: 0232 235111.

VAT
These VAT leaflets are available from your local CUSTOMS AND EXCISE office. Look under CUSTOMS AND EXCISE in your phone book.
Choosing Your Retail Scheme.
Filling in Your VAT Return.
Keeping Records and Accounts.
Overseas Traders and United Kingdom VAT.
Should I be Registered for VAT?
The VAT Guide (Notice 700) explains fully all the basic VAT rules and procedures.
Transfer of a Business as a Going Concern.
Visits from VAT Officers.
VAT – A Working Guide for Small Businesses by Ian Mills Published by the *Daily Telegraph.*

Chapter information sources
Davies and Chapman, Financial Advisers; Department of Social Security; Customs and Excise; Allan Butnick, Accountant; Citizens Advice Bureau; The Inland Revenue; *Know Your Rights*, Reader's Digest.

CHAPTER 6

Teleworkers and Outworkers

Don't fall into the trap of working un-social hours!

OUTWORKERS AND HOMEWORKERS

For the purposes of this book we are defining homeworkers and outworkers as separate, although they both work from home. The majority of homeworkers (our definition) are usually running their own business and selling and marketing the finished product.

The majority of outworkers (our definition) are working for a company and usually being paid for each item they produce and have no part of the selling process. The Department of Employment definition of a homeworker is:
'Someone who works from the home for an employer or contractor who supplies work and is responsible for marketing and selling the results.'

Generally firms class their outworkers as self-employed (**See page 23 Chapter 2 Starting your own Business**) rather than direct employees, because an employee has more rights. Thus a firm has less responsibility and fewer overheads if it gives work to someone who is self-employed. For this reason a lot of the information in this book is relevant to people who are working from home as self-employed and those working as outworkers who are also classed as self-employed, although the involvement in their work may stop at different points in the production process.

The job advertisement
Most outworkers' (see book definition as above) jobs are advertised in local newspapers.
Avoid at all cost advertisements that:

* Ask for the outworker to make a payment before the work starts.
* Ask for money for a 'starter kit' before you are even told what the work is.
* Describe schemes where you have to buy or rent equipment or raw materials and then sell the finished product yourself.

Be wary of advertisements that:
* Are vague about the nature of the work involved, e.g. mailing envelopes.
* Are found in the situations vacant or recruitment columns of local and national newspapers where they may not have been examined by the publishers and may not conform to the trading standards conditions.

The advertisement should contain the full details of the work and the conditions.

Is outworking legal?
It's perfectly legal for an outworker to work from home, providing that the work is safe and doesn't cause too much noise and nuisance to neighbours (**See page 212 Chapter 8 Your Home as Your Workplace**). You don't need planning permission as long as you:

* Mainly use your house as your home.
* Do not use large parts of your house for your homeworking.
* Do not cause a noticeable increase in the amount of traffic or people who call at your house and that you do not use, for example, more than one sewing machine at a time.
* If you are a council tenant you should inform your Council Housing Department that you are an outworker.
* If you have a mortgage agreement, it should not alter that agreement because the primary use of your property remains residential. Only if it is used for the purpose of a commercial business would mortgage interest tax relief be affected.

Disadvantages of doing outwork
* Pay may be low.
* You may have to work long, unsociable hours to earn a reasonable amount.
* You may be misled about your potential earnings, when the employers base their estimate on the work-rate of a highly skilled outworker or on the ideal rate that the employer would like to see.
* Work can be irregular as the supply can vary, especially for seasonal trades, such as toys, clothing.
* It can be an unreliable source of income.
* Space needed for any machinery and materials.

* You may have to work with dangerous, toxic substances.
* Work often repetitious.

Advantages
* Work done at home often means parents do not have to worry about alternative child care.
* Flexibility of working hours.
* Avoids commuting.
* Because of location and type, work done at home is often suitable for carers of elderly and disabled people.

TELEWORKING AND TELECOMMUTING
This involves people working either on a full- or part-time basis, from their home or a telecottage, and communicating with their office electronically rather than commuting to it physically.

The technology to teleworking need be no more complicated than the ordinary telephone line. Link a fax machine or portable computer through a modem – a modem is a small electronic device which converts a digital signal into analogue waves so that data can be sent down the phone line to another computer – and that telephone line becomes capable of carrying voice, data and pictures to anywhere in the world; and the massive network of cables and satellites is already in place and costs no more than a phone call to use.

Teleworking is already popular in France, Germany, the Netherlands, Scandinavia, Japan and the United States. It is now becoming highly successful in Britain. According to British Telecom, around 500,000 people work full-time from home via computers, and three times that number do some sort of part-time work. Teleworking is especially popular amongst disabled people, women with small children, people who prefer to live in remote areas and with companies who want to cut the cost of expensive city office space and paying workers weighting allowances. Some local authorities have already estimated that by the early part of the next century between one third and one half of all work could be undertaken remotely.

Teleworking, like all homeworking, isn't suitable for everyone's personality. Celia Pen, a teleworker who puts information into the BT Prestel system, finds it can be very lonely, 'Especially if I was working full time. I meet other people only through the PTS meetings at school.' Sheila has been an analysis programmer for three years. 'I go and see friends, but that isn't always convenient for them because they're working too. Friends come and see me, but if I'm busy I have to ask them to go away. I do get lonely.' **(See Chapter 10 Coping with working by Yourself and page 281 Chapter 11 Coping with Family and Friends.)**

As well as being capable of working alone, dedicated, flexible and adaptable, the teleworker also has to be technically competent.

By the very nature of the personal face-to-face contact, some jobs are unsuitable for teleworking, e.g. receptionist, counter-clerk, personal counsellor or demonstrator. Nor does it suit aspects of management that require personal supervision or work which has to be carried out near to its base. But jobs that supply a specific piece of work such as computer programming, data entry, book-keeping, accountancy, graphics, financial modelling, word-processing, estimating, invoicing, sales, auditing, equipment monitoring and maintenance are all highly suitable.

Some teleworkers like Sheila have equipment supplied by the company they work for. 'I have a terminal connected to a modem to a computer company and I ring up and dial in. If I have a work problem, I can ring in to a technical expert at the office or ring one of the five other teleworkers. I've met most of the people now that I talk to.'

Sheila is paid an hourly rate for her work: 'I send in time sheets saying what hours I've worked, because they vary. If I didn't do as many as twenty hours they would object and after a while something would be said.'

Other teleworkers are freelance and buy their own equipment. It should cost you around £300 to kit yourself up with a basic second-hand word-processor, database and spreadsheet capabilities.

Celia is a self-employed teleworker with her own equipment, 'But if either one of my major contracts fell through I would seriously have to consider if my nine-year-old terminal was too old and if I could carry on.' She is commissioned by the companies she works for and paid by the job. 'If the work's continuous then I'm paid monthly or by the screenful. I don't get paid holidays, sick pay, health insurance or a minimum wage. I pay my own National Insurance stamps. I fit the work around our holidays, or the company finds someone to cover.' **(See Chapter 5 Tax, Insurance and Pensions.)**

Space is critical to teleworking. You generally need somewhere to put the equipment, e.g. a spare room, garage (damp free and with electricity) or loft. The equipment is better off away from children who will be tempted to play with it.

The secret of successful teleworking lies with the training, both of the teleworker and their managers. There are various books and organisations dealing with teleworking, which you should read and contact before you begin (**See Help Section this Chapter**).

OUTWORKERS GETTING A FAIR DEAL

There is no foolproof way of finding out if your employment terms and pay are fair, and what you are willing to accept depends on how desperate you are for work. But there are some basic facts you can look into easily such as:

* At the factory you can ask as much as you like about piece rates, hourly rates, average weekly earnings, who pays tax and National Insurance and if the work will be regular.
* Contact the Trade Union that covers that industry. They will know whether the company is unionised and may also have some information about pay and conditions for outworkers.
* Contact your nearest Outworkers Campaign organisation – it will be in your local phone directory – who may have some information about the firm from other outworkers.

Sally is an outworker who codes questions for a market research firm. 'The company trusts me to say how many hours I've worked. I'm paid £5.50 a hour and I pay my own tax and National Insurance. I get paid by cheque straight away. I think the pay's good, but the work's seasonal so you can't plan. I got into debt when I didn't have any work for six weeks, I find it hard to budget.'

Outworkers' agreements

Any agreement, written or verbal, between an employer and employee about work is a contract (**See page 74 Chapter 3 You, Your Company and the Law**), and such agreements are binding and enforceable by law. Many firms who employ outworkers try to avoid entering into an employer/employee relationship and will usually try to establish that the status of the homeworker is self-employed. They'll do this by asking you to sign a statement to this effect. Even if you both agree that you are self-employed, a court may decide that you are an employee. To prove that you are an employee and not self-employed, you will need to show that your employer has control over your work, i.e. if you lose your job, or did not do a certain amount of work, if the work is collected and delivered at regular intervals, if the location of the work is interchangeable – if, for instance, someone is assembling machine parts at home, they could perform the same job on a production line in the employer's factory.

Keeping work records
A lot of outworkers don't even know the name and address of their employer, who often provides them with no paperwork or formal record of their employment, let alone a contract or regular pay slips. Even though your employment is informal, you must keep records of your work and your hours. The best way to do this is to buy a receipt book (**See page 121 Chapter 4 You and Your Money**), available from any stationers, and record all your work in duplicate. Make sure you get a signature for any that is taken away, so that you have evidence of what you have done. The reason for this is to avoid major problems if you ever have a dispute over non-payment.

TAX AND NATIONAL INSURANCE
(**See also Chapter 5 Tax, Insurance and Pensions**.) If your employer decides to treat you as a self-employed person it means that although you work for someone you are responsible for paying your own tax and National Insurance contributions. The cost of contributions changes every year in April.

There are differences between being employed and self-employed when it comes to paying your tax and National Insurance contributions (**See Chapter 2 Starting Your Own Business**). If you are an employee, it is your employer's responsibility to deduct tax if you earn more than the tax threshold. He will also have to deduct National Insurance contributions if you earn more than a certain amount gross each week (check with your local Social Security office for current figures). If you are an employee, you are covered for National Insurance benefit whether or not you earn enough to pay National Insurance.

If you are classed as self-employed, it is your responsibility to ensure that you pay tax if you earn more than the tax threshold (check with your local Tax Office for current figures). If you are a single parent, you should pay tax only if your earnings minus your expenses are over the current amount (check with your local Tax Office). If you are married but your partner is not claiming all their tax allowance, for example if they are unemployed, you can claim a higher tax allowance. This means you pay tax only if you are earning over the current amount per week after expenses.

If you are being treated as a self-employed person, depending on your earnings limit, you will have to pay Class 2 National Insurance contributions (**See page 151 Chapter 5 Tax, Insurance and Pensions**), which count towards basic contributory benefits only such as: sickness, invalidity and pension. They do not entitle you to Unemployment Benefit or Industrial Injuries. But you should check, because if you have paid Class 1 contributions in the previous relevant year, you may be eligible. You can pay either by direct debit or by buying a weekly National Insurance stamp from your post office and sticking it on to a contribution card. If you have paid enough stamps, you can claim all National Insurance Benefits, except Unemployment Benefit. If you earn less than a certain amount every year (check for up-to-date figure), you do not have to pay National Insurance contributions and you can apply for an exemption certificate. The problem with that is that if you don't pay contributions you may lose some benefit, and if you don't pay over a long period of time you may even lose your entitlement to a state retirement pension (**See page 149 Chapter 5 Tax, Insurance and Pensions**).

Class 1 National Insurance contributions entitle you to contributory benefits such as sickness, unemployment, maternity allowance and full pension. But it depends on how many contributions you have paid in the previous two years.

If you are not sure whether you will earn enough money in a year to pay National Insurance contributions, keep a record of your wages and put aside money to pay for your National Insurance stamps. At the end of the year you may find that you have earned more than the National Insurance threshold, (check for recent figures), and then you will be able to pay the stamp in one amount.

Outworker expenses
Before you start work it's important to find out what your work expenses will be, because you may discover that you don't need to pay tax or National Insurance as your earnings are below the

thresholds, or that you should be paying less tax because your work expenses should be tax free. Here are some examples of typical work expenses:

Small tools.
Oil.
Polish.
Rubber mats or other materials.
Extra laundry costs of special clothing.
Running a machine, extra electricity.
Lighting and heating your workroom.
Rent and rates for work.
Room or storage space.
Bus fares, petrol for collections and deliveries.
Telephone calls.

In theory your employer should pay an allowance on top of earnings to cover work expenses. In practice very few do and so you may have to claim for work expenses against tax and National Insurance contributions. When you first start work, you should keep a regular diary of all your possible work expenses (see previous list), showing items and cost – e.g. extra laundry £2 – and the total. Take your electricity, gas or telephone bills, the ones you think will be most affected by your type of homeworking, and compare them with bills for the same quarter the previous year when you weren't using machinery or additional heating. The increase should give you a rough idea of what your additional expenses will be. If you claim these expenses against tax you should save about a quarter, 25 per cent at the current rate. If you are going to claim for National Insurance contributions exemption you should send a copy of your expenses to your local DSS **(See page 153 Chapter 5 Tax, Insurance and Pensions)**.

Outworkers' statutory sick pay

If you are an employee and earn more than £41 a week, you are entitled to Statutory Sick Pay from your employer, but only after the first three days of being ill; you will then be paid for a maximum of eight weeks in any one year. After that you should apply for Sickness Benefit by getting form SP 1T from your employer and sending it with a medical certificate to your local DSS office. The amount you will be paid depends on what you are earning at the time you are unable to work through illness, provided you:

* Have not been on State Benefit within the last eight weeks.
* Are not pregnant (or within eleven weeks before a baby is due).

There are some other conditions, so you should check with your local Social Security office.

If you earn less than £41 a week you do not have to pay National Insurance contributions, but you are not entitled to Statutory Sick Pay or Sickness Benefit, although you are entitled to Income Support.

OUTWORKERS' WAGES COUNCILS
Wages Councils offer protection to some outworkers and homeworkers, regardless of whether they are employees or self-employed. If you are covered by a Wages Council your employer has legal obligations under the Wages Act 1986, the main ones of which are:

* You must be paid at least the statutory minimum rate.
* Records adequate to show whether workers have been paid at least the statutory minimum must be maintained and kept for at least three years.
* The records must be produced for inspection when requested.
* Notices of proposals and of Wages Orders issued by Wages Councils must be displayed where they can be easily seen and read by workers – copies must be sent to homeworkers. If requested by a Wages Inspector, employers must provide any other information to do with the enforcement of a Wages Order.

But not all homeworkers' trades are covered. For example, general clothing is covered but electronics is not. The packing of greetings cards and many other packing and assembly jobs in various industries do not come under Wages Councils. One of the most important Wages Councils for homeworkers is Clothing Manufacturing, because it is a trade that employs thousands of women, and the Clothing Manufacturing Wages Order covers most sewing workers.

The first thing you should do is check whether or not your trade is covered by a Wages Council and then check whether the particular job that you do comes under its remit. For instance, some jobs in toy manufacturing are said by the Wages Inspectorate not to come under its scope – for example, where the work is assembling goods which are not manufactured by the company. If you are unsure whether your job is covered get advice from the Wages Inspectorate (**See Help Section this Chapter for addresses and phone numbers**). If the question is complicated, they will get an opinion from the Treasury Solicitor. There are some jobs that fall either side of the dividing line, such as the dispute as to whether the assembly of Christmas crackers is covered under the Toy Manufacturing Wages Council's provision.

If your pay is under the minimum level of earnings, the firm you work for may be breaking the law and you should get in touch with your Wages Inspectorate who will make enquiries without mentioning your name or involving you. On the form there is a special box where you can indicate that you don't want to reveal your identity. If you don't want your employer to know, then don't tell your fellow workers. The Inspectorate normally deals directly with the person making the complaint, although if you give written permission they will deal with a representative. If you are being under-paid the Wages Inspector will visit your employer, inspect his records and interview a representative sample of workers. You will normally be included in this if you made the original complaint.

If the Inspectors find that an employer is under-paying, they will try to get the correct rate paid and negotiate any substantial arrears. You shouldn't accept anything less, even though both the Inspector and your employer may well try to persuade you to. The best practical way to help recover any money which may be owed to you is to join a Trade Union (**See page 183 this Chapter**). If you don't know which Union covers your trade, contact the Low Pay Unit Rights Office or the TUC.

Wages Councils cover trades such as:

* Toy manufacturing.
* Made-up textiles.
* Fur.
* Boot and shoe repairing.
* Button manufacturing.
* Hat, cap and millinery.
* Linen and cotton handkerchief and household goods and linen piece goods.
* Ostrich and fancy feathers and artificial flowers.

* Perambulator and invalid carriage.
* Retail and bespoke tailoring.
* Rope, twine and net.
* Sack and bag.

There are various trades not covered by wages councils, such as knitting and work with knitted fabrics, stockings, tights, socks and others.

Your employer should pay an additional cost for such things as heating, lighting, electricity, tools, equipment and phone calls, etc. If you are not covered by a Wages Council you may have to pay these additional costs yourself unless you make an agreement with your employer before you start, stating that he will be liable for them. If you are not sure whether you or your trade are covered by a Wages Council, contact your nearest Wages Inspectorate or, in Northern Ireland, the office of Wages Councils.

Wages councils' rates 1991/92
Nearly 2.5 million workers are covered by wages councils which set minimum rates of pay for workers twenty-one and over, in certain industries. The list below gives the current Wages Council hourly rates, which normally increase yearly.

* GENERAL WASTE MATERIALS RECLAMATION: from July 1991 minimum rate £2.50, weekly rate for 39 hours £97.50.
* TOY MANUFACTURING: from 17 June 1991, minimum rate £2.52, weekly rate for 39 hours £98.28.
* AERATED WATER: from January 1991, minimum rate £2.69, weekly rate for 39 hours £108.81.
* BOOT AND SHOE REPAIRING: from 11 February 1991, minimum rate £2.77, weekly rate for 39 hours £108.03.
* HAT, CAP AND MILLINERY: from 1 April 1991, minimum rate £2.54, weekly rate for 39 hours £99.06.
* RETAIL AND BESPOKE TAILORING: from 31 March 1991, minimum rate £2.96, weekly rate for 39 hours £115.44.
* MADE-UP TEXTILES: from October 1990, minimum rate £2.42, weekly rate for 39 hours £94.38.
* LINEN AND COTTON HANDKERCHIEF AND HOUSEHOLD GOODS AND LINEN PIECE GOODS: from July 1991, basic £2.60, weekly rate for 39 hours £101.40.
* LICENSED NON-RESIDENTIAL: from January 1991, minimum rate £2.74, weekly rate for 39 hours £106.86.

* CLOTHING MANUFACTURING: from 4 February 1991 minimum rate £2.4875, weekly rate for 39 hours £97.01.
* RETAIL TRADE (NON-FOOD) Workers employed in the retail sale of books, stationery, clothing, textiles, household, office and garden furniture and implements, ironmongery, tools, household items made from wood, glass, pottery or china, electrical and gas appliances used in the home, bicycles, prams, toys and games, leather goods, paint, wallpaper, brushes and cleaning materials used in the home. Drivers, clerks, warehouse staff, cleaners and workers employed in the alteration of clothing, including homeworkers, are also covered. From 1 April 1991, basic rate £2.955. Weekly rate for 39 hours £115.25.
* CAFES & PLACES OF REFRESHMENT (UNLICENSED): from 10 June 1991 basic £2.80 for all time worked up to and including 39 hours in any week, overtime £4.20. Accommodation daily limit 20p.
* HAIRDRESSING: from 8 April 1991, minimum rate £2.66, weekly rate for 40 hours £106.40.
* LAUNDRY: from 20 February 1990, minimum rate £2.785, weekly rate for 39 hours £108.62.
* ROPE, TWINE AND NET: from July 1991, minimum weekly rate £2.565, weekly rate for 39 hours £100.04.
* PERAMBULATOR AND INVALID CARRIAGE: from 8 April 1991, minimum rate £2.91, weekly rate for 39 hours £113.49.
* FUR: from 25 January 1991, minimum rate £2.60, weekly rate for 39 hours £101.40.
* BUTTON MANUFACTURING: from 27 May 1991, basic £2.46, weekly rate for 39 hours £95.94.
* SACK AND BAG: from 27 May 1991, minimum rate £2.53, weekly rate for 39 hours £98.67.
* OSTRICH, AND FANCY FEATHERS AND ARTIFICIAL FLOWERS: from 1 January 1991, minimum rate £2.54, weekly rate for 39 hours £99.06.
* COTTON WASTE RECLAMATION: from 15 April 1991, minimum rate £2.53, weekly rate for 39 hours £98.67.
* COFFIN FURNITURE AND CEREMENT MAKING: from 1 December 1991, minimum rate £3.05, weekly rate for 39 hours £118.95.

[Source information: Department of Employment and Low Pay Unit Manchester.]

TRADE UNIONS

Some outworkers' jobs are covered by Trade Unions. There are advantages and disadvantages to being a Trade Union member. The disadvantage is that you have to pay a weekly subscription fee, the cost varying from Union to Union. Some have lower rates if you work for twenty-one hours or less, but you may not be eligible for all the benefits offered by the Union. (Check before joining or deciding on your level of subscription.)

The advantage is that you can get free legal advice and possibly assistance with an Industrial Tribunal if you should lose your job, as well as certain sickness and death benefits. You will also get free information about particular firms, rates of pay and general help and support.

If a lot of outworkers who work for the same company join a Union, or if they belong to the same Union as the factory workers, the Union can seek recognition and negotiate rights on their behalf. Before joining a Union you should realise that you may not have the same employment protection as a full-time worker. It depends on how your employment is defined, i.e. if you are defined as an employee and you get dismissed for joining a Union, your Union can claim unfair dismissal.

Some Trade Unions that cover outworkers' trades:
* National Union of Tailor and Garment Workers is a section of the General, Municipal, Boilermakers and Allied Trades Union (GMB): 85p a week or 42p a week if you work 20 hours or less.
* National Union of Knitwear, Footwear and Apparel Trades: 90p per week.
* Transport and General Workers Union (TGWU): £1.10p a week or 60p a week part-time.
* General, Municipal, Boilermakers and Allied Trades Union (GMB): £1.15p per week or 55p for part-time (less than 21 hours).
* Union of Shop, Distributive and Allied Workers (USDAW): 90p or 68p part-time.

Your employer does not have to know that you have joined a Trade Union.

OUTWORKERS' RIGHTS
Under the existing law, almost all employment rights such as unfair dismissal, redundancy or maternity rights are dependent on whether you are classified as employed or self-employed. An outworker has to have had regular employment to prove employee status. The majority of employers classify their homeworkers as self-employed, which means that the homeworkers are responsible for paying their own tax and National Insurance.

If you are an outworker, you do not have a legal entitlement to paid holidays, but you should try to negotiate some form of payment with your employers. In theory you have the same employment rights as other workers, but because of being isolated and vulnerable, you may find it difficult to enforce these rights, even though you are entitled to them. You should know that ALL workers have the following rights:

All workers' rights
* The right to join a Trade Union and not be sacked or victimised for doing so.
* Women must be paid the same rate as men when they are doing the same or similar work or work of equal value for the same employer.
* Employers cannot discriminate on grounds of race or sex when taking on or promoting workers, or when paying different rates. They cannot sack a woman for being black or being a woman.
* Paid time off for antenatal care.

If you work sixteen hours or more each week you also have the following rights at work
* You are entitled to a pay slip which shows your wages before deductions, the amounts deducted for tax, National Insurance, etc. and your wages after deductions.
* After one month's employment, you are entitled to at least one week's notice of dismissal. After two years you become entitled to more notice.
* After thirteen weeks at work you are entitled to a written statement of the main terms and conditions of your employment, including pay, hours, holidays, sick pay, pension arrangements, grievance and dismissal procedures. No change

in your contract can be made without notice, unless you or your Union agrees.
* If you have worked for the same employer for two years by eleven weeks before the expected birth of your baby, you have the right to return to work after the baby is born, unless your employer employs fewer than six workers.
* If you have worked for the same employer for two years you are protected against unfair dismissal.
* If you have been in your job for at least two years after your eighteenth birthday and you are made redundant, you will be entitled to some redundancy pay.

If an outworker works between eight and sixteen hours a week they get the above employment rights after five years in the same job, i.e. working for the same employer.

INDUSTRIAL TRIBUNALS

Industrial Tribunals are very useful. They are independent judicial bodies which were set up to provide an informal, quick, inexpensive and accessible way of settling certain types of dispute between employers and employees. The disputes they cover range from equal pay and sexual or racial discrimination, to unlawful deductions from wages. But the majority of cases come under the unfair dismissal and redundancy payments provisions of the Employment Protection (Consolidation) Act 1978.

The tribunal is so informal that if you want you can present your case yourself. There is no rule that says you have to have someone to represent you, but if you feel uneasy about doing it then you can use either a solicitor or a Trade Union official.

If you think you have a case, go to either your Trade Union, local Job Centre, Unemployment or Benefit Office and get an application form for an Industrial Tribunal. It will tell you if your case is covered and the various time limits set. If you have any difficulty filling in the form, go to your local Citizens Advice Bureau or Trade Union (**See Help Section for addresses and phone numbers**) and they will help.

If you are dissatisfied with the decision of the tribunal, you can appeal – but only on a point of law. In England and Wales the Employment Appeal Tribunal (ET) holds preliminary hearings of all cases which do not appear to the registrar to disclose an error of law.

Depending on your financial circumstances, you may be able to get legal advice for preparing your application from a solicitor, without incurring any cost. A leaflet about this legal assistance scheme, Legal Aid for Civil and Criminal Cases, is available free from employment offices and Job Centres (**See Help Section this Chapter for addresses and phone numbers**). Also check with your Trade Union, who will give you free advice and representation if they think you have a case.

CHAPTER 6
HELP SECTION

Homeworkers
HOMEWORKING GROUP PROJECTS AND HOMEWORKING OFFICERS:
THE LOW PAY UNIT 9 Upper Berkeley Street, London, W1H 7PE.
  Tel: 071 262 7278.
Coventry Homeworking Officer. Tel: 0203 831285.
Greenwich Homeworkers Project. Tel: 081 854 9841.
Haringey Homeworking Officer. Tel: 081 975 9700.
Lambeth Homeworkers Project. Tel: 071 671 6811.
Leicester Outworkers Campaign. Tel: 0533 470940.
London Homeworkers Training Centre. Tel: 071 793 0350.
Manchester Homeworking Group. Tel: 061 953 4024.
National Homeworking Unit. Tel: 021 643 6352.
Northern Homeworking Group. Tel: 091 489 5515.
Nottingham Outwork Support Group. Tel: 0602 586515.
Rochdale Homeworking Assistant. Tel: 0706 514377.
Wakefield Homeworking Support Officer. Tel: 0924 295820/1/2.
West Yorkshire Homeworking Group. Tel: 0532 444937.

Wages inspectorate
Cumberland House, 200 Broad Street, Birmingham, B15 1SP.
  Tel: 021 631 3300.
The Pithay, Bristol, BS1 2NQ. Tel: 0272 273710.
127 George Street, Edinburgh, EH2 4JN. Tel: 031 220 2777.
Room 309, City House, Leeds, LS1 4JH. Tel: 0532 438232.
83–117 Euston Rd, London, NW1 2RA. Tel: 071 387 2511.
2nd Floor, Alexandra House, 14–22 Parsonage Gardens, Manchester, M3 2JS. Tel: 061 832 6506.
Broadacre House, Market Street East, Newcastle-upon-Tyne, NE1 6XN. Tel: 091 232 1881.
Outworkers Campaign, 116 St Peter's Road, Leicester, LE2 1DE.
  Tel: 0533 470940.

Booklets and articles
'Employment Rights Briefing, Who Is An Employer?' published by Leicester Low Pay Campaign by Mike Stock in *Adviser* 6 October 1987.

The Forgotten Workers by B. C. Roxby, Leicester Low Pay Unit.

Advisory conciliation and arbitration service (ACAS)
27 Wilton Street, London, SW1X 7AZ. Tel: 071 210 3000.
Booklets: *This is ACAS. Conciliation Between Individuals and Employers*.

Teleworkers
TELECOMMUTING POWERHOUSE CO. 27 Old Gloucester Street, London, WC1N 3XX. Tel: 071 404 5011. A National and worldwide organisation whose first priority is consciousness-raising, by example, of the possibilities of telecommuting in the UK for large sections of the community. Plus 'networking' of individuals, at home and abroad, into telecottages or small groups who can work together either from home or remote offices. Independent advice. Funded only by members. Registration of people's skills is free. Quarterly newsletter. £12 annually.
The Managers Guide to Teleworking by Francis Kinsman. For copies and more information write to: BRITISH TELECOM 2A Southwark Bridge Road, London, SE1 9BA. Call free on 0800 800 800.

Health
REPETITIVE STRAIN INJURY (RSI) ASSOCIATION Christ Church, Redford Way, Uxbridge, Middlesex UB8 1SZ. Tel: 0895 238663. Send £1.50 plus large sae with a 34p stamp for their helpful factpack with more addresses and phone numbers.
VDU Hazards Factpack and *An Office-Worker's Guide to RSI* £2.50 and £3.00 respectively, available from: City Centre Project, 32 Featherstone Street, London, EC1Y 8QX. Tel: 071 608 1338.
(See Chapter 9 Health and Fitness at Home.)

Chapter information sources
Low Pay Unit; Wages Council; National Homeworking Unit; Citizens Advice Bureau; ACAS.

CHAPTER 7
Selling and Marketing

MARKETING
If you are working from home for someone else, you don't have to worry about marketing (**See page 171 Chapter 6 Teleworkers and Outworkers**), but if you are working for yourself then marketing is the key to the success of any business idea. It is the formula that provides the right goods or services to the right customer at the right price. You will need to work just as hard on the basics of marketing when you are just starting as when you are more established. First ask yourself three basic questions which cover the main things you need to know:

* **Customers** – can I get enough of them, and will they pay me enough to be profitable?
* **Competitors** – will I be able to compete with those businesses already in the market?
* **Operations** – do I have the ability and resources to meet the needs of the customer?

Marketing takes the blame for a lot of business failures. But often it's because the owners of the business misjudged the market, so sales fell short of expectations which meant the cash flow wasn't sufficient.

When Judy decided to start a business making and selling lunchtime sandwiches to offices, she discovered that what she liked in her sandwiches wasn't necessarily what was going to sell. 'I love avocado, so I made some avocado sandwiches only to find that the people I was trying to sell them to hadn't ever tried it and didn't want to. They said that if they were paying for it, they didn't want to find they disliked it. So it's the good old favourites that sell – cheese and pickle, chicken and tuna, mostly on brown bread.'

Some people believe they don't need 'to market' their product, and that it is just what the customers want. But it doesn't necessarily work like that, and a product may fail to take off simply because you aren't able to make enough. Judging how effective your marketing is isn't difficult. You know if you're spending all day trying to sell to reluctant customers, or if your phone is constantly ringing with repeat orders. When Rachael started making ice-cream, she didn't even have a phone for doing her market research. 'It was a bit of a joke. I took ten 10p pieces, went to the phone box in town and made ten phone calls to restaurants and hotels, telling them I made an additive-free ice-cream. Six out of the ten said they were interested. I thought that wasn't bad. Now I do a flavour that's a monthly special, and if it goes well it joins the range. That's my way of doing market research.'

The questions to ask
When dealing with marketing there are key questions that you should explore:

* Try to define your market and estimate its size.
* Ask yourself if you are expecting to trade locally, or if your product is something that can be sold anywhere – maybe even exported?
* Try and define who your customers are, where they come from, who their buyers are and if they buy regularly, seasonally or at trade shows?
* Assess your competitors. Try to find out why their products sell. Can you at least equal or at best beat:
    * Their quality.
    * Their delivery service.
    * Their price (**See page 39 Chapter 2 Starting your own Business**).
* Is there a gap in that field for your product?
* Do you have the skill and the finance to beat the competition?
* Can you produce regularly and be available to correct any problems?
* Have you or someone else produced and distributed leaflets or advertisements?
* Is it possible to get a story about your business in the local media, radio, newspaper or magazine?
* Do you visit or exhibit at trade shows?

When David started performing as a professional magician and hypnotist he decided to test the area to see where he could get work. He and an illusionist colleague hired a hall in the local community centre and put on a show. 'We discovered it was the wrong venue; it was too far on the outskirts of town. Only about fifty people turned up and the weather was terrible. After we'd paid for the hall we were left with £15 each.' He felt it was worth finding out that if he was going to book his own venues, he would have to choose the locations differently.

Jane, like a lot of people running their own businesses from home, decided to advertise. Because she runs a business selling garden manure, she targeted her advertisements specifically to gardening magazines. In a recent *Which?* magazine report on organic composts, Jane's 'Lady Muck' brand came in the top five. 'All this hassle,' she smiled, 'and it's beginning to be worth it.'

Jane also gives talks to gardening clubs, the Women's Institute and the Women's Guild. 'I talk about my product, my pet subject which is earthworms, and I tell them funny stories. I charge between £15 and £20 an hour. But I really do it because it's a cheap way of advertising. I get a lot of orders, and of course gardening clubs get discount for buying in bulk. It's only January and I've got fifty talks booked for this year already.'

Research

Go to your local library and collect lists of potential customers from local newspaper advertisements, trade directories, and trade magazines (**See page 43 Chapter 2 Starting your own Business**). If your market consists of consumers rather than specialist business customers, then a good source of information regarding the purchasing power of different groups is the HMSO Family Expenditure Surveys (FES) available from your local reference library or on sale at the HMSO book shop (**See Help Section, Chapter 2 for addresses and phone numbers**). If you compare this to the types of area in which your customers live, you will get some idea of the spending power and population of a particular district. It's important that you find out if your 'catchment' area is appropriate to your business idea. For example, your business won't get off the ground if you are putting leaflets through letter boxes of retired people, offering them a child-minding service!

When Judy was starting her sandwich-making business she walked round the local industrial estate, trying to find a suitable outlet. 'I went furthest away from the town, because I thought they wouldn't have anywhere to go to buy their lunch and it would be perfect for me. But I was wrong. The men were mostly mechanics and didn't have any money on them, plus I couldn't ever seem to catch them when they were there. They were either going in to collect equipment or going out on calls.' Judy went back into town and concentrated on going round the streets in the business district. 'I went through loads of streets and they'd say no, they'd already got someone who delivered food. I discovered it wasn't just the food, but there was a sort of unwritten rule that you couldn't muscle in on someone else's patch. It's very competitive. Eventually I stumbled on a street of offices that didn't already have anyone selling sandwiches.'

The only way really to get an insight into your local business competitors is to visit them. But don't let on that you are thinking of opening the same type of business. It's relatively simple. For example, if it's a restaurant that serves the same type of food in the same price range as you are considering, then go in as an ordinary customer, study the menu, service, decor and have a meal. With other businesses you can try to get a job with them or become a client.

If the business is a limited company, you can do a company search (**See page 73 Chapter 3 You, Your Company and the Law**), which will tell you who and how many company directors there are and give you a set of the last year's company accounts, so you can see how they are trading and what their profits and losses are.

To find your local competitors, contact your local Chamber of Commerce, who will have a list of its members – they will also be listed in your Thomson's and Yellow Pages phone directory.

Preparing promotional material
You will need business cards and leaflets to leave with your customers. When Rachael's ice-creams started to sell, she was doing three deliveries a week. She now supplies to fifty restaurants and hotels in a radius of twenty-five miles. 'I was driving so much that I decided to have a logo designed for the ice-cream cartons and I stuck it on to the side of my car myself. I got ten new customers from that alone.'

Leaflets, business cards and a logo don't have to look super slick. In fact there are times, especially for work done at home, when they can be a positive disadvantage. For example, if you are selling your own home-grown produce or craft work at your garden gate, prices chalked up on a blackboard, with a hand-drawn carrot or tea cup, suggest that you aren't part of a large organisation with expensive overheads, so you must be offering a bargain. In this instance slick business cards would be saying the opposite. But if you are running something like a word-processing service, then you would be expected to be slick and professional and your business cards and leaflets should reflect that image.

Jerry found that when he started working from home he didn't have to worry at first about getting business. Like a lot of people who have left large companies where they have worked for a long time, he had built up a solid contact list. When he left, a lot of them went to see him. But gradually things have slowed down, so Jerry designed some leaflets on his desk-top publisher and had them professionally printed. 'They're for pension managers, and there's a corporate image leaflet to go on stands in dentists' and doctors' surgeries.'

Not all promotional material is printed. In David's case, because he is a professional performer he decided to have some photographs taken of himself to send out to clubs and agents. 'I set up the lights in the spare room and my wife clicked the camera shutter.'

Because David had done a photography course he decided to make the photographs look a little bit different, by putting a magic gleam coming out of his eye to emphasise the fact that he's a hypnotist. One thousand 10 × 8 inch prints with his name on cost him £135.

Making simple graphics
The image of your business that you want to get across to customers, clients and potential clients is very important. For that reason you should have business cards, a logo, labels, leaflets and a letter-heading, all of which should say more about what you do than just giving your address.

If you feel confident you can save money by designing your own logo, which can follow through on all your stationery and calling cards. It's fairly simple. You'll need a sharp pair of paper-cutting scissors, scalpel, steel ruler to use as a straight edge for cutting and white typewriter correction fluid to paint out any mistakes. For jobs up to A3 size, which is twice the size of normal A4 typing paper, you will need a plastic drawing board with a T-square and a set square, plus some felt-tip pens in different thicknesses: 0.1 mm is the finest, 0.5 mm is the equivalent of a thick ball-point pen and so on up the scale.

Letraset comes in a range of rub-down lettering styles that look like print, and there is a full range of type sizes, tints and coloured sheets. If you need to stick paper to paper don't use water-based glue, because it will wrinkle. Use something like Pritt Stick or rubber gum which you can remove with lighter fluid. Type and drawings can be reduced or enlarged on an ordinary photocopier to the size you need for your design. Cut it out and paste it up on card for your finished artwork, which can be duplicated again in quantity on a photocopier or printed for better quality. If you want to use an illustration and you see one that you think fits your business, don't pinch it, but phone the publication and ask for permission to reproduce it. They'll probably say yes, but want a small fee. The best thing is to have a go at doing your own; it doesn't need to be very artistic – it often works if it's something really simple.

If you have a carbon ribbon in your typewriter, it will produce excellent quality simple text. A word-processor is even better, and you can justify the text on the right-hand side of the column of type, which makes it look even more professional. If you have several thousand pounds, a desk-top publishing computer with a laser printer will do everything, including the drawings. It will allow you to create layouts with columns of type and a variety of headlines in different typefaces.

If you don't want to do DIY graphics, you'll find plenty of companies advertised in the Yellow Pages, *Exchange and Mart* and in the business pages of daily newspapers which offer a design service as well as cheap photocopying and quality printing. For example 5,000 A4 colour leaflets with design and type can cost as little as £200. The companies which offer these services provide helpful booklets showing exactly how to specify your design and cost out your print run.

If you just want a small number in one colour, photocopying at your local corner shop may be cheaper. Try one colour on a tinted page to enhance simple leaflets. The latest generation of laser copiers reproduce immaculate full colour from flat artwork, photographic prints or slides. But individual full-colour copies can be expensive.

SELLING

You've just made your first batch of country home-made ice-cream or just put the finishing touches to your first clock. Whatever it is, you are now at the stage when the object or product is finally finished and you have to go out and try to sell it.

If you enjoy performing, then the hype and banter of selling will be right up your street. But if you don't, and your ears go red when you walk into a room and you chew your bottom lip when you talk about yourself, then this bit could be living hell for you and you had better think about giving the job to someone else. Having said that, there are people who started off hating selling, feeling it was their real bugbear, but who persevered and have ended up enjoying it and doing it very successfully. So maybe you shouldn't shy away immediately, or give up instantly, even if it doesn't strike you as being something you were born for. Necessity is a great driving force. At first Jane hated cold-calling. 'I had no marketing experience whatsoever, but I had to earn a living and I just had to get on with it. That's the best way. Before seeing anyone I had to hype myself up. It made me feel like an upmarket beggar, but then I'd think, "What the hell! Let's go in there and do it." I've had to work hard to get people to take me seriously.'

Rachael makes home made ice-cream. At first, she also hated cold calling. 'I still do, but it's not as bad. I used to say that before I knocked on the door they could hear my knees knocking, and chefs can be very temperamental.'

If you drop in on prospective customers unannounced, you may catch their eye and their interest. Good salesmen reckon that once their foot is in the door they can't fail. But it's a gamble – you could catch the chef when his sauce has just curdled, or the potter when he's in the middle of crafting a delicate piece. This walk-in technique could just as easily put a prospective customer off. If someone's run off their feet they will simply see you as a nuisance, or not professional enough to make a prior appointment. It's usually best to phone first, briefly introduce yourself and your business, and make an appointment. The added benefit to this is that once they have agreed to see you, it means they are potentially interested in what you are offering. It saves a lot of wasted journeys, wasted petrol and the disappointment of repeatedly being rejected, which isn't good for anyone's confidence.

Like a lot of people just starting in business, Rachael had doubts about her product. 'I was trying untried flavours and had only my own opinion to rely on. I would say to customers, "I hope you like it," instead of being more positive. After a month my first customer told me to stop apologising, because I'd deliver it and say that I hoped it was all right.'

The person you're going to sell to, unlike your family and friends, probably isn't going to tell you how clever you are or wonder why you've been hiding your talent for so long. They will want to know the price you are asking, if you can deliver and in what amount, if your object fits into their racking system and if you have any literature. And then, after all that, they might shatter your enthusiasm by telling you that they've got something just the same which isn't selling, or they'll find fault with a clasp, a flavour, packaging, colour or simply tell you it was last year's fashion fad. Don't dismiss them. Listen to what they have to say. They know, because they are dealing with customers and seeing new merchandise all the time. Of course you can't go around changing details to suit every buyer, but if enough of them say the same thing, then it just might be time seriously to consider making changes.

Before you made your prototype you should have researched things such as retail outlet shelving, racking and display systems, so that your product would fit into them. The cheapest and most effective way to test the market without getting into a large financial outlay is to persuade a few local outlets – you don't need a lot – to take some of your prototype samples. In this way you get real customer feedback at grass-roots level.

Once you have established a business relationship, you have to judge whether or not it is appropriate to invite your client out for drinks or lunch. Some people thrive on putting socialising and business together, while others make a rule that the two should never meet. It's a very personal decision, but people who build up trust are known to go on working together for years.

Some people find that their product will sell in limited numbers almost without having to push it. 'I thought I would have to learn to sell,' says Sasha. 'But you don't really need to; things sell themselves. I was told I could go to large departmental stores and try to persuade them to take my picture frames, but I knew they would pay me badly and I wouldn't get my money for a long time. So I decided to sell at craft fairs and markets, where you just sell something and get your money straight away. It's simple. But you have to make things that are light and easy to carry around.'

Mail order
A lot of people who work from home sell their goods through mail order. One of the drawbacks with this is space, and before you start you should consider if you have somewhere dry, damp proof and accessible for storing large amounts of your product. A jumper may be a relatively small object, but not when you have 300 of them plus packaging materials! You also have to be able to carry the cost of large production or print runs of your product and the cost of packaging materials, before you have sold anything.

But if you have taken all that into consideration, then the next thing to be aware of is that with mail order there are certain legal rules that have to be followed. You must remember that your customers' rights are the same as if they were buying from a shop. If you offer to supply goods on approval, the prospective customer will be expected to pay for the return of any unwanted goods, unless you state otherwise in your advertisement.

Mail order advertisements
What you're selling must conform to the description that you put in your advertisement, so be careful how you write it. There is no point in writing flowery prose, which either exaggerates or gives untrue information. It may sound good but it isn't the truth. The goods have to fit the purpose they were made for and be of merchandisable quality, and the advertisement must describe them and what they do correctly. You must make it clear whether customers can try your merchandise before buying it, subject to it remaining undamaged. If no indication is given, it will be assumed that you have given permission for the customer to try it out. If you want to operate either an 'on approval' or 'sale or return' basis, it means that if the customer is not satisfied they have to return the goods within seven to fourteen days and you have to send them their money back.

In the main wording of your advertisement, you should put the true name or business names and full address where the business is managed and where you can be contacted during normal business hours. This does not prevent you from also putting in another address where you want your customers to send their orders. This address need not be in full – for example it can be a box or freepost number.

You should indicate the time within which you undertake to fulfil orders or appropriate services. You should never take longer than twenty-eight days to fulfil an order, except if you make it clear that a series of items is to be despatched in sequence and put the intervals between consignments. In this instance, only the first delivery needs to be within twenty-eight days. The only difference to this is when, at the discretion of the publisher, the advertisement is permitted to say a time which is in excess of the twenty-eight days, during which despatch will take place. This is relevant only to plants and goods that are bespoke and made-to-measure.

You must make it clear in your advertisement if the manufacture of the goods is not going to be a commercial proposition unless there is sufficient response. If they have to be specially manufactured, the media may want to see examples of similar work or models that are going to be supplied.

If it is clear that you cannot fulfil an order within the time stated in the advertisement, then you should immediately contact the customers and offer them a refund. If they decide to wait for their goods, then you must either give them a firm date when they will be despatched, or report to them at intervals of not more than fourteen days how the order is progressing.

You are under an obligation to return all money paid in advance by the customer when:

1. Unwanted goods are returned, undamaged, within seven working days of their receipt.
2. When attention is drawn to the benefit of a money-back guarantee (however expressed) and no limit is placed in the advertisement upon the period during which time such a guarantee is effective. In such a case you should be prepared to make a refund at any reasonable time, having regard to the nature of the product, i.e. with regard to perishable goods. For example, money could not be refunded on four-week-old yoghurt.
3. When the customer expresses a wish to be reimbursed because of a delay in the fulfilment of the order.
4. When, for whatever reason, the product received by the customer does not conform to the description of it in the advertise-

ment. Or when the advertiser is in breach of his contractual obligations. In such cases the customer should not be expected to bear the cost of return postage or carriage.

Exports
If you think your product is something that might sell overseas, the Department of Trade (**See Help Section this Chapter**) offers practical help and support for exporters at each stage of their trading process. They will give you information on such things as: finding a suitable representative to handle your products in overseas markets; financial support for visits abroad to allow you to find out about the export potential for your product; financial and commercial support to groups of British companies exhibiting at overseas trade fairs and support for participation in overseas seminars and store promotions. They also have access to information on products, trade statistics and specialist market knowledge. They will provide advance notice of overseas trade opportunities and give free professional advice to help you to decide whether you require a specific market survey. In addition they give financial support for overseas market research, advice to exporters on foreign technical requirements and a publicity service to help assess the commercial viability of new British products.

THE SIMPLER TRADE PROCEDURES BOARD offers help to cut down on all the red tape involved in exporting. The EXPORT CREDIT GUARANTEE DEPARTMENT helps ensure you get paid for your goods. For all export services, contact your nearest DTI regional office – look under TRADE AND INDUSTRY DEPARTMENT in your local phone book (**See also Help Section this Chapter**).

Selling in the single European market
Europe is on our doorstep. It's easily accessible and certainly something you should think about. If you're considering exporting, you should know about the Single European Market. Information can be obtained from the BUSINESS CO-OPERATIVE NETWORK (BC-Net), which helps firms liaise with other companies across Europe to enable them to establish partnerships and make contacts. The DTI's (The Department of Trade and Industry) EUROPE OPEN FOR BUSINESS has an information service which includes a 24-hour hot-line on 081 200 1992. They also have an on-line database of single market measures, a range of free regularly

updated fact sheets, booklets, plus videos and guidelines (**See Help Section this Chapter for addresses and phone numbers**).

CHAPTER 7
HELP SECTION

Advertising

DIRECTORY PUBLISHERS ASSOCIATION 147–149 Gloucester Terrace, London, W2 6DX. Tel: 071 723 7328.

THE BRITISH CODE OF ADVERTISING PRACTICE Brook House, 2–16 Torrington Place, London, WC1E 7HN. Tel: 071 580 5555.

BRITISH RATE AND DATA An encyclopedia of almost all UK advertising media. Contact: Maclean Hunter House, Chalk Lane, Cockfosters Road, Barnet, Hertfordshire, EN4 0BU. Tel: 081 441 6644.

ITP BUSINESS MAGAZINES Greater London House, Hampstead Road, London, NW1 7QZ. Tel: 071 387 6611.

DIRECT RESPONSE MAGAZINE 4 Market Place, Hertford, SG14 1EB. Tel: 0992 5011770.

THE POST OFFICE DIRECT MAIL SECTION Room 221, 148–166 Old Street, London, EC1V 9HQ. Tel: 071 250 2351.

ASSOCIATION OF FREE NEWSPAPERS LTD 27 Brunswick Square, Gloucester, GL1 1UN. Tel: 0452 308100.

IPC MAGAZINES Kings Reach Tower, Stamford Street, London, SE1 9LS. Tel: 071 261 5000.

ASSOCIATION OF MAIL ORDER PUBLISHERS LTD 1 New Burlington Street, London, W1X 1FD. Tel: 071 437 0706.

THE MARKETING SOCIETY LTD 206 Worple Road, London, SW20 8PN. Tel: 081 879 3464.

OUTDOOR ADVERTISING ASSOCIATION OF GREAT BRITAIN 21 Tothill Street, London, SW1H 9LL. Tel: 081 222 7988.

PERIODICAL PUBLISHERS ASSOCIATION LTD 15–19 Kingsway, London, WC2B 6UN. Tel: 071 379 6268.

RADIO MARKETING BUREAU Radio House, 46 Westbourne Grove, London, W2 5SH. Tel: 071 727 2646.

Craft fairs

If you make crafts, then craft fairs and county shows can be an inexpensive way of selling them. Craft fairs are held all over the country, especially in the summer. The majority rent stalls out, while the more permanent ones have them to buy. Your local authority will be able to tell you when, where and who to contact.

THE COMPLETE GUIDE TO WORKING FROM HOME

For more information go to your local library and look in the ANNUAL CRAFTSMAN'S DIRECTORY. In Northern Ireland LEDU publishes THE GUIDE TO CRAFTS AND CRAFTSMEN.

Craft fairs are also listed in *Exchange and Mart*.

Selling in the single European market

BRITISH OVERSEAS TRADE BOARD Department of Trade and Industry, 1–19 Victoria Street, London, SW1H 0ET. Tel: 071 215 5000. The BOTB offers advice and assistance relating to overseas markets.

BRITISH STANDARDS INSTITUTION 2 Park Street, London, W1A 2BS. Tel: 071 629 9000. Offers special help to exporters on standards in other countries.

CENTRAL OFFICE OF INFORMATION Hercules Road, London, SE1 7DU. Tel: 071 928 2345. Their overseas publicity service provides help in making your product better known overseas.

DEPARTMENT OF TRADE AND INDUSTRY 1–19 Victoria Street, London, SW1H 0ET. Tel: 071 215 5000. For advice on exporting (ask for BOTB) trade statistics, company law, etc.

EXPORT CREDITS GUARANTEE DEPARTMENT 50 Ludgate Hill, London, EC4M 7AY. Tel: 071 382 7000. Also: New Crown Buildings, Cathays Park, Cardiff, CF1 3NH. Tel: 0222 824100. Or contact any of the Department's regional offices, which are located in Belfast, Birmingham, Bristol, Cambridge, City of London, Croydon, Glasgow, Leeds and Manchester. ECGD offers insurance cover for export payment risks.

EUROPEAN HOT LINE (DTI) 081 200 1992.

European Information Centres:

Belfast Centre	0232 491031.
Birmingham Centre	021 454 6171.
Bradford Centre	0274 754262.
Brighton Centre	0273 220870.
Bristol Centre	0272 737373.
Cardiff Centre	0222 229525.
Exeter Centre	0392 214085.
Glasgow Centre	041 221 0999.
Hull Centre	0482 465940.
Inverness Centre	0463 234121.
Leeds Centre	0532 832600.
Leicester Centre	0522 554464.

SELLING AND MARKETING

Liverpool Centre	051 298 1928.
London Centre	071 489 1922.
Maidstone Centre	0622 696126.
Manchester Centre	061 236 3210.
Mold Centre	0352 2121, ext. 2494.
Newcastle-upon-Tyne Centre	091 261 5131.
Norwich Centre	0603 625977.
Nottingham Centre	0602 222414.
Sheffield Centre	0742 532126.
Slough Centre	0753 77877.
Southampton Centre	0703 832866.
Stafford Centre	0785 59528.
Telford Centre	0952 588766.

Marketing

MARKET RESEARCH SOCIETY 175 Oxford Street, London, W1R 1TA. Tel: 071 439 2585.

INSTITUTE OF MARKETING Moor Hall, Cookham, Maidenhead, Berks, SL6 9QH. Tel: 06285 24922. Offers courses, publications and advice on all aspects of marketing.

Banks and accountants often have literature outlining the key points in marketing. INNOVATION CENTRES offer assistance with marketing as well as the technical and commercial aspects of innovation. There are fourteen Innovation Centres, details available from: Mr A. Hurst, Secretary, Association of Innovation Executives, Centre for Product Development, The Lenton Business Centre, Lenton Boulevard, Nottingham, N47 2BY. Tel: 0602 782200.

Chapter information sources

LiveWire UK; Thomson Small Business Guide; Enterprise Allowance; Department of Trade and Industry; Citizens Advice Bureau.

CHAPTER 8

Your Home As Your Workplace

Are you sitting comfortably?

HOME SWEET HOME
There are a lot of advantages to using your own home to work from. Your overheads are low, you don't have to pay rent, rates, heating and lighting on separate office premises, neither do you have the inconvenience of travelling, apart from rolling out of bed!

The disadvantages are that it can be difficult to get away from your work, or in fact to get started. You may feel lonely and isolated (**See page 265 Chapter 10 Coping with Working by Yourself**) and you may find that because of the type of work you do, operating from home means that you have to reduce your range of services, like Pamela who is a solicitor practising from home. She decided not to do criminal work: 'I didn't want criminals coming to my home and I decided not to do matrimonial work either, because it would just be too depressing on my own.'

You may have to use noisy machinery, which means you can work only certain hours so that the noise doesn't affect your neighbours (**See page 212 this Chapter**) or other members of your family, or you may find that your home simply isn't big enough to accommodate you and your working equipment and supplies without having to utilise another space like a garage, spare bedroom or loft.

Having taken those aspects into consideration, you had better take a good look at your home – not the new shag pile carpet in the hall, but something less obvious: your renting and mortgage agreements.

Rented accommodation
If your home is rented, then you must check with your tenancy agreement or get permission from your landlord to use your home for business purposes. There may be a clause in your agreement which forbids any business use, in which case don't ignore it or you could be evicted for breach of tenancy. If there isn't anything

in the agreement that mentions business use, then carry on, but if the primary purpose of the agreement changes from being residential to business accommodation, then you could be evicted.

Home owners
If you own your own home, there may be restrictions in the title deeds of your mortgage agreement, about whether the premises can be used for business purposes. There isn't any formal guidance for mortgage companies about using your home as your workplace. You will find that individual building societies and mortgage companies will have their own rules and regulations, so you should check. It is very rare for a mortgage company not to allow someone to work from home, but it does depend on the type of business and whether it involves alterations to the character of the property. If there are restrictions, approach your mortgage company and ask them if they will change the terms of your agreement – they may decide to change your mortgage to a semi-commercial one. If you carry on a business without permission from your mortgage company, you could find that they have the right to take possession of your home because you have broken the terms of your original agreement.

Planning permission
If you own your own home and use it for business purposes, you may have to pay Capital Gains Tax when you move. Capital Gains Tax is payable only when you use part of your home exclusively for your business (**See Help Section page 166 Chapter 5 Tax, Insurance and Pensions**). It is not payable if you work at home but use the same room as living accommodation, or if, for example, the room you use as an office is also a spare bedroom.

If you want to make alterations so that you can service or repair goods, or if you have customers coming to the house, then you may need to apply for planning permission to change the use of your premises. But you don't automatically need to do this just because you are working from home, for although you may be *running* a business from home you may not be *carrying out* your business from home. For example, if you are running a decorating or plumbing business, but you do the decorating or plumbing elsewhere and use your home only for doing the paper work, then you do not need planning permission. You do not have to be the owner of the property to make an application for planning permission. If you are not the owner, or if you are only part owner, you will have to inform the owner or whoever shares ownership with you. This includes any leaseholder whose lease still has seven or more years to run. It isn't necessary to make an application yourself, and you can appoint an agent, such as a town planner, an architect, a solicitor, a surveyor or a builder, who can make the application on your behalf. But obviously it is cheaper for you to do it yourself. Whether or not you need planning permission depends on the nature and the extent of your business. but remember:

Planning permission is not usually needed if:	**Planning permission is usually needed if:**
The character and use of the building remain essentially residential.	The character and use of the building do not remain essentially residential.

A change of character or use will probably arise if the answer to any of the following questions is yes:

* Will your home no longer be used substantially as a private residence?
* Will your business result in a marked rise in traffic or people calling?
* Will the business involve any activities unusual in a residential area?
* Will your business disturb your neighbours at unreasonable hours or be particularly noisy or smelly? (**See page 212 this Chapter**).

There is usually a fee for an application for planning permission; the amount varies according to the type of development proposed, so you should contact your local council. The fee is not refundable if planning permission is refused. Some applications are exempt from fees, such as if a previous application has been withdrawn or refused. The government has in fact encouraged local authorities to relax the requirements for planning permission, so if you are in any doubt, contact your local Planning department for information and advice (**See page 238 Help Section this Chapter**). If you do need planning permission, it will take between four weeks to three months, so start preparing your application well in advance.

The planning department of your local council will be able to give you further information and advice. They will also have copies of the development plans for your area, with relevant Acts, Orders and Government policies (**See page 238 Help Section this Chapter**).

Neighbours
Always discuss your business activities with your neighbours and be aware of any noise you make – it doesn't have to be as obviously deafening as a cement mixer. Loud machinery or typing can be deafening through thin walls in the quiet of the night or early hours of the morning. If you use your home for business purposes without the relevant planning permission, you can be ordered to stop. However, this is very unlikely unless your neighbours have complained (**See page 172 Chapter 6 Teleworkers and Outworkers**).

GETTING ORGANISED
When you work from home running your own business, you will quickly discover that because you have to be your own secretary, managing director, telephonist, office cleaner and key worker you had better get yourself organised, or you are going to end up going round in circles trying to remember what you have to do next. Making notes isn't a bad system when you have to remember a dental appointment or to buy some more tea, but when it comes down to client meetings, orders to be delivered, invoices to be sent, book-keeping and filing to be done, letters to write and reply to, stock to order and so on, a little list stuck to the door of the fridge isn't the answer.

A system
To combat the notes and lists on the fridge door syndrome, buy an organiser – either a book type or an electronic one, it makes no difference. Or you can make one yourself with a three-holed ring binder and some paper, but include in it a yearly, monthly and weekly calendar. Buy or make a wallchart planner; they are large enough to see at a glance and are a good organisational aid. You can fill in the spaces not just with appointments and deadlines, but also with personal aims that you want to achieve by a

certain date. Great for planning ahead.

Filing
A pinboard can be useful for displaying business cards and other items that have to be attended to immediately; when dealt with they should be filed. But don't let it turn into an art gallery of family photographs and cards. Do not throw away any business papers. File them. You never know when you may have to refer to them, or use them as evidence in a dispute. Whenever you think, I've called them, I've paid that, I've replied to that, stop yourself from screwing the evidence into a ball and discarding it. File it instead. The tax man can ask to see paperwork up to six years later. Unfortunately things do get lost in the post, people do deny you ever paid them, or that they received your complaint on the date you wrote it, so make a note of postage dates and get a postage receipt from the post office, or send important items by registered post or recorded delivery.

File all letters and keep a copy of your replies. Check reference numbers and make a note of changes of address.

Memory jogger
Keep pen and pencil in the car, by your bed, in your coat pocket or bag so that wherever you are you can jot things down as you remember them. It's surprising what you remember while waiting at the supermarket check-out, or sitting in the car wash!

Address books
Keep your address book and contact books up to date. If it helps you to find things more immediately keep two, one for business and one for family and friends. Photocopy all address books in case they should get stolen, lost or damaged. An address book of work contacts gathered over the years can be invaluable.

Messages
Keep a large message pad by the telephone or by the answer machine. All messages must be timed and dated and it's a good idea either to have an in-tray specifically for them, or to put them on a metal spike. You can make your own out of a wire coat hanger and a cork. It may sound a bit DIY but it works and who is going to see it? Keep all messages and check at the end of the week if you have returned all the calls. Transfer any new phone

numbers to your address book and then file the messages in an appropriate file in case you should ever need to refer to them.

MAKING CONTACT

Use telephone directories to find phone numbers and addresses; they are the most obvious source and the cheapest, but tend to be overlooked. The majority of people and organisations are not ex-directory.

The post

Use the post to communicate; it is cheap and reliable. With a first-class stamp mail will usually get there if you allow twenty-four hours. For businesses there are other postal services.

Intelpost

This is a combined fax and express messenger service for those occasions when you need to send a fax to someone who may or may not have a fax machine. Via Intelpost, messages are delivered the same day to most addresses in the UK and to many countries world-wide via the 112 nationwide offices (**See page 239 Help Section this Chapter**).

Business reply services and freepost

Both of these services give people the incentive to get in touch with you, because there is no need for them to put a stamp on the reply envelope. Business reply is designed mainly for business-to-business communications, and companies tend to use it for direct mail and financial transactions. If your business is consumer orientated, then you would be better off with Freepost. Both services are offered under licence and both carry the same annual licence and handling fees. There is an annual fee for each return-address that you want to use. For both services you have to pay a fee plus an advanced payment based on the estimated number of replies. (**See page 239 Help Section this Chapter**).

Admail

This is specifically designed for companies that use direct-response advertising. It is a redirection service (with or without reply-paid postage) enabling you to receive orders and enquiries at an address which is different from the one you use in your promotional material. For example, you may live in Winchester but might want a prestigious address in W1. Admail will divert your mail from the W1 sorting office and have it delivered to your actual address. When you take out an Admail contract, you are given a user-number to incorporate in the address you chose to publicise **(See page 239 Help Section this Chapter)**.

PO boxes
Private boxes are generally for people who prefer to collect their mail rather than having it delivered, although there is a delivery service. A PO box can be useful if, for example, you live in a block of flats and the porter might not want to sort out your business mail, or you simply don't want the general public to know your real address. The latter may be especially relevant if you are selling mail order and don't want to be troubled at home by customers calling in **(See page 239 Help Section this Chapter)**.

Messenger services
If you have parcels and bulky envelopes which need to be sent in a hurry, there are several different types of messenger services such as: motorbike, pedal cyclist, van or mini-cab. The larger courier services will deliver packages world-wide via plane. If you think you are going to use a messenger service frequently, then it's more convenient to open an account which you pay at the end of every month. Shop around for a good deal. Price and reliability vary.

STATIONERY
Check that you always have a supply of stamps (send non-urgent mail second-class), a variety of different-sized envelopes, paper, staples and sticky tape. There's nothing wrong with recycling envelopes, cardboard boxes or jiffy bags (just cover the front with a sticky address label), paperclips, files, binders, spines for binders, elastic bands, string, brown wrapping paper, etc., it all helps keep down the cost. If you have the space keep a cupboard, drawer or shelf specifically for all your stationery. It means you know where things are, and you don't have to scrabble around when you want a piece of notepaper, or rush down to the newsagent for an expensive and ineffectual Snoopy rubber every time you want to erase something. Don't have everything just slushing around in the bottom of a drawer, keep small items such as elastic bands, paperclips, drawing pins, and staples in containers such as

left-over glass or plastic yogurt pots. Make sure your stationery cupboard is kept well stocked.

Mathematics
Buy yourself an inexpensive calculator, or ask for one for your birthday. Don't rely on using your children's. They take them to school just when you need them. Make sure it does percentages. There are a lot of basic models on the market and they are invaluable when you are doing your invoices or trying to place an order over the phone and have to do a quick calculation.

TIME MANAGEMENT
Keep an appointments diary up to date, so that you can see how your week pans out and where you have to be.

To save time and energy, try to make all your appointments on only one or two days of the week, so that those are your out days and you can put everything else to one side.

Jot down phone numbers which you should later transfer to your address book, or reference numbers which you have to keep referring to during your work. Don't let your work space become a tip for all sorts of junk. Clear it and do your filing at the end of every day.

On your list of things to do the following day, never write more that you can possibly achieve in that time, or you will only get disheartened at the end of the day when you see what you haven't done. Either that or you will beat yourself into a frazzle trying to get everything finished. Don't put off the things you don't want to do, or you will only find yourself writing them on the following day's list and the day after that. Anything that has appeared on a list more than three times seriously has to be done and must take top priority. No more putting off.

Write down your aims, both long- and short-term, but be realistic; stay out of the realms of fantasy. Fantasy aims should be confined to long baths or hot beaches! Next to your aims, write down what you need to achieve them, what actions are required and in what timescale. Put your aims in order of priority. You can buy diary pages with aims and goals written out in headed columns; this may be helpful to you.

YOUR HOME AS YOUR WORKPLACE

Appointments
When making appointments, be aware of how valuable your time is and try not to travel during the rush hours. Allow plenty of time. There is no point in arriving at a meeting flustered and exhausted. Plan your route before you leave, and carry a pocket road map and train and bus map (make sure they are up to date). If you are travelling by car allow parking time, make sure you have change for parking meters, or make a note of where the nearest car parks are situated. If you are travelling by public transport, allow for delays. It may be easier travelling by public transport rather than trying to park a car. If you are going on a longer journey, you can save your energy by not driving and taking the train, leaving you time to read through or write your meeting notes.

Whenever possible try to make your day's appointments in geographic order – those in the same area after each other – so that you don't end up running from one side of town to the other and back on yourself again. If you have to make a delivery, do it first.

Don't necessarily agree to a meeting where it suits the other person. Of course be flexible, but try to arrange a time and place that is mutually convenient, or you could find yourself having to kill hours before the next appointment. Leave time to grab a light lunch, or have a quiet cup of tea, so that you aren't exhausted. There's nothing worse than sitting through a meeting with a rumbling stomach. Make a note of where the nearest public lavatories are on your route and use them when you are near one, not wait until you are desperate. Department stores can be a boon.

Business lunches can be a waste of valuable time, costly and fattening. Breakfast or tea-time meetings are far more constructive. They don't drag on, no one drinks alcohol, they aren't fattening as long as you skip the tea-time cream buns and the breakfast eggs and bacon, and they are cheaper than lunch.

Try not to have to carry around too much; it can be very tiring. Only take with you what you need for that day.

The diary
Keep a family diary up to date as well as your work diary so that you can see quickly whether or not your meeting is going to collide with the school play or taking your son to the dentist. It's important that each member of the family, if they are old enough,

is responsible for filling in times and dates of their various activities and appointments. If they don't write them down no one can be expected to remember. If it helps, use different coloured pens for each person's entry. Keep pens by the diary. You will have to fill in the entries for young children.

Working from home means that there are times when your plans, however well organised, go out of the window. For example, however much your planner said that today you were going to complete an order and type outstanding invoices, if the washing-machine floods over the floor, you have no choice but to deal with it. So call the plumber, mop up the floor and then turn your back on it and get on with your work. If you weren't there you wouldn't be able to move the furniture and take up the carpet. Be careful not to exaggerate minor disasters into events that write off the whole day. I mean the cat being stung on the nose by a bee doesn't mean you have to drop everything. You know when you're using an event to get you out of doing work.

Credit cards
It can save you a lot of hassle if you photocopy your credit cards. If they are stolen or lost you can quote instantly their numbers and expiry dates so that they can be cancelled – and the police know what they are looking for. Keep the photocopies in a safe place. This is also useful if you join a credit card security scheme. The scheme will have a list of your various credit cards, but it may be that you have just either cancelled one or received a new one and not informed the credit card security company, but at least you have photocopied it. There are a number of different security card systems, some run by large chain stores and credit card companies. They all require a membership fee. You contact them immediately you are aware of missing your credit cards and they will cancel them for you on your behalf. Some also offer a returning lost keys service. Shop around before you decide.

Time-keeping
When you work from home you can choose if you want to work nine-to-five office hours. If those don't suit you or your family, then break up your work time differently. Marjorie has chosen to start work at five in the morning (she doesn't work with noisy machinery), stops three hours later for breakfast and a shower, continues working again and finishes her day at three in the after-

noon, when she mentally switches off by preparing the evening meal, or going shopping. If you want to work very early or very late, don't forget about others around you, including your neighbours, who may be sleeping while you are making a noise.

It's better to work when you are at your peak. If you get sluggish at certain times during the day make those your break times. Gary starts work at 9a.m. although he makes phone calls before then. 'In the summer I cut the lawn with my mobile phone in my pocket. I took two calls.'

Flexibility in working times may be great for you. Rosemary likes to start work at 5a.m. every morning. 'I put on a track suit and get started. I stop between eight and eight-thirty to shower, get dressed and put on my make-up, then I'm ready to continue the day's work.'

But this sort of flexibility may not be so great for your family, so you will have to negotiate with them if it causes conflict. If you have children to look after during the day, you may find your working times are dictated by them. You work while they are at school or sleeping. Tricia is an outworker, and finds she is unable to work with her two young children around. 'I work when they've gone to bed. It means I finish around one in the morning. Of course my children wake up at six the following morning, so I'm exhausted and sometimes really grumpy and short with them.'

Some people's work is seasonal, so they are working flat out at certain times of the year and are more relaxed at other times. When you aren't flat out, use that time to recharge your batteries. Be nice to yourself; do all the things you have neglected; have fun as well as doing the filing and painting your work area. Establish new customers, do some cold calling, organise advertising and leafleting. Put that logo on the side of your car, shampoo your office carpet, restock the stationery cupboard or just go and have a facial.

Some people prefer to work only so many days a week and spend other days on a hobby, or with their family. Your work schedule is entirely up to you. It can be tailor-made. But if you know you are no good without a disciplined routine, then start work at nine and finish at five, five days a week. Be careful not to let days drift by with not a lot of work to show for them. However you choose to work, set yourself a work load that you will achieve by the end of the week and make sure you do it. If you know you have a week of family commitments, make allowances for them in the rest of your schedule.

RESOURCES MANAGEMENT

When you are your own boss or you are working for someone who isn't at your side to make sure you're getting on with the job, you have to motivate yourself. You also don't have a team of people to fall back on for help when you're rushed off your feet, when you're feeling below par or you're simply not well. You have to be self driven (**See page 270 Chapter 10 Coping with Working by Yourself**). To do that you have to have one major commodity – energy, or the work simply won't get done. You can conserve your energy by practising time management when you're working and a different sort of time management for your non-working activities. With energy you have to use a war-time expression which was blazened across posters all over Britain; SAVE IT! Only we aren't talking about saving electricity and coal, we're talking about *your* energy. There are various ways you can save your energy when you aren't working.

Food

If you can do something more quickly and easily and simply by using an appliance like a microwave, then use it. Food processors grate cheese and salad vegetables more quickly and better than you can and save you crying over the onions. They also make quick, fresh, delicious soups and drinks. It's quicker to use kitchen scissors for chopping. Ready-made pastry is indistinguishable from homemade and easier and quicker. Cheat with a casserole sauce by using a tin of soup. Tomato purée or tinned tomatoes blended in a machine are just as delicious as steeping and peeling fresh tomatoes. You don't have to remember to soak dried beans overnight, but can reduce the soaking time to two hours by using boiling water, and it's even easier if you use tinned beans. Convenience food is expensive, but it can be useful when you are just too tired to start cooking. But don't fall back on eating junk (**See page 253 Chapter 9 Health and Fitness At Home**).

Try to find recipes that you like which are nourishing and can be made quickly and easily. Anyway, not having rich sauces and fattening cakes is far healthier.

Washing
Use a washing machine or a service wash at your local launderette rather than wasting time handwashing. When you buy clothes check that they can be thrown into the washing machine and, even better, don't need ironing. Don't spend all your time wearing things that have to be dry cleaned; it's both expensive and time-consuming taking and collecting them. Sheets, towels and underwear certainly don't need to be ironed, so save your energy for your business. If other members of your family need things ironed, don't stop them from doing it and don't feel guilty.

Shopping
Save your decision-making for the big decisions, not over which flavour Bonios Rover prefers or what colour kitchen roll you fancy. When you go shopping always have a list and stick to it. It saves time and money and prevents impulse buying. If you have the space to store and you can afford it, bulk buy; it saves all those trips to the shops for every day essentials where every time you go you spend more money and take up more time.

Housework
When you have a tidy-round make a rule. Either put it away, throw it away or store it. Gary thinks that he and his wife have virtually reversed roles, for she goes out to work whilst he runs his insurance business from home. 'I don't cook, but I do load and unload the washing machine and get my own lunch.'

Children who are old enough should be responsible for tidying their own rooms. You are not their servant and they should be proud of their own area. If they choose to have it like a pig sty let them, until the day you decide to go in with the black plastic garden sack and your motto 'Put it away, throw it away or store it'. But warn them of what you are going to do and when, giving them a chance to tidy up first. **(See page 296 Chapter 11 Coping with Family and Friends)**.

Worrying
Worrying is a waste of valuable energy, especially if you tend to do it at bedtime when you need the rest. One of the ways to dispel worries and put them into proportion is to make a list of all the things you have been worrying about. Opposite each worry write down how the worry has changed since you have been

worrying about it. Nine times out of ten you will find worrying hasn't changed anything. It should show you how negative worrying can be, and how it uses up your valuable energy.

A WORK SPACE

When you work from home, it sometimes isn't easy to find a space to work in. A place that you can call your own, where you and your work things won't be disturbed. Gerry has moved his work area around the house three times in the last two years. 'I started off in the play room, between the kitchen and the dining room. As I got more clients it really wasn't big enough. Then I moved to the extension off the dining room, but it's south facing and got too hot. It was my wife who suggested I took over the lounge. It took me ten days to move everything. Half a day to move all the leads. The electric points were luckily in the right place, but I had to get phone plugs put in.'

The perfect place is somewhere you can get away from at the end of the day. Rosemary, who runs a typesetting business, works in the spare bedroom, 'Which means I don't interfere with anyone.' It is ideal if you can find somewhere where you don't keep catching a glimpse of work still to be done, or you may be tempted to get on and do it. Pamela works on the dining-room table, with the computer on one end and the files on the other. She wishes she could escape from her work at the end of the day. 'I find work weighs on me. Because I work in the dining room, we now eat in the kitchen, but I can see the files lying there and even when I unplug the phone I can hear the answer machine click on. I wish we could move somewhere where I could work in the garage or the loft space.'

If possible most people want to work in a place that is quiet, airy and comfortable. A place where your bits and pieces won't get broken or made dirty. A place where you don't have to put your work things away at the end of every day. It sounds like a perfect place and it may not exist. Sasha makes satin picture frames in her small sitting room. 'I have to control the mess, partly because the material has to be kept clean and partly because I don't want to see it when I'm not working. I finish work about seven in the evening and all the bits and pieces have a place. When the work is put away my room changes; it isn't a work room any more.'

Certainly most people who work from home don't need an

impressively spacious place to work in. Some homeworkers don't mind where they work, and even choose the dining room table because they enjoy having the family around them. Others need to get away from noise, families and the television and be alone. Some have no choice, if their home isn't large enough for them to be able to have a place of their own to work in, and where they work is often where they and their families live.

There are homeworkers like Ken D'Cruz, who with four other people, plus drawing boards, computers, laser printer, TV, radio and records, runs a design team from his bedroom. 'It's all a matter of co-operation not space. I have been known to go to bed with people working round me, or I've been woken up at four in the morning with someone coming to use the computer.'

Other people work in the kitchen, clearing their work things away when they have to cook, like Cilla, who is an indexer. 'I used to change the babies' nappies on one end of the kitchen table and proof-read manuscripts and do indexing on the other end.'

Some people work on the dining-room table, pushing their work to one side when it's meal times. Others are lucky enough to have a spare bedroom, play room, walk-in larder, hall, garden shed, garage or loft extension which they have converted into a workplace, giving them all the advantages of being able to separate themselves from the rest of the house and being able to shut the door on it all at the end of the working day.

Work furniture
If you are lucky enough to have a place you can work in and you don't have to share it with the rest of your family, then you can usually furnish it with bits and pieces from around the house. Rosemary relies heavily on modern technology to send information down the line to the printers. She is lucky enough to have a room of her own, a spare bedroom which she has furnished from bits and pieces. 'I have two computers, a fax, printers and four desks. One desk was bought, one was a sideboard and the other was a kitchen table.'

A trestle table (they come in varying heights and you can always saw the legs down) previously used for pasting wallpaper will make a perfectly good desk or work-table. The length of it provides a good space for laying out files, fabric, patterns, etc. Old chests of drawers or cupboards are good for storing files and you can use the top to put the telephone, answer machine, fax, photocopier or computer printer on. Gerry built up his office furniture bit by bit. 'I now have one desk-top and two lap-top computers, fax, laser printer, two answer machines and two telephone lines, three grey metal filing cabinets, two huge steel cabinets and I work at a computer table. I bought new stuff. I bought a computer while I was still going out to work, but unless you're in manufacturing you don't have to go mad and buy everything overnight. I worked out that all the equipment in my office is worth about £18,000, but it's all insured.'

On the other hand Ken, the designer, was advised not to buy all new equipment, so most of his is leased.

If you are using machinery that is heavy, make sure you stand it on something sturdy enough to take the weight. If the machinery is noisy, stand it on a piece of carpet. A doubled-up blanket or tablecloth will deaden the sound and vibration. Cover the top of an old table with PVC; it will brighten it up, prevent you from getting splinters, you can wipe it down to keep it clean and it doesn't matter if you mark it.

Second-hand equipment
You don't need to splash out and buy brand new work furniture. Bankrupt office furniture sales, garage sales, junk shops, and fire damage sales are the best places to buy cheap serviceable filing cabinets, metal cupboards and desks. If you want to buy new, then there are a number of mail order catalogue companies that sell office furniture and supplies at reduced prices (**See page 238 Help Section Chapter**). Rachael bought all her ice-cream-making equipment second hand, including her pasteurisation machine. 'I was very lucky; I was given a demonstration model freezer box by the company I went to buy one off. It fits nicely in the back of my car to make my deliveries.'

DIY household furniture is perfectly good, although the desks aren't generally large enough. It is important that if your work involves sitting behind a desk, especially if you use a VDU, you do not save money at the cost of your health. Wrong positioning of computer screens and keyboards is the cause of Repetitive Strain Injury – now the most common industrial injury in the United States (**See page 246 Chapter 9 Health and Fitness at Home**). You can adapt the bedroom furniture for office use, but don't stand heavy printers or machinery on it. It often isn't solid enough to take the weight.

You can utilise everyday objects for your office: for example, a wicker bread basket can be used for storing pencils, pens, staplers, etc. Christmas biscuit tins are useful for keeping small things such as glue, stamps, typewriter correcting fluid or sewing materials. You can keep drawing pins and paper clips in an old partitioned sewing or make-up box. Heavy-duty cardboard filing cabinets or concertina files won't last forever, but used carefully are fairly substantial for storing papers in. Plastic food containers will hold small tools, sewing equipment or pieces of machinery. Metal foil frozen-food trays and plastic soup containers are useful for mixing paint in or for storing small nuts and screws or fabric scraps. All supermarket cardboard boxes are great for storage, if you have to put your work things away when you finish at night. If you have one, the cupboard under the stairs, loft, unused outside lavatory, back of a garage, cellar or garden shed, spare room wardrobe, old toy box or picnic hamper provide great storage space for larger items; but make sure if you are using anywhere outside, or a space that isn't generally in use, that you check it for damp and rain or things might get damaged.

Communications
When you're working from home you have to be accessible to the outside working world, otherwise you'll miss work and deadlines and find that clients, after tearing their hair out trying to contact you, might give up and use someone else who was easily at hand. It's the stuff nightmares are made of. But in fact it's easy, possible and fairly inexpensive to link a modem up to a computer and send data and text down a telephone line to a client, employer or supplier. Fax and cellular technology is changing all the time and new telephonic tricks like call diversion have made it much simpler for the home-based worker to stay in constant touch.

When you're just setting up an office at home, the cost of a fax machine or a computer may make your hair stand on end and create difficulties with cash flow, so before you commit your capital think seriously about what type of equipment would be most useful to your business and the type you would feel happiest using. You don't have to go wild and buy everything outright, but could look into leasing and renting, bearing in mind that with most rental deals you get a maintenance package.

The telephone and your business
The simple old telephone isn't the simple old telephone any more when you are running a business. Before you order one, think about how you're going to use it and what you need it for, because there is a wide range of options and a lot of new services for the homeworker and the small business. Do you want to be able to take notes whilst you talk? If so, you should look at the handsfree facility. Should you have another line installed for business calls? In addition, there are time-savers such as memory store and last number redial.

First, ring your operator to find out if your exchange is digital. According to British Telecom, two exchanges every working day are being modernised. If yours if one of them, it will give you a greater choice of services. You can have the CALL DIVERSION facility, which means that your phone calls can be re-routed to wherever you are – even to your mobile phone – just by tapping in a short code. The advantage is that without employing help you have freedom to leave the office, even though you may be expecting an important call, and you don't have to rely on an answering machine.

There is a CALL WAITING facility, which alerts you to incoming calls on the line by a discreet bleep, which means you can put your first caller on hold while you check the identity of the second one.

If you're too busy to make a meeting THREE-WAY CALL can be a useful option. This facility allows you to talk to two callers at once, which can be a great time saver, especially if, for example, you are discussing something like building plans which always involve more than one person and all of them in different locations.

When it comes to the phone bill the CHARGE ADVICE service is a great help to a small business. If you have to make a lot of long-distance calls which you then have to charge to individual clients, you need an accurate way of assessing the cost of the call. All you do is key in the appropriate number and the operator will contact you after you have made your call and tell you exactly what you have spent. This can save you money, as we all have a tendency to under-charge long-distance phone calls.

A separate business line
When you are working from home with a family around and your business is dependent on the telephone carrying both incoming

and outgoing calls, you should have a separate telephone line installed. It will also help to differentiate private calls from business ones, so that children can be told they are not allowed to use your business line, or answer it (**See page 288 Chapter 11 Coping with Family and Friends**) and private phone calls don't engage your business line. It also helps you to be able to 'shut up shop', which you can do by simply putting your business answer machine on your business telephone line when you want to stop work, or avoid being interrupted if you're under pressure. Another advantage is that you are automatically included in the Business and Services Phone Book.

Phone systems
With a phone system you can transfer calls to different extensions and use phones around the house as an intercom system. The advantages are: intercom, bell-off and a sufficient number of extensions.

Answer machines
These are invaluable to people who run their own business from home who want to be accessible at all times and don't have a secretary. You can put the machine on when you're out at a meeting or walking the dog, when you're at home hurriedly trying to meet an order deadline, or just having a quiet cup of coffee, and you won't have to worry about missing anything. You can get answer phones that have the additional facility of remote interrogation, which allows you to listen to your messages from any telephone, anywhere. This is important if you have to do a lot of travelling or are out during the day. For example, if you're at lunch you can phone in to your answer machine between the soup and chicken pie and check whether that all-important call has got through.

It's better to have a large-capacity tape for receiving messages, for there is nothing worse than your client trying to leave complicated instructions in a set time limit of ten seconds and having to keep calling back with the rest of the message. To sum up, advantages are: remote interrogation, remote message change, two-way record which allows the recording of tricky instructions during a conversation rather than writing it down, and a large-capacity tape.

The fax

There are currently 700,000 fax machines in Britain and thirty-four million sheets of fax are sent every working day. There are a lot of advantages to having a fax. It speeds up the movement of paperwork, information and documents and faxing an invoice can speed up cash flow. You can fax not only text but detailed plans, maps, drawings, diagrams and designs to over eight million fax users around the world over the telephone network. Sending a fax costs the same as a phone call, plus you can use off peak rates. Customers can call you free or for the cost of a local call and leave their order or message if you link your fax to your 0800/0345 number so you're always open for business. If you use a fax to check stock or delivery details, it means you are able to close a deal immediately with your suppliers. If you accept an order by fax, you are able to match last-minute demand with last-minute supply. You can also send fax messages twenty-four hours a day regardless of time zones.

There is a debate as to whether or not a fax counts as a legal document, but it depends on whether or not the recipients acknowledge (verbally or in writing) that they have received it and recognise the signature on it. If the receipt is acknowledged it counts as a legal document, but remember to take a photocopy of the fax as the print tends to fade.

You may find that a lot of clients may expect you to have a fax and in the long run it's easier and cheaper than using the one at the local newspaper shop. Look for a fax machine with copying facilities, memory, fine setting for detailed documents and auto-redial. You can get a fax with a built-in answering machine or a fax with a switch for plugging in an answering machine; it depends on your requirements. Both are ideal if you don't want to have a separate phone line for the fax and answering machine. A fax with a switch for plugging in an answering machine is more flexible as both the fax and the answering machine can be upgraded. But a combined answering machine can often work out cheaper. You can rent or lease – and remember that the cost of fax machines is constantly coming down.

Mobile communications

A mobile phone is essential if you do a lot of travelling. There's either the hands-free set which is fitted into your car, allowing you to talk and drive in safety, or a handset which you can carry around with you, and with which you can make and receive calls to and from anywhere in the world. Alternatively there's the pager: there's the simple one which alerts you to call your office, one that displays messages on-screen, or a Voicebank which is a computerised telephone message service on which up to ten callers can leave messages at a time, and using a special code you can check them from any telephone (**See page 227 this Chapter**).

Personal computer
It's probably essential in a modern office, and even more so when you're working from home where people are often alone, to have a computer which can give you access to a word-processor, database and even be an accounting aid. A computer connected to a modem will give you access to all kinds of on-line database information such as news, travel information, share prices – and you can even do your shopping down the line. A modem is a small electronic device, about the size of this book, which enables you to send information from your computer down the phone to another computer anywhere in the country. It is ideal if your work depends on transmitting or receiving information from one PC/database to another, which is especially relevant to a lot of teleworkers. If you know you're wary of modern technology then look for a computer with a PC starter pack, or with a teach-yourself video – these are available. A lot of local authority adult education classes include lessons in word-processing and computers.

Getting plugged in
Working from home generally means using more electrical appliances than normal, such as word-processors, computers, freezers, machinery, tools and heaters. It's easy to overload the electricity circuit in your house, particularly if you don't have a ring main. If you live in an old property you must have all your electric circuits checked before you start, to make sure they are safe and can carry the extra load. Inadequate wiring can blow, if, for instance, you are using an electric typewriter and keeping your feet warm at the same time with a fan heater going full blast.

One homeworker who lives in an idyllic old cottage in the country wondered why her shower tingled. When she called in an electrician to install another freezer for frozen gâteaux, he discovered that the wires were so old that the outer rubber protection had perished, and that the system wasn't even earthed. She could have been electrocuted! Once you are sure that your electrical circuits are up to modern standards, you'll probably discover that you haven't got enough sockets so you'll have to get more fitted. Put a socket near each desk or work-table area. Budget for a desk lamp, fax, computer or word-processor, printer, answer machine, etc. If you use a small workshop you'll need a socket circuit breaker for safety: it prevents fuses blowing or you from getting an electric shock if, for example, you should accidentally cut through a power cable with your circular saw.

If your equipment doesn't use a great deal of electricity, like electric typewriters, computers or power hand tools, you can run them off an extension block with additional 'gang' sockets. If you need to connect only low-power equipment such as a computer, printer or fax machine, you are better off with a neat 'mini gang' that can be hidden behind the furniture. This is much safer than a 'Christmas tree' of adaptors. For safety always switch off any machinery at the wall socket when you have finished or if you're interrupted. If a plug should get hot and start to smell, call in an electrician. If you have an employer with an employment contract that states that they are responsible, get them to check it.

The light comes shining through
If it's possible, natural light is the best light to work by. If you are using electric lights, they should not be directed at your work and should not dazzle you. If you are using a desk angle-poise light, keep it tilted downwards and not at your work. If you have an overhead central light, beware of working in your own shadow. When daylight changes, especially in the winter when it starts to get dark in the afternoon, remember to switch on your light. Halogen lights are the kindest to the eyes.

WORK VISITORS
With forms of communication such as fax, telephone and the post, meetings aren't necessary very often these days. Work equipment or products can be collected and delivered. If the distance is too far for you to travel or you don't have a car, then you can use the parcel post or delivery service (**See Post Section this Chapter**). Make sure you register anything valuable. If you aren't always at home then ask a neighbour to take in any deliveries for you, or give an alternative address from which you can collect.

If you have to have meetings with customers, clients, or your work associates, try not to meet them at home. Having business people tramping through your house usually means you have to lock up the dog, get the children deeply involved in something and tidy up. You probably don't want to bother with any of those things when you have work to do. Suggest you meet at a convenient café, pub, wine bar, tea shop, hotel foyer, station waiting-room or their office. Try to avoid meeting in a restaurant unless you know of one that's inexpensive and closes early.

It can also be difficult if you don't have a space for meetings. You may work on the end of the kitchen table, in the cupboard under the stairs or the bedroom. Some people are very understanding and really don't mind climbing over your bed to get to talk to you, or slipping on a piece of Lego, but others just might object and think you aren't very organised or business-like. It can also throw you when you are trying to understand something or put your point of view to be interrupted by your children or the dog mounting the sofa.

Before you decide where at home you are going to work, stop and think if you are going to have many work visitors. If people are just going to drop things off, then working in a tiny cramped area that is also shared with the family is fine. But if you are going to have regular work meetings it could be difficult. If you have no choice as to where in the home you work, then you are going to have to be organised. If you have children, try to make the meeting either during school or nursery hours, bedtime or nap times – this only works if your children have a predictable sleeping pattern. Or arrange for them to be with a friend or relative, either in their house or yours (**See page 292 Chapter 11 Coping with Family and Friends**). Make sure you have walked the dog, so that it doesn't pester everyone, and shut it out of the way, along with the cat, just in case your work visitors are allergic or frightened of animals (**See page 294 Chapter 11 Coping with Family and Friends**).

Turn off any food you may be cooking. Tidy your work space. Put on your answer machine. If you don't have an answer machine take the phone off the hook. If you can't because you're expecting an important work call, you must be prepared to be brief and firmly fend off all personal callers. Even though your visitors may be pleased to see that you are so busy you have to eat where you work, you should clear away any left-over food and cold cups of coffee. If you aren't happy about people smoking where you work, you must ask them not to. There are a lot of offices out of the home which are designated 'no smoking'. If you work in the kitchen or a part of the house which is used by the rest of the family, you are going to have to do some housework before your visitors arrive, even if it means using the black plastic sack to drop things into (**See page 297 Chapter 11 Coping with Family and Friends**). Be careful not to tidy round frantically and then be unable to find things when you need them later. Try to avoid having a work meeting in your home during lunch time, for the last thing you want to have to do is to prepare food or spend money on ready-made meals.

If you have a separate area or table that you can sit round so much the better. Make sure you have spare chairs, tea, coffee, milk, sugar, mineral water, lavatory paper, perhaps biscuits and some unchipped mugs or cups. If unchipped china is a rarity in your house and you have meetings often, keep some away from everyday use. If you work in your bedroom make the bed and clear away any discarded clothes. A tidy bedroom can be a perfectly acceptable place to sit and talk, but not if the floor is covered in underwear and there's wet washing hanging over the radiator. If you have children in your work-room with you, clear away their toys into the toy box. If you work in the kitchen, tidy away kitchen utensils and any old takeaway food cartons and wash up. However cramped your work-space may be, and if it doubles up as a living area and your work-room, try to make it a pleasant, tidy, business-like environment to have a meeting in.

ALL DRESSED UP

You can choose what you want to wear when you work at home; there is no uniform. You don't really have to make much of an effort unless you are meeting either with a client or your bank manager or you are out pressing the flesh or, as it is more commonly know, cold calling, trying to drum up trade (**See page 197 Chapter 7 Selling and Marketing**). But if you decide that you want to look like Madonna while you type out your invoices or make your pots of jam, the choice is yours. If you want to stun the dog or confuse the children by wearing something sequinned and slinky, who's to stop you? You don't have to worry about whether or not you're fashionable, or if your work colleagues are wondering why you're wearing the same skirt four days running. You don't have to glue yourself to the morning weather forecast to see if you need to put on your wellington boots, thermal vest or a sun dress, or all three, and you can't envy what others are wearing and convince yourself you have to go and buy an identical outfit – because you won't see them. Of course it's best to avoid the other extreme of deciding that working at home means no one's going to see you and so you can slob around all day in a stained dressing gown, sloppy slippers, with your hair in curlers and your face concealed behind a rejuvenating mud mask. It's bad for morale and there could be that unexpected visitor.

Clothes to wear at home
If you choose not to wear make-up at home, put on a coating of moisturiser, because your skin doesn't dry out just under make-up. Make sure your hair is clean and fresh and you're showered and smell nice. There's nothing more likely to make you want to hurl yourself off the roof of the garden shed than when you catch a glimpse of yourself in the mirror looking greasy, grubby and grim, at the same time as the client cancels an order, the bank manager's screaming, the cat's licked one of your cream cakes and the computer has taken to having a mind of its own. Some homeworkers like to change in the early evening, as if they're shedding their work clothes and therefore their work persona. Some homeworkers are early risers, like Mary who starts work at six in the morning wearing a tracksuit, stops work at eight for breakfast and a shower and changes into more formal working clothes.

Others prefer to work in the type of clothes they would wear if they were going out to work, like Pamela who is a solicitor. 'I don't bother to dress up. I just wear comfortable clothes, but not a tracksuit in case a client should drop in. I think that would look too casual for a solicitor.' You have the choice – just feel good about yourself, both inside and out.

Check the regulations with the Health and Safety Commission **(See Help Section Chapter 3 You, Your Company and the Law)** as to whether or not you should be wearing protective clothing. If you should be wearing a mask because you are working with chemical substances, for example, when stripping old furniture, also wear goggles to protect anything splashing into your eyes. Overalls and rubber gloves will protect your skin and your clothes, but you should also work with plenty of ventilation. Most DIY stores now sell protective clothing and masks.

If you're sitting at a word processor all day, avoid tight clothes such as jeans, skirts or dresses with a tight waist band which will restrict the base of your rib case as you sag in the middle with hours of sitting in the same position (**See page 245 Chapter 9 Health and Fitness at Home and pages 224 and 236 this Chapter**). Tight trousers will restrict your groin movement as well as your waist and will become very uncomfortable. Don't wear shoes that will cramp your feet, because you may find that with hours of sitting your feet develop a tendency to swell.

Make sure you wear clothes that suit the type of work you're doing. If your business is cooking, have a supply of aprons and catering overalls. Don't wear clothes with baggy sleeves or long neck ties that are a fire hazard, unhygienic and will get stained. Don't wear clothes made from heavy fabrics or woollens that will be too hot for working in a kitchen. Look for fabrics that don't stain easily and can be thrown into the washing machine. The most practical and hygienic wear which also prevents you from ruining your clothes is an easily washable nylon overall. If, for hygiene reasons, you have to wear a hat, make sure it is a hat that actually does cover your head. There are plenty of catering hats available from catering suppliers which also allow for long hair to be tucked up inside them.

If your work involves giving your hands rough wear and tear, protect them with heavy-duty thick rubber gloves which you'll find in garden centres or DIY shops. You will also find tough hard-wearing overalls which are perfect for decorating or mechanical work. If your business means you walk dogs, stand on your feet all day or simply travel a lot on public transport, wear comfortable shoes.

Clothes for going out
If you have a business appointment, listen to the weather forecast to give you a rough idea on how to dress. There is no point in dragging around a heavy coat or umbrella when you don't need them. A day out is not the time to break in new shoes or to totter about on very high heels, or open-toed sandals that let your toes drag in the dust. If you're going to appointments you don't have to forsake fashion for comfort. Maybe you should think about buying more expensive shoes in order to get the right fit and a style which also offers comfort. If you need them, wear support stockings; no one will ever know the difference.

When you go to see clients or the bank manager look business like. The fact that you know what you want and are a professional person should come over as soon as you enter a room. If you are unsure of your wardrobe or feel it's full of reject clothes bought on grey days buy yourself a couple of business outfits, or one skirt or pair of trousers, and two alternative jackets, preferably in dark colours, which you can brighten up with a shirt or interesting tie. People notice the top half of you more than the bottom half, but that isn't any reason to go out in down-at-heel shoes, threadbare trousers, or torn tights.

Clothes counselling
If you are unsure of your image, invest in a meeting with a colour co-ordinating counsellor. Tell them what you do, the type of people you will be meeting and your life-style, and they will help you to adapt your existing wardrobe perhaps with a few additions. For the very unsure they'll even go shopping with you and give you on-the-spot advice. We all make mistakes with clothes. If we didn't, the second-hand clothes shops and charity shops wouldn't be bulging with the rejected contents of people's wardrobes. Don't tell me it's all to do with weight gain and loss! And tailors wouldn't have orders to alter new trousers which were bought in a moment of desperation, to make them fit. Men as well as women are known to buy clothes that they get home and hate!

Briefcases
If you really intend to look professional, throw away the supermarket carrier bag and invest in a briefcase for carrying papers, samples, etc. There is a wide price range, from leather or hide of one sort of another, to plastic, vinyl and very good fake. They're all perfectly fashionable because the briefcase has managed to avoid fashion changes, so it will last for years. Choose one that suits your needs in terms of practicality, either top or side opening – but with the side opening sort be aware that they aren't easy to undo with one hand if you need to get at your railway ticket in a hurry. A pilot's brief case is large enough to double up as an overnight bag. Make sure it opens wide enough for you to be able to get out anything bulky, such as samples. If you only carry papers, don't buy anything too large, or you will be tempted to fill it and then find it too bulky or heavy to carry around. A

briefcase looks as if you mean business and allows you to be more organised.

ARE YOU SITTING COMFORTABLY?

In 1988 381.5 million working days in the UK were lost through back problems, and back-related illnesses are reported to have risen by 40 per cent in the last five years. There's nothing worse than sitting uncomfortably, especially when you're in the same position for hours. Because of the type of work they do, a great many homeworkers sit for most of the day at work-tables, desks, computers and word-processors. This can often result in signs of physical strain such as backaches, headaches, neck and shoulder tension and Repetitive Strain Injury. The cause of all of these conditions is a culmination of things, but the root of the problem is often how you are sitting and the height you are working at.

Eight out of ten people suffer from disorders caused by strain. Constant strain on discs and joints in your lumbar region (which is your spine) can often result in serious back problems. A lot of us work sitting on chairs which give inadequate support for the small of the back, thus putting extra strain on the front part of the discs and with it the risk of slipped discs. Desk work for most of us means leaning forward, bent over. Experts recommend that work surfaces for writing and paper work should be 28½ inches (72.5 centimetres) from the floor. For typing and computers the work surface should be between 24 and 27 inches (61 and 68 centimetres) from the floor and computer monitors and copy-holders should be 16 to 28 inches (40 to 71 centimetres) from your face.

Before you start work, experiment with your seating. If you need to support your back, particularly your lower back, do so either by using a rolled-up towel, a small cushion, a piece of foam rubber, or you can buy a commercially made back roll. Seat edges should not cut into the backs of your legs. Try using a foot rest – you can make one by adapting an old box or telephone directory or, again, by buying a commercially made one which will be height-adjustable. Test if your chair is the correct height for your work-surface by putting your chair sideways on – the arm of the chair should be level with the edge of the table or desk-top. You can raise the height of your work-desk, table or chair by using wooden cubes with holes that the desk leg will fit into. You can either make or buy them. Don't sit with your legs crossed. Never sit lower than the space you are working at. **(See page 246 Chapter 9 Health and Fitness At Home.**

Don't let the filing get on top of you!

CHAPTER 8
HELP SECTION

Office furniture supplies and design
PEGGY PRENDEVILLE INTERIOR DESIGNER 10 Colman's Court, 45 Morris Road, London E14 6NQ. Tel: 071 515 5134.

MISCO Mail order office suppliers across the country. Inexpensive, basic, office furniture, everything from work stations, printers, computers and all hi-tech accessories, freecall 0800 789000 for catalogue.

ESTIA Reasonably priced, modern design, adaptable, colourful office furniture. Mail order across the country. Tel: 071 636 5957 for catalogue. Or visit their showroom at: 5–7 Tottenham Court Road, London W1P 9PB.

CONRAN SHOP 81 Fulham Road, London SW3 6RD. Tel: 071 589 7401. Not cheap. Streamlined Mosquito desk in ripple sycamore £1,795. Or in plywood and aluminium £1,575. Steel studio tech desks with steel tops £95.

IKEA, Drury Way, 255 North Circular Road, NW10 0QJ. Tel: 081 451 5566. Europa Boulevard, Warrington, Tel: 0925 55889. Park Lane, Wednesbury, West Midlands, Tel: 021 526 5232. Sells low cost, Swedish self-assembly workstations. Tabletops and legs can be bought separately for custom-made combinations. White melamine tabletop £16, tubular chrome trestle legs £13 each.

REJECT SHOP For branches tel: 071 736 7474. Inexpensive, fixed five-shelf units, mobile trolleys, hi-tech four-shelf computer stations.

Planning permission booklets and information
The planning department of your local council will give you information and advice on planning permission. They will also have copies of the development plans for your area, which will contain local policies that may be useful to you. You can also look at the

relevant Acts and Orders and Government policies as set out in *Planning Policy Guidance Notes and Circulars*. A list of circulars (Index of Exant Circulars) is also available. Copies of these can be purchased from any book shop which stocks government publications, or ordered by telephone from HMSO PUBLICATIONS CENTRE Tel: 071 873 9090. They may also be available at your local reference library.

A Step by Step Guide to Planning Permission for Small Businesses. Department of the Environment and the Welsh Office.

ROYAL INSTITUTION OF CHARTERED SURVEYORS 12 Great George Street, London, SW1P 3AD. Tel: 071 222 7000.

RURAL DEVELOPMENT COMMISSION 11 Cowley Street, London SW1P 3NB. Tel: 071 276 6969. 141 Castle Street, Salisbury, Wilts, SP1 3TP. Tel: 0722 336255.

ROYAL TOWN PLANNING INSTITUTE, 26 Portland Place, London, W1N 4BE. Tel: 071 636 9107.

DEVELOPMENT BOARD FOR RURAL WALES, Ladywell House, Newtown, Powys, SY16 1JB. Tel: 0686 626965.

The post

How to Send Things of Value Through the Post, leaflet from your local Post Office.

LOCAL THOMSON'S DIRECTORIES

Head Office: Tel: 0252 516111.

Thomson's Regional Offices:

9th floor, 51–53 Hagley Road, Edgbaston, Birmingham, B16 8QJ. Tel: 021 456 3000.

3rd Floor, 1 Bridewell Street, Bristol, BS1 2QG. Tel: 0272 279188.

3rd Floor, Bovril House, Southbury Road, Enfield, EN1 1LY. Tel: 081 366 9606.

Thames Plaza, 5 Pinetrees, Chertsey Lane, Staines, TW18 3DR.Tel: 0784 469940.

Black Horse House, 8–10 Leigh Road, Eastleigh, Hants, SO5 4FH. Tel: 0703 644033.

6th Floor, Anderston House, 389 Argyll Street, Glasgow, G2 8LR. Tel: 041 248 7277.

6th Floor, Wade House, The Merrion Centre, Leeds, LS2 8PB. Tel: 0532 444677.

Clarendon House, Stamford New Road, Altrincham, Cheshire, WA14 1BT. Tel: 061 927 7557.

Venture House, 15–17 High Street, Purley, Surrey CR8 2YW. Tel: 081 668 2023.

Seating and relaxation

THE ALEXANDER TECHNIQUE is a way of becoming aware of balance, posture and movement in everyday activities. The technique is popularly supposed to be concerned with posture and relaxation. Lessons are individual lasting thirty to forty minutes, they recommend a foundation of twenty to thirty lessons spread over three to five months. Cost varies between £5–£10 per lesson. For a list of names and addresses of teachers who have graduated write, enclosing SAE to: SOCIETY OF TEACHERS OF THE ALEXANDER TECHNIQUE 10 London House, Fulham Road, London SW10 9EL. Tel: 071 351 0828.

AUTOGENIC TRAINING is a series of mental exercises that ease the physical symptoms of stress. Once you have learnt the method you can benefit from it whenever you need to. THE BRITISH ASSOCIATON OF AUTOGENIC TRAINING AND THERAPY 101 Harley Street, London, W1N 1DF. Tel: 071 935 1811.

YOGA readjusts the way you stand and sit so that you are correctly aligned. Will alleviate backache and headaches, with the added advantage that stretched muscles are healthier muscles. By adding yoga to a sedentary life-style you can achieve both strength and the ability to relax. BRITISH WHEEL OF YOGA will give you the names of reputable qualified teachers. Tel: 0529 306851.

THE BACK STORE 330 King Street, London, W6 0RR. Tel: 081 741 5022. Mail order across the country, but they will not send chairs.

THE BACK SHOP 24 New Cavendish Street, London, W1M 7LH. Tel: 071 935 9120. Deliver to England, Scotland, Wales, Northern Ireland and the Isles of Shetland, Orkney, Man, Anglesey, Scilly and Wight. Both companies have a range of ergonomically designed office chairs, desks, lecterns, computer mounts and levellers. They will also help to plan your office.

AROMATHERAPY, REFLEXOLOGY AND SHIATSU are all based on massage techniques using vital points of the body to release energy. AROMATHERAPY ASSOCIATES 68 Maltings Place, Bagleys Lane, London, SW6 2BY. Tel: 071 731 8129. BRITISH SCHOOL OF REFLEXOLOGY 92 Sheering Road, Old Harlow, Essex, CN17 0JW. Tel: 0279 429060. THE BAYLEY SCHOOL OF REFLEXOLOGY Monks Orchard, Whitbourne, Worcester, WR6 5RB. Tel: 0886 21207.

REPETITIVE STRAIN INJURY (RSI) ASSOCIATION Christ Church, Redford Way, Uxbridge, Middlesex UB8 1SZ. Tel: 0895 238663. Send £1.50 plus large SAE with a 34p stamp for their helpful factpack with more addresses and phone numbers. *VDU Hazards Factpack* and *An Office-Worker's Guide to RSI* £2.50 and £3.00 respectively, available from: City Centre Project, 32 Featherstone Street, London, EC1Y 8QX. Tel: 071 608 1338. *VDU Terminal Sickness: Computer Health Risks and How to Protect Yourself*, Green Print (**See also Help Section Chapter 9 Health and Fitness at Home, for further addresses**).

Telephones and communications

BRITISH TELECOM products, free call 0800 800 800. Information on British Telecom Chargecard free call 0800 800 838.

CHANGING WORK PATTERNS, National Economic Development Unit, 1986 Institute of Manpower Studies.

PRINTACALL TM48E call VIDCALL ELECTRONICS LTD 14 Newbridge Road, Tiptree, Essex, CO5 0HS. Tel: 0621 819094. To enable you to keep tabs on the cost and number of phone calls you make.

REMOTE WORKING UNITS FOR DISABLED PEOPLE Information Technology Division 1985, Department of Trade and Industry.

Tomorrow's Workplace the manager's guide to teleworking by Francis Kinsman, from BRITISH TELECOM.

Car telephones and mobile phones

CBA TELECOMMUNICATIONS Tel: 0276 691811.
COLEMAN MILNE Tel: 0942 815600.
HOOPER Tel: 071 624 8833.
MIKE WELLS AUDIO Tel: 071 381 4742.
PANASONIC BUSINESS SYSTEMS UK Tel: 0344 853 912.
MOTOROLA Tel: 0256 790 207.
RACAL VODAFONE Tel: 0635 33251.
VIDCALL ELECTRONICS LTD 14 Newbridge Road, Tiptree, Essex CO5

0HS. Tel: 0621 819094. This small machine helps you to keep tabs on the cost and number of phone calls you make, which is invaluable for your costing and if you are billing your client.

Chapter information sources
A Step-by-Step Guide to Planning Permission for Small Businesses, Department of the Environment; National Homeworking Unit; The Post Office; The Back Store; British Telecom, The Quentin Bell Organisation; *Working at Home: The Dream That's Becoming a Trend* by Lindsey O'Connor, Harvest House.

CHAPTER 9

Health and Fitness at Home

Work's much more fun when everyone feels FIT!!

FITNESS FOR THE HOMEWORKER
When you're self-employed and working from home, your health and well-being is vitally important to keeping your business and workload under control. When you're a one-person outfit, ill health can result in lost orders, unhappy clients, discontented customers and a lack of follow-up business. Even if you are able to crawl out of bed to work, your paperwork and the day-to-day jobs of running a business single-handed will be neglected and mount up. Invariably you will have no one to fall back on. This bleak scenario can get bleaker if you consider that if you are ill you won't be able to earn any money, whilst your running costs will continue to mount. So it cannot be emphasised enough that if you want to be successful you have to consider your body and your mind as much as you do your cash flow.

TAKING A BREAK
In order not to get tired or slow down in your concentration, you must take regular breaks, just as factory workers do. Even just ten or fifteen minutes every hour and a half will do the trick. Move away from your work area, do something else, so that you get some movement in different parts of your body. Get up and make yourself a warm drink; get up to answer the telephone rather than have it near at hand; or go to get some stationery. Maybe you can arrange to be able to move to another work space to do a different job; for example, you may type at a desk, but move to a table to handwrite your letters and packages.

Even when you are not moving around, you should change your sitting position, even if it's only slightly, every five minutes. If you suffer from back and neck tension at the end of a long day hunched over a desk, (**See page 236 Chapter 8 Your Home as Your Workplace**) try relieving it by finding a place where you can be quiet, and lie flat on the floor. Tilt your pelvis up to make sure all your spine is on the floor and there is no space between your lower back and the floor. Tuck your chin in to lengthen your spine and lie still, with your palms upwards and your eyes closed for a few minutes.

There are many alternative methods for relieving tension and stress and bringing about a feeling of well-being, such as yoga, the Alexander Technique, Autogenic Training, Aromatherapy, Reflexology and Shiatsu (**See Help Section this Chapter**).

REPETITIVE STRAIN INJURY (RSI)

Repetitive Strain Injury is a major health hazard for people who spend most of their day working on a computer keyboard. The name RSI is an umbrella term for a variety of industrial injuries, although the condition is usually felt in the tendons and muscles of the wrists and arms. It is caused by overuse of these tendons and muscles and also those in the neck – not through actual use of the keyboard, but through bad seating and positioning.

RSI does not occur out of the blue but develops in stages. First symptoms are aches in the fingers, wrists and arms while you are actually working at the keyboard and which disappear when you stop working. If you ignore these warning signs, you could develop stage two symptoms: the aches and pains do not disappear when you stop work and can be severe enough to prevent you sleeping. Full-blown RSI is so severe that as well as preventing you from working, even the simplest domestic task such as picking up a kettle or buttoning up clothes can become impossible.

How to avoid RSI

When it is your livelihood which could be at risk, prevention is obviously better than cure and it is worth taking some time and expense before you start working on your keyboard, to safeguard your health.

* Most ordinary desks are not suitable for VDU (Visual Display Unit)/keyboard use; they are often too small so that you have to sit in a cramped position and are not of a suitable height. It is worth investing in a purpose-made table.
* Chairs for use with VDUs are specially designed to be adjustable for correct posture. They should have back-rest adjustment and support as well as height adjustment. It is better to have a chair without arms.

Once you are working on a keyboard, the single most important rule

HEALTH AND FITNESS AT HOME

is to take frequent breaks. Experts recommend that short breaks of five minutes every half-hour or so are better than ten minute breaks every two hours. Try to exercise your arms, shoulders and neck during some of the breaks by moving them about. **(See page 224 Chapter 8 Your Home As Your Workplace**.)

If you are unlucky enough to experience any of the symptoms of RSI, act quickly and see your doctor. In the early stages RSI is curable, but later on it may take months or years to clear up, during which time working with a keyboard will certainly be impossible. (**For RSI Association, see page 258 Help Section this Chapter**).

OTHER HEALTH PRECAUTIONS FOR COMPUTER WORKING

Glare from reflected light causes eye-strain and headaches. To avoid glare you should:

* Have blinds or curtains which diffuse bright sunlight.
* Place your screen at right-angles to windows so that both direct and reflected glare are avoided.
* Avoid wearing white clothes which may reflect back at you.
* Make sure your desk has a dull, non-reflective surface.

It is also advisable to have an eye-test if you have not recently had one, before beginning to work with a VDU. Around 30 per cent of the population have undiagnosed eyesight deficiencies which will be shown up by VDU working and cause eye-strain related problems. If you already wear glasses or contact lenses, you should check that these are suitable for VDU work.

EXERCISE

Regardless of age, most people who work from home lead fairly sedentary lives. They don't even use their energy pushing and shoving in the train, running for the bus, walking to the office or struggling up those five flights of stairs because the lift has broken. Homeworkers are generally people who sit slumped over a desk, table or drawing board from the moment they get out of bed. Their most frequent form of exercise is boiling the kettle. At the end of the day they'll wonder why they're stiff, their back hurts, shoulders ache, neck has cramp and knees have set. It's time to get away from that sitting position and get moving. You don't have to throw yourself into marathon running or the worry of wondering if you dare show your thighs at the local aerobics class. Ordinary general exercise which gets you moving and increases your heart rate, will help to keep your joints and muscles supple, healthy, strong and your body slim. Exercise also has another known key use: it helps to relieve stress, which affects people who work from home just as much as out-of-homeworkers – possibly more so because homeworkers don't have colleagues to share things with. Working from home is the perfect excuse to do no physical exercise at all, but once you start you'll wonder how you ever managed to get through a day without it. Janet runs a printing business from her spare bedroom but makes the time to go swimming three times a week, cycling three miles to the pool and three miles back, as well as walking the dog for twenty minutes every day. If you aren't a natural lover of exercise like Janet, then it's important to choose a form of exercise that you enjoy. It may be doing you good, but it has to be fun as well.

Walking
Good brisk walking is a way of strengthening the heart and lungs and improving cardiac resistance. In some studies of different forms of exercise, walking has come out better at pushing up the heart rate than cycling or running. Other scientific studies confirm the notion that walking helps clarify mental processes. At Purdue University in America, after giving subjects psychological tests to determine their decision-making abilities, researchers put people into a fitness programme in which regular walking was a central feature. They found that after six months they had improved their decision-making skills 60 per cent more than subjects in the control group who did not exercise. Walking also helps to clear the mind and relieve tension, which is something homeworkers tend to suffer from because they don't have colleagues around to share work problems with.

Brisk walking is the form of exercise that is the least likely to cause injury, is inexpensive to practise and natural, as well as being something you can do to fit your work timetable. It will lift your spirits or calm you, will keep your weight down, tone your muscles and reduce risk of heart and lung disease.

If you need motivation to walk and you have a dog, then you have the perfect answer. But that doesn't mean you take Fido out and stand in the middle of the park while he rushes around chasing a ball, or that you both amble about for ten minutes. If you're a dog-walker, make sure you walk briskly and for a set time, at least an hour. Both you and the dog will feel the benefit. If you don't own a dog, don't rush out and get one, for there are plenty of dog-owners who go out to work all day and would be only too relieved to lend you their dog for a brisk daily walk.

If you aren't a dog-lover or simply don't own one, make sure you walk rather than drive or take transport for a trip to the post office with the day's mail or to buy stamps, to the newspaper shop, bank, shops, stationers or to a client meeting. A lot of homeworkers get their exercise from walking their children to and from school. After a while, start walking briskly for twenty to thirty minutes two or three times a week, you will soon build up stamina and find you are less tired. Aim to walk a mile in fifteen minutes. If you have the choice, walking in the park or countryside can be more pleasant than through busy streets, but wherever you walk make sure you have strong, comfortable, low-heeled shoes and warm socks, especially if you are going walking in the countryside at weekends (**See Help Section this Chapter**).

Cycling

Try cycling to your errands. It's a cheap and easy way to get around, although not recommended if you're collecting a lot of stock or taking bundles of letters or parcels to the post office. If you are going to cycle in busy streets, make sure you really do know your Highway Code. It's a good idea to take a cycling proficiency test; contact your local authority for more information. Make sure you wear light-coloured clothing, a reflective chestband, crash helmet and if you are cycling in rush-hour traffic you might prefer to wear a face mask to filter some of the fumes, but remember to change the filter regularly or it will do more harm than good. You can buy all of these from any cycling or sports shop. DIY shops also sell face masks. If you cycle at night make sure that all your lights work. Don't cycle in a full skirt that will billow out, or in high-heeled shoes, or carry a child on the cross bar. Cycling won't do much for your suppleness if you're young, but if you're older it'll keep you moving. You can join a cycling club, or go cycling with friends at weekends (**See Help Section this Chapter**).

Swimming

Swimming is excellent for building your stamina, and especially good if you're overweight or suffer from backache or stiffness (**See page 236 Chapter 8 Your Home As Your Workplace**). It's also a great way of waking you up, either before you start work in the morning or when you're feeling sluggish in the middle of the afternoon. You don't have to buy a fancy swimming costume and most pools have heated changing rooms, showers and hairdryers. If you can't swim, don't worry; you can learn at any age and most local pools have swimming classes for adults only, or can arrange individual private tuition for the really nervous. They also have parent-and-baby or parent-and-toddler classes. You can go swimming with friends or swim alone. It can be great fun, and if you want to be really adventurous a lot of local pools now have water chutes, slides and wave machines (**See Help Section this Chapter**).

Running

You will see joggers and runners on any tow path, common, park or even pavement. Over the last few years it has become a very popular way of getting fit. Running or jogging is fun, it's free, and your only overheads are a pair of good running shoes which give you support, plus a track suit, but you don't have to wear anything fashionable. You can run or jog at any time, either during the day when you need a break from work, first thing in the morning to get you started or to round off a day's work before your evening meal. Don't overdo it at first or you may risk injury to your feet, ankles and hips. Run on soft surfaces; whenever possible you're better off on grass. If you have arthritis in your legs, hips or back or if you are overweight, you should try cycling or swimming instead. Be careful in traffic. If you jog at night wear light-coloured clothing and a reflector chest-band or ankle straps. You don't always have to jog alone; there are lots of athletic clubs which don't just cater for high performers (**See Help Section this Chapter**).

Apart from the sports suggested, there are other activities to choose from that get you moving about, such as: golf, bowling, badminton, tennis, squash, weight-training, judo, martial arts, exercise classes, dance, or if you prefer you can exercise at home using either an exercise instruction chart or one of the many exercise videos on the market. Whichever you choose, don't overdo it. Do just as much as you need to feel the benefit.

HEALTHY EATING

It's very easy when you're working at home on your own to get into the habit of not eating properly. You'll make the excuse that you're too busy to have a nutritious lunch (no one's talking about a four-course meal here), too preoccupied to eat healthily, or you just can't be bothered to get food when it's only for you. Brenda finds that when she gets lonely and fed up with work she eats: 'I'm a chocoholic.'

You might have had a gourmet, love-hate relationship with your workplace canteen or local café, but at least it was somewhere to fall into for a hot meal, half-acceptable salad or a sandwich. You might even have complained about it, but at least it got you away from work and gave you a defined break in which you could either socialise with your colleagues and eat food that you hadn't had to prepare, or simply work on through. Now you find you no longer have that opportunity, neither do you have work companions to share a meal with and let's face it, for most of us eating is a social event. Not many people really enjoy and savour their food, or make the conscious effort to prepare it with such detail when they are going to eat alone.

So what do you do at lunch time when you work from home? Tricia works through lunch with a sandwich and the newspaper. Jane has breakfast but doesn't stop for lunch. 'I just drink coffee and pick my way through the day.'

You might prowl around the fridge like a leopard studying the leftovers, picking at bits of cold this and sticking your finger in a bit of that and then shoving a half-eaten something into the microwave. Or you walk around eating, while reading the newspaper, watching the lunch-time news on the TV or flicking through junk mail, eating as quickly as possible to get it over with, because you don't want to sit and acknowledge that you are eating alone. The only thing more depressing than eating leftovers is eating them on your own.

In between meals, when the work's going badly or you're just fed up with it, you'll hurl yourself into the bread bin or biscuit tin because bread fills you up and the sugar in the biscuits gives you instant energy – but it's not sustained, which means that an hour later you're back at the biscuit tin again. And you'll wonder why you've started to gain weight since you've been working at home.

You may find it difficult, but you have to try to be as disciplined about eating properly and at set times as you are about organising your work schedule. If some of your motivations for getting down to work are money, success and a feeling of achievement, then your motivation for regular, healthy eating should be because you want to look good, feel good and have the stamina to keep going. Remember, when you're working for yourself, nobody pays you when you're ill.

Breakfast

I'm sure you've read it a million times before, but breakfast is an important meal and shouldn't be missed. Working at home with breakfast so easily available you can choose at what point you decide to stop for it. If you are one of those people who gets up and starts work at five in the morning, you may only need a hot drink or some fruit juice to get you going and prefer to stop for breakfast around eight or nine. Or you may have breakfast the moment you wake up and then start work. But don't delay it so that it collides with or even replaces your lunch. Breakfast should be tasty and nutritious, and shouldn't consist of your children's or partner's left-over soggy cereal or toast crusts, or a cigarette and a cup of sweet tea, or nothing at all. People who work from home tend to miss breakfast because they think they aren't travelling anywhere and can grab something later. They do. It's usually a mid-morning packet of tooth-destroying, calorie-packed sweet biscuits, which give an instant shot of energy and not a lot else.

Your breakfast should be either wholemeal toast, unsweetened muesli, two Weetabix, two shredded wheats, puffed wheat, porridge, cornflakes or other cereal. If you have a juicer there's nothing like freshly squeezed fruit juice; if not, the shop variety is great.

Lunch

If you have eaten a proper breakfast, then you shouldn't be starving and prepared to eat any old rubbish at lunch time. Lunch doesn't have to be anything fancy, costly or take long to prepare for it to be nutritious. Rosemary and her husband run a typesetting business together: 'We have the same thing for lunch more or less every day, cheese, biscuits and fruit. I never eat between meals.'

Baked beans on toast, for example, are especially good for you. Buy the beans with less salt and sugar and have wholemeal toast with just a scraping of either butter or margarine. Potatoes in their jackets are easy to cook and if you have a microwave they can be done very quickly. Low-fat fillings such as cottage cheese or chilli con carne without the butter, or tuna salad are better for you. Or try fish fingers, grilled rather than fried, with frozen peas, which have more nutritious goodness in them than fresh ones that have been lying about in the supermarket losing their vitamin C. If you're going to make a quick spaghetti bolognese, make sure the minced meat isn't too fatty – and it's better to have less sauce and more wholewheat spaghetti. There's nothing to beat a fresh crunchy salad with pulses, such as lentils, haricot beans, red kidney beans, black-eyed beans or chickpeas which you could try eating cold with a light vinaigrette dressing, or add them to casseroles or stews. If you don't want to spend time cooking beans, buy tinned ones which are already cooked, but rinse them in a sieve first to get rid of the salt that they are in. All these easy light snack meals are also good for children and perfect for tea time.

Fast food
There is such a thing as healthy fast food, here are a few examples:

Fresh Fruit.
Raw vegetables.
Frozen vegetables.
Baked beans.
Baked potatoes.
Fish fingers and frozen fish, grilled or baked rather than fried.
Tinned fish.
Plain yogurt.
Cooked eggs.
Wholegrain breakfast cereals which don't necessarily have to be eaten at breakfast time.

If you fancy a sandwich, make it with good bread such as wholemeal and just a scraping of low-fat spread. Put in fillings such as:

Tuna.
Low fat cream cheese.

Mashed banana.
Grated apple.
Grated raw carrot.
Half-fat hard cheese.
Crisp salad.

Finish your lunch with fresh fruit or unsweetened yogurt, not tinned sweetened fruit, cakes, sweets or biscuits. Try drinking unsweetened tea or coffee, preferably decaffeinated coffee, and if you take sugar try to cut down gradually. Buy low-calorie soft drinks or unsweetened fruit juices, preferably ones that dilute with water.

Junk foods to avoid
These foods should be avoided because they have no roughage and too much salt and animal fats.

Burgers.
Fish and chips.
Sausage rolls.
Chips.
Vegetable or meat samosas.
Meat pies.
Meat pasties.
Salami.
Crisps.

Be aware that most prepared foods have too much salt (only buy tinned vegetables that say 'unsalted') plus they have additives, watch out for those E numbers!

Snacks
If you eat sensibly there is no reason why you can't work through the day with all the energy you need, without picking at leftovers and molesting the fridge. If you fancy a mid-morning or mid-day snack try fruit, or crunchy vegetables. It's best to have a small dish of them scrubbed and peeled ready in the fridge. Prepare them in the morning before you start work, so they are handy to nibble when you feel peckish. If you have to stop and scrub a carrot or wash the celery you just won't bother. The foolproof way to avoid eating junk food is simply not to buy it. If it isn't there you aren't tempted, especially when the work is going slowly or you're bored. You will also be doing the rest of the family a

favour. They don't really need it either and think what treats you can buy with the money you save!

Healthy snacks
You shouldn't need to eat between meals if you have a proper lunch and breakfast. If you are going to snack, stick to the healthy snacking list below and you can add to it a little bowl of sunflower or pumpkin seeds – toasted they are yummy – which are delicious to dip into.

> Fresh fruit.
> Raw vegetables; thin strips of: carrots, celery, cauliflower, cucumber, green and red pepper, mustard and cress, alfalfa sprouts.
> Pitta bread (plain, or filled with something like mashed banana or salad).
> Natural yogurt with fresh fruit.
> Unsweetened breakfast cereals, with skimmed milk.
> Unsweetened fruit juice.
> Bread with either low-fat spread or a scraping of butter.
> Unsweetened biscuits or popping corn with a little grated cheese.

Always try to eat away from where you work. It not only keeps your work clean – I have experienced greasy stains on papers and tea-time honey sticking together the keys of my word-processor – but it also gets you away from your work environment, so that you can return to it fresh. Always sit down to eat; don't eat wandering around. Try simply to enjoy your meal, which you have chosen and taken special care to prepare. Don't try and rush it, or get it over by reading or watching television at the same time. It may be time you would use to catch up on the news on the radio, or in the paper, but your meal is the most important thing and you should eat it without taking your mind off it. Sit somewhere comfortable. If you have a garden or balcony and the weather's good, put your meal on a tray and take it outside. Don't rush to get through it, unless you really do have a serious deadline to beat with your workload. Once a week meet a friend (**See page 283 Chapter 11 Coping with Family and Friends**) or invite someone round for lunch, but don't drag lunch-time into the afternoon. Be disciplined about your work-times.

CHAPTER 9
HELP SECTION

Exercise
CYCLISTS TOURING CLUB Cotterell House, 69 Meadrow, Godalming, Surrey, GU7 3HS. Tel: 0483 417217.
BRITISH CYCLING FEDERATION 36 Rockingham Road, Kettering, Northants, NN16 8HG. Tel: 0536 412211.
BRITISH SPORTS ASSOCIATION FOR THE DISABLED (BSAD) Mary Glen Haig Suite, 34 Osnaburgh Street, London, NW1 3ND. Tel: 071 383 7277.
EXERCISE classes in England, Wales and Scotland. For details contact THE LOOK AFTER YOURSELF PROJECT CENTRE Christ Church college, Canterbury, Kent, CT1 1QU. Tel: 0227 455687.
LAWN TENNIS ASSOCIATION, The Queen's Club, London, W14 9EG. Tel: 071 385 2366.
THE RAMBLERS ASSOCIATION, 1–5 Wandsworth Road, London, SW8 2XX. Tel: 071 582 6878.
AMATEUR SWIMMING ASSOCIATION, Harold Fern House, Derby Square, Loughborough, LE11 0AL. Tel: 0509 230431.
SQUASH RACKETS ASSOCIATION LTD, Westpoint, 33–34 Warple Way, London, W3 0RQ. Tel: 081 746 1616.
RACE WALKING ASSOCIATION, 9 Whitehouse Court, Rectory Road, Sutton Coldfield, West Midlands, B75 7SD. Tel: 021 329 3505.
Or contact your local ADULT EDUCATION INSTITUTE (Listed in your local phonebook under the name of your local authority or LEISURE AND RECREATION DEPARTMENT). If you want more general information about a specific sport ring the SPORTS COUNCIL REGIONAL OFFICE that serves your area, and they will put you in touch with the right organisation:

EAST MIDLANDS: covers Derbyshire, Nottinghamshire, Lincolnshire, Leicestershire and Northamptonshire. Tel: 0602 821887.

EASTERN REGION: covers Bedfordshire, Hertfordshire, Cambridgeshire, Suffolk, Norfolk and Essex. Tel: 0234 345222.

GREATER LONDON AND SOUTH EAST: covers Greater London, Surrey,

Kent and East and West Sussex. Tel: 081 778 8600.

NORTH WEST: covers Lancashire, Cheshire, Greater Manchester and Merseyside. Tel: 061 834 0338.

NORTHERN: covers Northumberland, Cumbria, Durham, Cleveland, Tyne and Weir. Tel: 091 384 9595.

NORTHERN IRELAND: Tel: 0232 381 222

SCOTLAND: Tel: 031 317 7200

SOUTH WEST: covers Avon, Cornwall, Devon, Dorset, Somerset, Wiltshire and Gloucestershire. Tel: 0460 73491.

SOUTHERN REGION: covers Hampshire, Isle of Wight, Berkshire, Buckinghamshire and Oxfordshire. Tel: 0734 483311.

WALES: Tel: 0222 397571.

WEST MIDLANDS: covers the West Midlands, Hereford and Worcester, Shropshire, and Warwickshire. Tel: 021 456 3444.

YORKSHIRE AND HUMBERSIDE: covers West, South and North Yorkshire and Humberside. Tel: 0532 436443.

Articles and booklets
Suggested reading: de Vries Herbert *On Exercise for Relieving Anxiety & Tension*, Executive Health, September 1982 XVIII (12).
Sporting Mind, Sporting Body Cambridge University Press 1984.
Walking, Nature's True – And Painless – Elixir Executive Health, June 1984 XX (9).

Healthy eating
For booklets on healthy eating contact your local HEALTH EDUCATION COUNCIL, listed in the phone book under the name of your LOCAL DISTRICT HEALTH AUTHORITY.
DAIRY PRODUCE ADVISORY SERVICE Milk Marketing Board, Thames Ditton, Surrey, KT7. Tel: 081 398 4101.
Eat Your Way To Health: The Bircher–Benner Approach To

Nutrition, Allen & Unwin, 1984.
HEALTH EDUCATION AUTHORITY Hamilton House, Mabledon Place, London, WC1H 9TX. Tel: 071 387 9528.
Healthier Eating – Good Foods Guide available from The Coronary Prevention Group, 60 Great Ormond Street, London, WC1N 3HR. Tel: 071 833 3687.
HEALTHY EATING, details from: Learning Materials Service, The Open University, PO Box 188, Milton Keynes, MK7 6AA.
Raw Energy by Leslie and Susan Kenton, Century, 1984.
Raw Energy Recipes by Leslie and Susan Kenton, Century, 1985.
Food and Your Heart and *Food Should Be Fun*. Both available from The British Heart Foundation, 14 Fitzhardinge Street, London, W1H 9PL. Tel: 071 935 0185.
Sarah Brown's Vegetarian Cookbook, Dorling Kindersley, 1987.
The Right Food For Your Kids by Louise Templeton, Century, 1985.
Further publications from: The Vegetarian Society of the United Kingdom Ltd, Parkdale, Dunham Road, Altrincham, Cheshire, WA14 4QG. Tel: 061 928 0793. The Vegan Society Ltd, 33–35 George Street, Oxford, OX1 2AY. Tel: 0865 722166. The Vegan Shop, 86 Tilehurst Road, Reading, Berks, RG3 2LU.

Health
REPETITIVE STRAIN INJURY. RSI ASSOCIATION, Christ Church, Redford Way, Uxbridge, Middlesex, UB8 1SZ. Tel: 0895 238663. Send £1.50 plus large SAE with a 34p stamp for their helpful factpack with more addresses and phone numbers.
VDU Hazards Factpack and *An Office-Worker's Guide to RSI* £2.50 and £3.00 respectively, available from: City Centre Project, 32 Featherstone Street, London, EC1Y 8QX. Tel: 071 608 1338.
Also contact TUC 23–28 Great Russell Street, London, WC1B 3LS. Tel: 071 636 4030. Your Trade Union, where appropriate, will probably have booklets and advice that you can be sent.

Relaxation
By adding yoga to a sedentary life-style you can achieve both strength and the ability to relax.
AROMATHERAPY, REFLEXOLOGY AND SHIATSU are all based on massage techniques using vital points of the body to release energy.
AROMATHERAPY ASSOCIATES 68 Maltings Place, Bagleys Lane,

London, SW6 2BY. Tel: 071 731 8129.
BRITISH SCHOOL OF REFLEXOLOGY Tel: 0279 429060.
THE BAYLEY SCHOOL OF REFLEXOLOGY Monks Orchard, Whitbourne, Worcester, WR6 5RB. Tel: 0886 21207.
The BRITISH WHEEL OF YOGA will give you the names of reputable qualified teachers. Tel: 0529 306851.

Chapter information sources
British Heart Foundation; The Health Education Authority; *Ageless Ageing – The Natural Way to Stay Young* by Leslie Kenton, Century.

CHAPTER 10

Coping with Working by Yourself

WE'RE ALL DIFFERENT

You will have been spurred on by the dream that working from home can be the idyll of working by the log fire, taking the dog for gentle walks between meetings, seeing more of your family and being free of all that commuting and office routine to get on with what you want to do. It can be, but only if you are organised and emotionally prepared. Prepared not only for the realisation of those nice fantasies, but also for the occasional feelings that some homeworkers complain about – of isolation, loneliness, an inability to 'get going' on the work at hand and to keep set working hours, lack of discipline, and depression because there is no one to fall back on when the going gets tough. You need to be aware that we are all different and that for some people these feelings predominate because they do not have the right character or psychological make-up to work at home on their own. These people need the physical presence of others around them, feeling that they are part of a team, the noise and hassle, the cut and thrust and politics of office life. And you have to consider that you may be one of them.

Allan, for example, stopped working in an office in central London and moved into a front room in his house in a suburban cul-de-sac. Although he was able to work with the window open, something he had always wanted to be able to do, his phone calls now undisturbed by ambulance and police sirens and no interruptions from office colleagues, he hated the silence and the lack of physical presence of other people. Even the lunch-time news on the television or the noise of the radio in the background didn't bring him relief. Eventually the silence and feeling of isolation so enveloped him that he gave up working from home and returned to an office in central London. He remembers his expedition into homeworking with horror.

When Sheila was working from home she found she missed the comradeship of being able to wander into a colleague's office to throw around ideas or debate a work problem; this was something she had just taken for granted. Liz missed socialising, even the casual conversation over the photocopier. Steven complained that he simply couldn't get started. He found self-motivation impossible. Sally, like a lot of homeworkers, had the opposite problem, she didn't know when to stop. Her work started to creep into her family and social life, rather like the filing cabinets that started to take over her dining-room and the hall.

On the other hand very few of us are Trappist monks nor want to be, and we all sometimes need the stimulation of phone calls, a meeting, seeing a colleague for lunch or just playing truant. But as long as you are aware of the psychological pitfalls to working from home as well as the tremendous advantages, you will survive and you'll enjoy it and be tremendously productive.

Psychology
Alongside the benefits of working from home, people find that there are also the psychological effects of the changes in their work habits. Apart from an obvious need to earn an income, there are five basic reasons why people go out to work. Firstly work imposes a time structure on most people's lives. Not everyone has the necessary self-discipline or motivation to impose some form of time-management on themselves and working in a central place with others does, for a lot of people, reduce the opportunity to shirk responsibility. Working on your own means that the motivation to get the job done has to come from within; there isn't a boss behind you telling you to get on. Neither do you have anyone to delegate work to, so if you have deadlines, it's up to you and no one else to ensure they are met.

Going out to work also provides most of us with a regularly shared experience with other people outside the family group. Surveys have shown that work remains the single most important source of good friendships for people from all social backgrounds – additionally it gives individuals an alternative source of identity and reassurance. For many people work defines aspects of personal status and identity and some people thrive on the cut and thrust of the conventional work environment. Finally, work enforces activity and allows people scope to utilise experience, knowledge and talents. It's a fact that some people simply work better as part of a team.

WHY FEEL LONELY?

Working at home can be a lonely business. There's no getting away from it: you just did. You have successfully escaped the commuting, the gossip, the back-biting, the working relationships, the hurly-burly of office life and you have replaced it with your own company almost ninety-nine per cent of the time.

Sasha found she was often lonely. 'Working from home is like living on the moon and you live in your own head a lot. I went through a series of psychological evolutions, it forced me to come to terms with myself.' Before working from home she had always worked in the theatre as a dancer and then in wardrobe, which meant she was always on tour and home wasn't all that real. 'It was just somewhere to sleep, but working from home forced me to put down roots. It took me a while to deal with myself. If you go out to work you have people around to distract you. I don't really know why I missed them, because I never had conversations at work with people as interesting as the things I listen to on Radio 4. I used to hate the silence.'

There are times when it can feel that it's just you and perhaps the cat and the dog, various cups of tea, and the same four walls you work in and live in. It's fine when the work is going well. You give the cat a congratulatory stroke, treat yourself to another chocolate chip cookie and bless the fact that you can get so much done without the interruptions of other people's telephones and messages, other people's lives, office politics and all the other interruptions. But when the work is going badly, or you just don't feel like doing any and your self-motivation rating is zero it can be dire.

For a lot of people who work from home, money or the overdraft are great motivating factors. Others find there are times when they feel fairly negative about work, and that's when Sally relies on her husband to spur her on. 'He tells me to go for it. He's very assertive and it rubs off on me.' Other people prefer to have a deadline to work to, or find that as long as they keep working they're OK. It's when they stop that it's difficult to get going again. That's when the loneliness creeps up on you as the day wears on. You may then be tempted to spend the time interrupting other people, phoning friends, trying to make human contact between bouts of attempting some work. You tidy your work area, clean any equipment, write to a distant relative and finally go shopping for something you don't really need and isn't urgent. Sasha says she has become a radio freak in order to break the silence. 'I have it on all the time. It's made me very knowledgeable. I never put the television on during the day. I was going to buy a freezer but decided not to, because then I wouldn't have any reason to pop out for food. I don't see many people because I live on my own and I have no family. I rely on neighbours to pop in, but I don't pop into them.'

Annie finds the lack of company one of the disadvantages of working from home. 'I have friends who are solicitors like me and I call them if I have a work problem, but if I worked in an office and a problem came up I would simply drift into someone else's office to discuss things. I don't actually get lonely, though; I talk on the phone and my clients are nice. I go to school and meet other mums.'

Dr Anthony Fry is a consultant psychiatrist at London's Guy's Hospital and he thinks that there is something we can do for ourselves to alleviate all types of loneliness. We can build a network of good strong human links and ties which contribute to giving each of us a vital component in our lives which he calls a 'safe space'. He says that if we are starved of too many sustaining ingredients in our lives – such as good friends, loving family, a useful job, firm beliefs and commitments, as well as a safe and secure place to live – then it isn't long before our lives start to crumble. He isn't talking directly about working from home, but his prescription for survival in a threatening world (from *Safe Space*, Dent), I think, fits the bill.

* Belong to a group outside your family and work.
* Do not work so hard that you have no time for people.
* Challenge is best coped with if we have good families, friends and support.
* Never take your nearest and dearest for granted.
* Find an ally and a confidant.
* Take a minute's silence each day and test how you feel.
* Find out why someone makes you feel threatened.
* There is no substitute for love and tenderness.
* Encourage inner peace through faith, religion, meditation or even day-dreaming.
* Remember your television cannot listen to you, nor reply.

Socialising

Make a date, however busy you are, to meet a friend for a social lunch at least once a week. If you prefer, go shopping or to a movie with them. But these outings shouldn't be more than three times a week; anything over that and you're not socialising but running away, and the work will suffer.

Set work times

Have set work times. Don't just casually start work when you feel like it, or finish when you don't feel like doing any more. If you are used to working from nine to five then continue to keep those hours. But know when to stop and relax. Move to another room if possible. If it isn't, then go out, even if it's just a walk to the post box, to draw a line under your working day and return home to begin your social evening. Put on your answer machine if you have one, or firmly tell business callers to ring back at nine the following morning (**See page 218 Chapter 8 Your Home As Your Workplace**).

Hobbies

Join an evening or afternoon class or group where you will meet people, go somewhere different and do something that is nothing to do with your work (**See page 219 Chapter 9 Health and Fitness at Home**). Cultivate a hobby – anything from playing bridge to going to navigation classes.

Your family

Don't exclude your family from your business. If your children are old enough or at home from school on holiday, include them by allowing them to help you to do simple jobs (**See page 277 Chapter 11 Coping with Family and Friends**). Involve your partner either by asking him or her to help you do a job which you find difficult, such as the accounts, or to help you more directly by actually taking over some of the workload. At least show them what you are doing. Remind them that just because you are not going out of the house to work, you are still working (**See page 278 Chapter 11 Coping with Family and Friends**).

Activity

Go for a walk. Walking is a wonderful way to clear the mind. Or join an exercise class. It'll do you good physically, and it's amazing how different you'll find your mood is afterwards. Yoga or some other form of meditation may help you to relax. Take up a sport such as tennis or squash and join a club. Singing is a great way to relieve stress and tension and there are plenty of singing classes for this purpose. Juggling is becoming a popular stress reliever and there are now evening classes in it **(See Chapter 9 Health and Fitness at Home)**.

Change of scene
However busy you are, make time to do something different and meet different people. Don't lose contact with friends just because they are now out at work and you are at home so it is geographically more difficult to meet. Don't get lazy and decide you can't be bothered to make the effort. Put on your shoes and get out to meet them. **(See page 281 Chapter 11 Coping with Family and Friends.)**

Meeting a deadline
Of course, the other side of the coin is when you have work which has to be completed by a deadline and you're feeling lonely. It's then that you will have to use your self-discipline to put the loneliness and the silence on the back-burner. Once you get working, you'll forget about it until the job is done. Remind yourself how important the client is to you, and that if you don't complete the job on time you might not get work from them again. Remind yourself how much you are being paid. Remind yourself what you are going to do with the money. Look upon the work as a challenge to get it finished and out of the way and, when it is, congratulate yourself by calling up a friend and going out to meet them. Take your children out or go for a gentle stroll with your partner or, if you prefer, on your own with your day-dreams.

Handling loneliness
For some people the silence is the worst aspect of working from home and they become dedicated radio listeners. Other homeworkers say that when the work is going well they aren't aware of being alone, but when it's going badly they have to get out. Get to know your neighbours, for they may have lonely moments just like you. Get to know the local shop-keepers; small shops are usually more sociable places than supermarkets. If you have children, get involved in the school parents' association and help

to organise school events. Get involved in the local council, amateur dramatic society, preservation or historical organisations. There are plenty of local classes you can join, from rambling to yoga, swimming to squash. Your local library will have a list **(See Help Section Chapter 9).**

PUTTING OFF WORK
When you work from home you have a lot of choices. You can choose the hours you want to work, your lighting, your work space, your chair, when you want to take your lunch, if you want to work in your track-suit or evening dress – and the ultimate choice of whether you want to work or not. Putting it off is very easy when you work from home, because there are so many useless distractions and no one but yourself to shout at you to stop it. When the going gets rough anything other than work seems more attractive: such useful things as walking the dog in a blizzard, reading the telephone directory, picking the old grey mashed potato from the gas cooker, getting the cat's hairs out of the carpet, individually setting up a series of unnecessary templates on your Amstrad, studying your neighbour digging the garden, unbending forks that your son bent on his camping holiday, tidying your desk drawers by way of reading your thirty-year-old school reports; all this can successfully while away a morning and is very appealing when you are trying to put off working.

If there aren't enough mediocre little household jobs around, when you're really desperate you can always stoop as low as watching afternoon television. Of course you'll tell yourself it's only for research purposes for that little project you had in mind, or to distract your concentration so that you can return fresh to the challenge. That's after you've dusted and polished the TV set, moved it round the room and then put it back to where it started. Or you'll put the radio on just for background noise and end up listening to it, telling yourself that the news programmes are keeping you in touch with world events. Finally there's always the junk mail to read!

Cooking is another way of putting off working, but it at least has a constructive end. Eating or major snacking is a good time-waster. You'll trail around the kitchen opening cupboards, having a handful of muesli, a spoonful of custard, a mouthful of old Christmas cake, a finger in the cold baked beans, a ripped-off piece of bread dipped in pickle and then you wash it all down with numerous cups of coffee and decide it's too late to start work because it's lunch time.

In between snacking and watching the Test Match, you'll paint your nails, weigh yourself, mentally write your obituary and the invitation list to your funeral, polish any jewellery you wear with your cuffs, clean out your ears and then make patterns with the baby buds and during an idle trip to the bathroom you'll incorporate an unnecessary shave and floss your teeth. You'll be a paragon of hygiene when you're putting off working.

Unless you stop yourself you will also waste time worrying about your dry elbows, having the electric blanket cleaned, wondering if baldness is hereditary, whether life would have been different if you had married the person you went out with twenty years ago, does the cat have worms, is the garden shed subsiding, should you move somewhere larger/smaller, does the vet fancy you or was the dog the attraction? Not much work gets done when there's all that trivia to think about!

Self-discipline
When you work at home you have to discipline yourself because no one else is going to. It is especially important when you have work to do that you don't like, or you're tired, or you feel as if life is a bed of hot coals and you're wearing open-toed sandals. Then you have to give yourself a good talking to and fall back on a strict routine – otherwise the work just won't get done.

Deadlines
Some people say they work better when they are hitting a deadline and that when forced they will suddenly pull out all the stops and do the work. You know if you are one of those people who wastes days and weeks and then spends nights frantically getting the work finished. You might consider adapting this crippling routine and not force yourself so near the deadline so that you don't have to stay up working so many nights. After all, you may get the work done, but is it done to the correct standard, or is it just a little botched because you were tired and beating the clock?

Inspiring aids
It may be that you just need inspiration because you have forgotten what your goals were. Maybe some visual aids would spur you

on. For example, if you're worried about money, stick a particularly bad bank statement or an unfriendly letter from your bank manager to the screen of the TV; that should stop you watching it. Stick pictures of the people whose shape you envy to the front of the fridge/bread bin/cake tin/biscuit cupboard. Even better don't have cakes or biscuits in the house. Stick your work agreement or salary cheque on to your work area, write a list of priority things you have to do and put it where you can't avoid it. Stick a picture of your dream car, house, boat, dress, beach, where it will make you want to aim for it. Stick bills that have to be paid where you cannot miss them. If you have a favourite work quote, put it somewhere prominent. Stick to eating meals at regular times **(See page 251 Chapter 9 Health and Fitness at Home)**. If you're a phone addict, hide it. Ignore the housework: you're too busy to notice it and you know the dust can wait. It'll still be there when the work is finished, and so will the dirty washing, the hole in your sock, the broken zip, the weeds in the garden and the smudge on the TV screen. Try not to let your mind wander into worrying about trivia such as the dry rot on the rabbit's hutch. Pull it back to the job at hand. If you start to kill time, be aware of it. You have to be your own boss, supervisor and line manager.

This is when you have to shake out that old buddy of all homeworkers – self-discipline and its co-worker, self-motivation. The only day-dreaming you can do while you work is thinking about how nice you can be to yourself when you have finished.

WORKAHOLICS

If you have the opposite problem, and you don't know when to stop working (which is easily done when you work from home, because there isn't anyone to blow the whistle and you don't have to worry about missing the last train home) then you have to apply the self-discipline in the opposite direction, not to get you started but to get you to stop. Ralph has exactly that problem and finds it one of the disadvantages of working from home. 'I don't stop work; I'm happy to work on through the night because it's going well. There comes a point when the work's doing itself and then I don't want to leave – it's like magic. How can you stop? Unless you're disciplined you're always thinking about your next project, and you have to be disciplined not to let your work creep into your leisure time. I find that hard.' He is toying with the idea of having a studio built at the end of the garden and moving out of the house. 'Then, however much I wanted to work, I couldn't because my tools would be in there.'

Set yourself fixed working hours so that you know when you start and when you stop. Faithfully stick to them. No carrying on, however involved you are, or however well it's going. The work will still be there in the morning and with people like you so will the impetus. Make definite stops for meal and break times – no working through lunch and missing dinner. Do not eat at your desk (**See page 255 Chapter 9 Health and Fitness at Home**) and take yourself away from your work area. A break will help your concentration. If you can't sit still and do nothing, then go for a leisurely walk or cycle ride on a business errand, perhaps to the local post office or stationers. Or sit in the garden, play a game of tennis, go to a fitness or yoga class or watch the lunch-time news on the television. Put away feelings of guilt that you aren't working. Stop saying to yourself that you aren't doing anything, because you are doing something vital: you are recharging your inner batteries, relaxing your mind and feeding your body to return to work refreshed.

Stop work in the evening at a set time, and only go beyond that if you have a serious deadline to meet. Serious deadlines don't happen every day. When you stop work at lunch-time or in the evening, put on your answer machine and refuse to take any work calls. If you don't have an answer machine then you will have to tell work callers firmly but professionally to call you in the morning. If you worked in an office they wouldn't be able to talk to you at ten in the evening. If possible you should have an answer machine for your work telephone number and a separate line for private calls (**See page 226 Chapter 8 Your Home as your Workplace**).

When you stop work, shut your office door and don't go back in there until the next day. Don't even wander in there; it's a banned area. Don't bring work home into the rest of the house, either, and definitely not into the bedroom. When you stop work, you also have to stop thinking about it, unless you have a particularly sticky problem you need to discuss with your partner or a friend, but having discussed it, forget it.

CHAPTER 10
HELP SECTION

Psychology work-related stress – recommended reading
Safe Space by Dr Anthony Fry, Dent.
Living With Stress. A Consumer Publication.
Psychology at Work edited by Peter Warr, Penguin.
Thank God It's Money – Strategies for increasing job satisfaction by Charles Cameron and Suzanne Eluson, Ebury Press.
Training for Decisions by John Adair, Macdonald.
Getting Things Done – The ABCs of Time Management by Edwin C Bliss, Elm Tree Books.
I'm OK You're OK by Thomas A. Harris, Pan.

Your local library will have information on Adult Education Classes, Local Training, Social Activities and groups. (**See Chapter 2 for Further Information.**)

Chapter information sources
Safe Space by Dr Anthony Fry, Dent; *Working from Home – The Dream That's Becoming a Trend* by Lindsey O'Connor, Harvest House.

CHAPTER 11

Coping with Family and Friends

TEAM-WORK
No one can successfully be a one-person outfit, carrying all the burdens of work and home on their shoulders, and it's crazy and non-productive to try. Working from home means team-work and the team are the other members of your family. You have to learn to delegate. If you don't, both you and your work will eventually suffer and, in turn, your finances – and that will have an effect on your family.

As you obviously intend to be successful at working from home, you have to involve your family as your back-up team. That doesn't necessarily mean just your family that you live with, but also your extended family. It simply means you seeing them differently, as part of your team and helping them to see you as a working person, despite the fact that you are at home.

Organising the team
You may find it difficult to delegate at first, if you have always done everything yourself, and it can be frustrating watching someone else doing things differently or more slowly than you do them. The best thing is not to watch. There isn't any reason why children or partners can't do jobs around the house. During the school holidays Gerry's two children go to the local bakers and get lunch for them all. 'My twelve-year-old daughter will even type for me occasionally on a Sunday.'

It's probably easier if you all sit down and jointly devise a rota system for basic tasks, such as emptying the rubbish or vacuuming. Generally teenagers are happy to work for payment, so come to a financial arrangement over things like the ironing. Your working from home is going to change their lives as well as your own.

If your business can afford it, then there's no reason why you shouldn't employ someone to help clean the house. If your resources don't run to a cleaner every day or once a week, have someone in to do a monthly or a three-monthly spring clean. It's better than you stretching your energy.

Your partner
Partners, not business ones but life ones, may find it hard when you first start working from home to understand that you really are working. They have a tendency to collapse in through the front door groaning about their hard, exhausting, difficult, frustrating day, seemingly unaware that you might have had one too.

They might not say it, but they will presume that as you are at home it's easy for you to pop to the dry cleaners for them, collect their doctor's prescription, take the pets to the vet, do the shopping, go to the shoe menders, be interrupted by messengers, builders, plumbers, even their mother. As well as your work, you will probably get lumbered, if you aren't careful, by all those irritating little jobs that interrupt a working day. Your partner will presume that as you are there you can hold the fort – and you probably will. They will disappear off to work putting it all behind them, in the relaxed knowledge that you'll drop their dirty running gear into the washing machine for them, plan the evening menu, shovel up the dead bird under the bed, sort out the children – and all before you start work and they return home. They'll call you to say they're bringing their boss back for drinks, which is a code-word for you to flash round with the vacuum cleaner, dash out for a bag of peanuts, a bottle of wine, get the cat's hairs off the sofa and make sure the children are in bed before they arrive back. And you probably will.

You've probably got a conditioned reflex that makes you jump up from your work, even when you're struggling to get something finished, as soon as they return. You'll make them a drink, get dinner, bundle the children into the bath and run a comb through your hair, just so that you look as if you haven't been doing anything. And they'll probably think you haven't.

When everyone's dinner is over and they've told you all about their day and have either gone to bed or are relaxing in front of the television, you will go back to your workplace and carry on working at something you should probably have finished hours earlier. But could you have dealt with the guilt you might have felt as your partner prepared dinner, bathed the children, and popped to the late-night corner-shop to buy the milk you hadn't had time to get? By your behaviour, you probably fuel the belief that neither you nor your work is as important as someone who goes out of the house. You try to do everything, and the more you do it, the more other people will let you.

If this is your situation, then for your survival you have to sit down with your partner and explain what work you are doing. Show them exactly what you have to do. Tell them how much you earn, and if you are running a business make them feel part of it. Ask them to help at something they either might enjoy or are better skilled at than you are. Running a home is a team effort and you are not the leader of the team when you have work to do. The leadership alternates. Of course it is easier for you to deal with household jobs and household events simply because you are there, but if you have work to do, you *are* in your place of work, which although it is home to them, at that moment it isn't to you. You will then have to delegate your housework role and as you and your partner are part of a joint unit, both sharing the rewards of your work, you will have to divide the roles. Your partner will have to stop expecting you to do housework when you are a homeworker. That might not happen until you tell them.

Learning to delegate is the key. Gerry is at home running an insurance business, while his wife is out working as a teacher. 'I'm at home when the kids come in, and although I don't really do housework, I do put the washing machine on. I don't really cook but I get my own sandwich at lunch-time.'

Even if you don't have a big shift in the division of labour with your partner, at least you can work towards it by sharing the responsibility for household jobs. For example, the leaking lavatory needn't necessarily be your problem just because you're at home. Your partner can just as well ring round to find a plumber when they get to their place of work, interrupting their working day just as it would yours. There is no reason why they can't leave a little earlier in the morning or evening and collect their own dry cleaning.

You have to stop the presumption that because you are at home, your work is not important. It is important – to you, your boss, your client, your self-esteem, your career, your investment, your bank manager *and* to your partner.

HOMEWORKERS IN THE SAME HOME

If there's more than one of you working from home it can be tricky, especially if the two of you are involved in a personal relationship with each other. You have to remember the key to success and harmonious working time together is the following cliché: forget the arguments at the office door and forget the office at the bedroom door.

If you're both working together on the same projects, maybe even for the same people, you are a team. Neither of you can close the door on the housework **(See page 279 this Chapter)** and neither of you can get away from the other in the morning and return in the evening. So you had better be sure that you both have the same interests, see work in the same way, complement each other and are able to bounce ideas off one another, because there is no escape from a close working relationship like this.

You do have the advantage over most homeworkers that you won't be lonely. Sally and Harry are two homeworkers in the same house but Sally thinks they complement each other. 'We don't get on each other's nerves. We have the same interests and don't really need other people.' Harry paints in his studio upstairs while Sally works downstairs spinning goat's wool. 'After a while I get fidgety and take my wheel up to his studio to be with him, or he comes down with his paints to be with me and we talk while we work. We like to have each other around. We knock ideas off each other; for example, if he's got a particular commission we'll talk about it.'

The disadvantage is that neither of you is bringing mental input from the outside world into the life of the other. I rely on other people in my family who go out of the house to work to report back about life on the 'outside'. I enjoy them prattling on about their day, which is totally different from mine, and get vicarious pleasure hearing about their office gossip, even though I haven't ever met the people involved and don't particularly want to. I even get vaguely curious about what was being served in the canteen, because I didn't have to eat it. It's another world out there and when the time is right I enjoy hearing about it, even though I prefer to look at it as if it was down the far-away end of binoculars. Without that outside input, however trivial, you both have to be careful that you don't become too insular – as careful as a homeworker who lives alone. Sally and Harry live on Islay in Argyle, where they contend not only with working in the home together but living on an island. 'We talk about work a lot,' says Sally, 'but that's a way of life. Living on an island, I think we've lost the art of talking about anything but the immediate art of surviving. On the island there's no theatre, no cinema, no intimate little restaurant, none of the niceties of life. Because you don't have those outside things, you need to have a common bond.'

Make a rule not to talk work when work is finished. You don't both have to finish work at the same time – after all you might both be doing different kinds of work – but make sure it isn't always the same one who goes on, leaving the other to do the housework or make the meal. Remember the team. Take it in turns. If you have agreed that one of you prefers to cook and the other to clean, that choice is yours.

Make a rule to socialise, and not just with people you work for. Don't allow work to rule your life. Don't allow work to creep into every bit of your home, with files in the bedroom and the photocopier in the kitchen, but try to keep work things confined to one area (**See page 222 Chapter 8 Your Home as Your Workplace**). Although working together can give you a common bond, make sure it isn't the only bond. If you have children, you will have to make definite times when one or both of you is with them, and don't make them feel they live in your office – after all it is their home (**See page 286 this Chapter**).

FRIENDS VERSUS WORK

Friends don't tend to pop in and see you at your workplace when you go out to work. I think it's because they have to get past the daunting prospect of the receptionist at the front desk and then they're sure that as you are out at work they shouldn't be interrupting you.

But when you work from home, friends tend to see you as being available whenever they feel like a chat or decide just to drop in as they were passing. Ken, who runs a design business from his bedroom, find that friends drop by all the time. 'It's because they know someone's always here. I don't mind. They make tea, bring food, just hang around.'

Friends somehow forget that you told them you were working from home, as they bundle in, eager to show you what they bought at the sales, or to bend your ear about their new lover, diet, difficult spouse, irritable teenager. They somehow turn a blind eye to the piles of work they step over as they moan on, or sink into a chair surrounded by your orders, stock or invoices and they wait, panting, until you give in and make them a cup of coffee.

Of course, you say how lovely it is to see them but you are frantically busy, but they won't hear you. They'll have kicked off their shoes and be rummaging in their bags to show you their new purchase and finally you will either succumb, resigning yourself to the fact that you will have to work on into the night just so that you have the pleasure of being with them now, or you can suggest they make their own cup of tea, while you get on with your work.

Turning a blind eye
You either have to decide that you really would rather see your friend or relatives and that you will work late to make up for playing truant; or if you let them stay and make themselves a drink then you have to be impervious to the sounds of them clattering round your kitchen trying to find the cups.

Your working hours
If you don't want either of these things to happen, then you have to make it clear, very clear before they even get past the front door, that you are working. That you would love to see them some other time, but not during your working hours. And you tell them what your working hours are. Ken has found that once friends are in the house they ignore the fact that he's working, which can be especially difficult when he and colleagues are really busy. 'So now if we don't want to see anyone because we've got so much to do, we either pretend we're not in and don't answer the door, or if we think they can take it, we tell them we're busy.'

Utilising friends
Utilise these friends or members of your family who pop in by making them your co-workers. If you run a business that requires packers or unpackers or someone to perform other simple tasks, why not ask them to help? Instead of slumping into a chair ready to chat, they could start to pack! You'll find they either love it and ask for more, or disappear pretty fast, in which case they won't make a habit of popping in to kill their idle hours during your working day. If they have a skill, such as book-keeping or typing, then ask them if they would like to work for you. There's nothing like harnessing all that untapped energy; that's what friends are for.

Sticky spots – friends

There are two sticky spots in this fairly straightforward system of using them or losing them. One is when friends call when you are feeling either bored, stuck or lonely **(See Chapter 10 Coping with Working by Yourself)**. Then it isn't easy to say you'll see them some other time. Especially when they appear as saviours to rescue you from having to do the grotty work that you have been putting off, or just when you were sick of staring at your office walls, or when you didn't want to have to phone the client who still hasn't paid you **(See page 127 Chapter 4 You and Your Money)**.

How much nicer to sit chatting with friends, even if you aren't interested in what they have to say. It saves you from having to deal with that task you didn't want to do. And best of all, when they finally go and it's too late to do the job you had been putting off, you can blame it all on them and not yourself.

I know, I have done it. I've made all the excuses to no one but myself and I'll tell you, all that happens is that you have to face the job you were putting off either when they have gone, or the following day – because the job isn't going to go away. It just pops up on the top of another list. So you had better get to grips with it and use your friends not as a means of escape, but rather as a way of celebrating when your job is done.

Phone calls which come slap bang in the middle of working can be another distraction. The snag is that working from home generally means that you don't have anyone to filter your phone calls. You don't have a secretary to take messages or tell callers that you are unavailable, or in a meeting. If you have only one phone line, it's very easy to get caught up in social chit-chat or be interrupted when you are in the middle of a meeting or concentrating on a tricky piece of work. These calls not only take time, but they jam up your phone line if a customer or client is trying to get through. You have to be accessible, but to working people during work-time. This is just one of the reasons why it's a good idea to have a separate business telephone line, and if you have an answer machine leave it switched on to your personal number to fend off friends and relatives whom you can call back at your convenience. If you do that, don't be tempted to listen to the answer machine messages until you have finished work, or you will only end up phoning them back immediately. Make sure that people who matter, such as children and live-in partners, have both telephone numbers in case there is an emergency.

You just have to learn to be ruthless about your time and protect yourself from interruptions when you don't want any. It is best to tell your friends and family what your business hours are and stick to them.

Sticky spots – your family

The second sticky spot is your family. Rosemary, who runs a typesetting business from home, thinks that friends and relatives popping in can be difficult, but that relatives are the worst. 'I'm easy-going and tend to stop work, but my husband gets really ratty. My son and daughter-in-law think I want to see their new baby, and I do, but eventually I had to ask them not to come so often.'

Families have a way of not observing or respecting the other members' lives. They walk in in the middle of divorces, childbirth or nervous breakdowns, so why on earth shouldn't they walk in on you working? They will even bring with them their own arguments, upsets, hysterics. They always have done, so why shouldn't they do it now? What's work? If you tell them you're working, they'll suggest they are happy to wait until you're finished. Rosemary's mother used to come over and see her for the whole day, but she wasn't used to people working at home. 'She didn't understand the pressures. I had to be really cruel. But we worked out that I go to see her now and it's easier.'

Having someone standing or sitting silently next to you, waiting, can be just as off-putting to your concentration as them talking.

The reason they ignore your work is because no one has ever laid down any ground rules for fear of emotional blackmail, which is something a lot of families are expert at. You will find that working at home you are a perfect target for them either coming round or phoning to ask you something, or for giving you their opinion.

Here are just a few examples which you may recognise when you tell your family you have work to do:

'I know you said you didn't want to be interrupted when you were working, but I am your mother.'

'I know how busy you are, but it would be nice to talk to you now.'

'I know you have a lot of work on, but I'm lonely. But I don't want to worry you.'

'I don't know who to turn to; I've only got you.'
'Your father used to say you shouldn't ever bring work home.'
'I think it's damaging the children to see you doing all this work.'
'I think you should put us first; after all we are your family.'
'Since you've been working at home I can't get hold of you.'
'I won't keep you. I know you're working, but I just wanted to say . . . no, never mind. I know you're busy.'
'Look, for God's sake, I'm not just anyone interrupting you; I am your sister.'
'That little job that you do at home; is it really necessary?'
'Well, aren't you even going to make a cup of tea for your own brother?'
'Why can't you be like your cousin and get a proper job outside the house?'
'I'm not going to keep you. I know I shouldn't ring, but I just thought you should know the doctor's worried about me.'
'I know you're busy working, but when you've got a minute could you take me to have the cat put down? In your own time of course.'

If you worked outside the home, I doubt very much if any member of your family would turn up or telephone to say any of these or similar things at your place of work. They wouldn't dream of it, because they'd think you might get into trouble from your boss but they don't think working from home is serious. Working from home is just a hobby. Working from home makes you so accessible.

In these cases an answer machine (**See above**) is essential as a diversion, and you must not give members of your family your other phone number. If a separate phone line isn't possible, then you have to continue to be firm against all odds while you have work to do. You have to repeat your working hours, knowing they will probably choose not to hear you. If they appear on your doorstep, you have to put aside any thought that they are blood relatives, despite what they say, and treat them as everyone else who interrupts your working pattern. Be firm, tell them the hours that you work, and see them or talk to them out of those hours. Tell them everything you have to do, such as your work schedule, your payment, your clients. The more relaxed you appear to be, the more they think they can interrupt you. It may be easier for you to visit your family, rather than to have them visit you.

CHILDREN
When you are working from home you have to lay the ground rules early on, if you want you, your work and your family relationships to survive. If you don't lay ground rules, you'll find that you'll be grey and tired like an overstretched piece of elastic.

The fact is that home is home for the rest of your family, but for you it has the dual purpose of being home plus workplace – and that may be difficult for other people to understand. It may be especially difficult for them if they are used to your being there to do things for them. You must make it clear that although you are 'at home' it doesn't mean you are 'at home' for others. There are times when you are at home to work and sometimes that work may overstretch into family life. You will also have to make it clear that you have a work-space, even if it's only the end of the dining-room table, that you also have work equipment and that both of these may be out of bounds to them and deserve some respect. A lot of homeworkers report that their children don't interfere with their work equipment. 'I work with fragile materials at one end of the dining room table,' says Brian, who is a modeller, 'while my three young children play at the other end, and nothing's ever been broken.'

Other homeworkers like Jane have to do most of their paperwork when the children have gone to bed. 'I just can't trust them not to scribble over important documents.'

Working hours
One of the first ground rules you have to make clear to your children is what they are allowed to do and what they are not allowed to do while you are working, then everyone can establish a working–living pattern. If you have decided to work set business hours, make sure that everyone knows what they are, but explain that these are flexible. If you are trying to get work finished to a deadline, your hours will be longer. Write your work times on a large sheet of paper and stick it on the fridge door or somewhere where it can be seen and referred to either if there is a dispute or someone wants to interrupt those hours for a trivial reason. If you don't want to be interrupted when you are working, then put a 'Do Not Disturb' sign on your office door or stand it up on your work-area. If you have older children or another adult in the

house, you can try using the office door open/closed policy. If it's closed it means you are working and must not be interrupted unless it is a true emergency. Make it clear it is not an emergency when someone steals someone else's favourite toy!

When children watch you working, they learn very quickly which work actions signal that you are about to finish or don't need to concentrate so hard and can be interrupted and when you are concentrating and involved. For safety reasons the closed door policy works only if you have another person in the house who can keep a watchful eye on everything and everyone's needs, or if your children are old enough to look after themselves and just want to interrupt you in order to settle arguments. Pat makes curtains and cushion covers, working from her converted garage which backs on to her house. 'I try not to work when my son is home from school, but if I have to, then my son and I can see each other through the windows. He is twelve, so he's old enough to come into the garage if there's a real problem.'

Work equipment out of bounds

The next ground rule is about your work equipment. Make sure that your children know they are not allowed to touch it, whatever it is, from papers to machinery to interesting-looking tools or materials. Ann gives her children all her scrap paper and junk mail to draw over, as a way of deterring them from touching her important papers. They keep them in their own file marked 'scrap'.

But it isn't a matter of just keeping them off your papers. Sally codes questionnaires at home, and usually has to do her work when her two children, aged two and three, have gone to bed. 'I just can't trust them with all this huge amount of paper about, plus they affect my concentration.'

You have to try to make it clear that all work materials are out of bounds in all circumstances. They cannot even be borrowed and they certainly aren't there to be fiddled with or drawn over. They aren't out of bounds just because you say so – that doesn't appease a child's curiosity. They are out of bounds because:

* They are vital to your work – without them you are unemployed, which could affect your family's lifestyle.
* They are dangerous – explain in what way.
* They belong to your employer – explain the ethics of using someone else's equipment.

* They are very expensive – and a replacement just might have to come out of a child's pocket money.

If it's possible, store your materials away, preferably in something that locks, such as deep cupboards, filing cabinets, a blanket chest or a desk. The answer, if possible, is to have a separate workroom where you can close your work equipment away, perhaps even lock it, and that area is out of bounds to the children and their friends. You may have to explain to the children's friends the rules about your work area and work utensils and equipment, for none of us can honestly be responsible for the actions of our friends.

If you don't have a separate area, then you have to make it clear that it has to be hands off, not only because you don't want things lost, dirtied or damaged, but for safety reasons. It may be tedious for you, but a lot of the time you may have to put everything away. Before long, you will establish a quick packing-away routine at the end of every working day. You will find some hints on storage in Chapter 8.

Children versus the telephone
If you have two phone lines, your work phone should be the one that they are not allowed to use or answer (**See page 226 Chapter 8 Your Home as Your Workplace**). If you don't have a work phone line, then either they must be told they cannot answer the phone or teach them how to answer it correctly and politely, which isn't difficult. Linda has two young children who are used to her working from home. 'They know that when Mummy's working or on the phone they have to be quiet. They don't rush to pick up the phone and they know the difference between the work line and our private line.'

You can't change the rules and only allow children to use the phone or answer it to get you out of a jam, such as when you want them to say that you are unavailable or will call someone back later. Explain that when you are using your work telephone they have to be quiet and you must not be interrupted. A mobile phone can be the answer in these situations. 'When the children are playing,' says Pamela, who is a solicitor, 'I have been known to take the mobile phone and sit in the loo in order to be able to have a quiet conversation.'

You will have to tell children that they can use the phone for their personal calls only when you are not working. If you have teenagers who are addicted to using the telephone and impervious to time restrictions once they get talking on it, it may be necessary to refer them to the notice of your working hours and explain that customers or clients may be trying to get through to you during those times. Make sure that if your children are allowed to use your work telephone, they don't scribble on your work material or over any surfaces. Always keep a telephone message pad available.

All in the work pen together
If you work at home alone it isn't easy keeping an eye on very small children while you are working. You not only feel guilty but worry about their safety, which means spending a lot of time getting up and looking for them and trying to keep them safely occupied, at the same time protecting your work materials if you have them in the same room. This can create havoc with your work schedule and can result in you working nights when everyone is safely asleep, which will in turn affect your daytime schedule and your life. One interior designer, who works from home and wanted to keep her small daughter as near to her as possible, has designed a working area that is based on the principle of a huge playpen, inside which she works while her daughter plays.

The playpen is in fact a room within a room, covering 80 square feet (7.5 square metres). It is open at the top and can be anything between 3 feet (1 metre) and 5 feet (1½ metres) tall. The seven sides of the roofless pen are hinged so that the shape can be changed and if necessary taken apart for storage. The top edges are stepped and interrupted by domes and triangles to mimic a skyline, the walls are painted in colours and patterns. The playpen is made from medium-density fibre boards, while shelving adds stability near the entrance and provides storage for toys and books. It is the perfect way to keep an eye on children while you work. As the children grow older they can be left alone to play in the giant playpen. You could design and make your own giant playpen – it isn't difficult – or contact Ms Prendeville **(See page 238 Help Section Chapter 8)**.

Work play
Another alternative is to help children keep themselves constructively amused, which creates a learning process for them and a space to work in for you. But you have to plan ahead. Create a

box of 'special toys'. It can be that the box itself is special – use a cardboard box from the supermarket or a linen basket, paint it or stick on cutouts over the outside of their favourite symbols and characters. This box is only brought out when you are working. Occasionally change the contents, popping in surprises. You don't have to buy anything, but just put in something that isn't normally to be found in the box, so that it doesn't become predictable.

Don't put all their toys out, but keep some hidden and rotate them. Keep a button box. Children will spend hours colour-coding shapes and patterned buttons and threading them. Save all your junk mail for them to cut out and lick down the envelopes. Older children enjoy keeping a written diary which includes bus tickets, old stamps, supermarket receipts, junk mail, etc.

Give children their own 'work' area. Put them at a space near you so that they can work 'alongside' you with their own toy envelopes, plastic scissors, scrap paper, crayons, and other simple office supplies which they play with only when you are both working.

If you work in the kitchen preparing food, make sure you keep them away from any food or food preparation area (**See page 93 Chapter 3 You, Your Company and the Law**), but they could have their own tub of soapy water and wash up their own little plastic things.

Set up a 'messy area' using a large table if possible, where they can do finger painting, keep their own diary scrapbook up to date, make paperclip necklaces, paper chains, beads, decorate an old pair of trainers or old T shirt with fabric pens or special paint. In order to prevent you having to do a lot of extra clearing up afterwards, cover the floor with sheets of gardening plastic and the children in something old and washable. A piece of old sheeting cut into a large circle, like a cape, with a head-hole cut in the middle and the child popped through, will successfully cover them and can be thrown away afterwards.

In desperate times, you can fall back on rented videos or story-telling cassettes, but they don't always work, as Sally has discovered when she's been under pressure and has tried to work with her two children under four around. 'I've stuck them in front of videos, but after the third one they say they've had enough.'

It's a good idea to buy a few and keep them for 'special' times, so that the children will think watching a video is a treat and won't suffer overkill. Yet all children are different. Joyce, a computer programmer, finds that her son doesn't bother her – he has his friends and just wants her to be around. Linda, a solicitor with two small children, works from 9a.m. till 3p.m. and makes sure she has finished by the time she collects them from school. 'I just sign the post while they watch television. They know not to touch my papers or to write on anything, as I have always worked from home. It's their friends who are difficult.'

Mother's little helpers
Some people who work from home so that they can spend more time with their children organise their working day around them and when they are at school. Others say it isn't possible to juggle time between children and work under the same roof and that you end up giving neither your full attention. It *is* possible to do both if you are organised, and it's easier if you have children of school age as they usually spend a lot of time out of the house. In that case there's no reason why you can't get a lot of work done between them leaving in the morning and returning in the afternoon.

When you have young children, school holidays, especially the long ones, can be tricky. I can remember worrying about them, not because I didn't want to be with my son, but because I had to work out a system which allowed me to spend time with him, and also be able to do my work. I sometimes felt torn in half I sort of muddled through, but looking back I can see that the system worked. My mother didn't live far away and she came over to us. She loved it.

Occasionally he went and stayed with her; he visited his friends and sometimes stayed the night or they stayed with him; he went to friends who lived in the country. I paid an assortment of people to look after him – a foreign student, a divorced woman with three grown-up children, a retired policewoman, a nursery-school teacher who wanted pin money in the holidays and a girl who waitressed in the evenings. I organised the following day's activities, which meant ringing round the various children's events phone lines. If there wasn't anything on, it was a trip to the local park, friends, even a picnic. If it rained, out would come the 'make' books and the videos. My rule was always to stop work at tea-time and to continue when he had gone to bed.

When there was no one else to look after him, then he would have his 'play work' to do next to me, and I would get on with mine next to him. But on those days most of my work would get done when he had gone to bed. It wasn't easy for either of us. He knew I had work to do. I had explained to him, and he had seen my office. He had my reject paper for scribbling and adding to the papier mâché bowl. I felt guilty at the end of some days because I thought I hadn't seen enough of him. I felt pleased when I could hear him and his friends playing, or when he told me his adventures and I knew that we had devised a workable system. I had to shut my ears when I heard him and my mother or the foreign student having a dispute. If I hadn't, I would have been continually stopping work. If he came into my room and asked me to become involved, it was usually because he was losing! I would tell him I had to do my work and it was between him and the adult involved to sort things out. We might discuss the dispute at tea-time, though, when I had finished working.

His friends' mothers who didn't work invited him to join in day-trips, teas and overnight stays. I have to admit the secret is probably to let it be known that you are working from home.

Child care – under tens
Most people with children appreciate the difficulty of child care when you are working and they are not. If you know someone else who is working from home, then why not pool your resources to pay for someone to look after all your children? Or have a rota system amongst yourselves to take time off to look after them.

The extended family can really come into its own in these situations – mothers, brothers, mother-in-law, sisters, relatives or maybe a close friend who lives locally can help you out either by having the children, or coming over to you. Ask the other mothers that you meet at school, or a neighbour whose own family has grown up, if they will look after your children for a few hours a day. During the school holidays Linda, the solicitor, asks her mother to come over and look after the children. 'She understands about my working from home and even does the photocopying. My husband can be flexible with his working hours, so he takes the children out. They have friends who come over and they go up into the bedroom to play and I can get on.'

Older people are often ignored when they are perfectly able-bodied and desperate to feel they are of some use. Caring for a child is something that can work very well, helping their self-esteem and allowing you to work. You may feel you ought to pay

COPING WITH FAMILY AND FRIENDS

them, or to save them travelling, take the children to them a couple of days a week. These are arrangements you can discuss. If your family live some distance away, think about sending the children to them for a period of time during the school holidays.

If you have older children or your partner has flexible work times, then a system that allows you to work with their help can be devised. If not, you might have to fall back for part of the day on a well-organised local play group, relatives, a child minder or a full-time nursery school **(See page 298 Help Section this Chapter)**.

Child care – ten years plus
Older children are easier to fit your work around because they have their homework and, if organised properly, Girl Guides, Boy Scouts, piano, dancing, music and karate classes to give them a full out-of-school diary. These can be never-ending as long as you tap their interests and organise the travelling. It gives you space to work in and them a great deal of enjoyment as well as broadening their social circle.

Schedule one of your break periods for when they return from school, or have a blanket rule that you stop work once they arrive home because, unlike younger children, they may not need physically looking after, but they do need social interaction.

When there's no child care
If you can't arrange any of these child care alternatives, then you will have to organise your working day to fit around your children. If you have school-aged children, you work when they are at school and stop when they return. You may be able to continue working once they have settled into playing, watching television or doing their homework. Pre-school children take naps and go to bed early at a regular time. They can also be contained for safety's sake in either a joint giant playpen **(See page 289 this Chapter)** or in their own playpen plus toys in your room.

Do make sure that you either take a break when they return from school or stop work altogether once they arrive home.

The key words are organisation, forward-planning and knowing it's OK to ask for help **(See page 292 this Chapter)**.

Carers and the disabled
You may choose to work from home because you have either disabled children or relatives to care for. You should contact

your local Social Security office for information in respect of any financial assistance you may be entitled to.

If you are disabled, the Department of Employment may be able to put you in touch with employers who will provide you with regular work. The DOE (Department of Employment: see your local phone directory) can also loan you special information technology equipment which will enable you to work from home. If you decide you want to set up your own business, they can also provide a disabled person with a grant under their BUSINESS ON OWN ACCOUNT scheme (**See page 298 Help Section this Chapter**), which gives grants to purchase essential equipment and initial stock to start up a business.

WORK AND FOUR-LEGGED FRIENDS

Work and pets go together as well as summer sandals and snow. Never mind about the muddy paw prints all over the letter to the bank manager, which you had been embellishing for days. Sasha's two cats have a habit of sitting on her ironing board when she's pressing material for her picture frames. 'They sometimes leave paw prints on the satin, so to hide it I have to create a design over it with my satin flowers.'

It's when the cat throws up in the middle of your latest business plan and the dog decides to mount the sofa and give a free demonstration of the canine version of the *Joy of Sex*, with a Habitat two-seater, right in the middle of you trying to assure a new client what a professional organisation you run, that you have to admit this isn't good working practice.

One of the best examples of pet mayhem is when you are in the middle of a client meeting or in a frenzied panic trying to get an order out on time and the cat, moving triumphantly like Mike Tyson, walks into the room with a mouse's tail hanging nonchalantly between its clenched teeth. Only Genghis Khan could carry on regardless. Those of us who are a little more human will drop everything, forgetting about high finance and what it says in the small business plan brochures and hurtle round the house sending products, filing cabinets and clients flying, in a frenzied rescue attempt. If the mouse is still alive when you retrieve it, you will be unable to continue with work, because you will be sitting clutching a fountain pen filler, with the gasping mouse wrapped in cotton wool lying in a shoe box, while you try to drip droplets of brandy down its terrified little throat. If you fail to reach the mouse in time, you will also be unable to work because you will be trying not to gag up as you scoop the headless corpse into the nearest thing at hand, probably a copy of your latest accounts. You will then be unable to work because you'll be preoccupied with devising cat torture such as placing an unopened tin of Whiskas in its bowl or super-gluing up the cat flap.

When you have pets around, you will find you stop work. You have to give the dog its antibiotic pills, rescue the hamster that's fallen down the loo, the budgie who's got its head stuck inside its bell or decide whether it's possible to give the kiss of life to the goldfish floating on the top of the tank. None of this will improve your business, impress your bank manager or pay your income tax.

When the cat curls up on your desk in the warm air from the cooling system at the back of your xerox or computer, you'll think how cute. In fact the machine isn't only blowing out air, but sucking in air and with it the cat's fur. You'll discover this a few months later when the machine starts choking and the repair man hands you a large bill and a handful of kitty's tabby fur coat.

Pets are attracted to paper, especially when they're dirty or tired. What's just paper to them are order forms, instructions, bills, ingredients or accounts to you. Pets enjoy ambling across keyboards, writing more gobbledegook than you can imagine you did, and it isn't easy to recall what you had written just before they erased it. They leave dirty paw prints on spotless fabric, dip paws in pots of food and drag anything that's edible off your work surface. They love snooping inside bags and boxes, preferably turning them upside down and sleeping in them, regardless of what else is inside. With a flick of a paw they can send pens, pencils and any drawing equipment scattering over the floor. They'll eat cotton, needles – whoops, there goes another large vet's bill – climb over machinery, oblivious to the fact that it could probably skin them alive, and sharpen their claws on almost anything.

The truth is, that however well trained they are, it's not possible to predict the behaviour of pets all the time. You may have customers or clients who are not pet-lovers, who are allergic to them, frightened of them or simply don't want them around. Pets should be banned from all business meetings.

In the right place, pets are wonderful and the right place is not where you're working. The best thing you can do with them when you are working from home is either not to have any or not allow them in your work area. You also have to learn to ignore them, and what is even harder, they have to learn to be ignored. This will be about as easy as cutting bacon with a plastic airline knife. If it helps, gather your pets around you and break the hard rules to them: that you are not there for them during working hours and neither is your lap, desk, desk-chair, table, papers, pots, typewriter, computer, xerox, stock, boxes, or your clients.

The moment you start work, you have to pretend your pets don't exist. You will find that gradually their distraction rating will lessen. Feed them, walk them, talk to them, give them their pills, clean out their cage, hutch, tank and then shut them out of your work area and out of your mind.

HOUSEWORK FOR THE HOMEWORKER
If you work out of the home it's easy to slam the front door on the chaos of housework, but for people who work at home, escape isn't that easy. Some homeworkers are able to ignore an untidy house. They are impervious to the sight of mounting dust, washing-up, unmade beds and dirty clothes. It's great if you can be like that, because it means you are able just to get on with the work at hand. But if you aren't, and mess makes you feel guilty, or you are just a tidy person and cannot bear to be surrounded by untidiness, then you are either going to have to work in a room where you can close the door on the rest of the house and refuse to let it interfere with your work, employ a cleaner, get the family and your partner to do their share, or get organised.

You can try the box-under-the-table routine. This is where you put a large cardboard box under the kitchen, hall or dining-room table, whichever is the designated family dumping ground. At the end of every day put anything that has been left on the table and that shouldn't be there into the cardboard box. Warn the family you are going to do this and that if they are frantically looking for anything they might find it in the box. Also warn them that at the end of the week everything left in the box is going to be dumped in the dustbin. After a couple of goes at shovelling through the dustbin, trying to retrieve something they can't find, you might discover that the dumping ground becomes less popular. You can use the large-plastic-sack routine in the same way. Go round the house picking up everything that's on the floor and put it into the plastic sack. At the end of the week, warn them that the contents are going into the dustbin.

If unmade beds upset you, take half an hour before you start work each morning to make the beds and tidy round. But only half an hour, or it will become an hour and then the whole morning and you won't ever start working. On the other hand, you may prefer to use that half hour to wander round the park, go for a swim or prepare yourself in other ways for the work ahead. The choice is yours.

Take a day or an afternoon off every week specifically to do housework, if it bugs you. Make it the same time every week so that it falls into your work routine. Don't do housework at random such as cleaning the cooker when you get stuck, making the beds when you're bored, doing the washing up when the work's difficult. This is just using housework as a way of putting off your other work and you could end up with neither job getting done properly. Decide what's really important to you. You can't do everything, so just stick to the things that bug you. You have to decide that the rest will wait until you don't have so much work on. If your children are old enough, there's no reason why they shouldn't get into the habit of making their own beds and tidying their own rooms. They can earn their pocket money by doing small jobs around the house and being responsible for their own things. Ask your partner to help; there's no reason why they can't do housework as well as you, after all, you are both working.

If you find you just can't manage working and looking after the home, but neither can you live with untidiness, then you will have to employ someone to clean. Put this into your budget and see if you can afford to pay them and how much. You may find you can't afford a cleaner weekly, but maybe you can afford one fortnightly or once a month, or someone to spring clean every three months. If you have a friend that has a cleaner, discuss sharing. It may be easier to find someone in your street who is willing to clean once a week, if they are cleaning for someone else as well. If you know someone who has an au pair or foreign student looking after their children, ask if they want to earn some extra pin money cleaning for you in their time off.

CHAPTER 11
HELP SECTION

Carers
People working from home in order to care for ill or disabled relatives may find support and advice from:
CARERS NATIONAL ASSOCIATION 29 Chilworth Mews, London, W2 3RG Tel: 071 727 7776.
If you are unable to pick up any DSS leaflets locally, or if you need large quantities, you can order them from:
DSS Leaflets Unit, PO Box 21, Stanmore, Middlesex, HA7 1AY.
REMOTE WORKING UNITS FOR DISABLED PEOPLE Information Technology Division 1985 Department of Trade and Industry.

Childcare
GINGERBREAD 35 Wellington Street, London, WC2E 7BN. Tel: 071 240 0953.
MAMA (MEET-A-MUM ASSOCIATION) c/o Ms Briony Hallam, 58 Malden Avenue, South Norwood, London, SE25 4HS. Tel: 081 656 7318.
NATIONAL CHILDCARE CAMPAIGN/DAY CARE TRUST Kingsway Hall, Wild Court, London, WC2B 6ST. Tel: 071 405 5617. The trust gives information on finding day care, improving it and setting it up.
NORTHERN IRELAND PRE-SCHOOL PLAYGROUP ASSOCIATION Unit 3, Enterprise House, Boucher Crescent, Boucher Road, Belfast, BT12 6HU. Tel: 0232 662825.
NATIONAL CHILDMINDING ASSOCIATION 8 Masons Hill, Bromley, BR2 9EY. Tel: 081 464 6164.
NATIONAL COUNCIL FOR ONE-PARENT FAMILIES 255 Kentish Town Road, London, NW5 2LX. Tel: 071 267 1361.
PRE-SCHOOL PLAY GROUPS ASSOCIATION 61–63 Kings Cross Road, London, WC1X 9LL. Tel: 071 833 0991.
PLAY MATTERS – NATIONAL TOY LIBRARIES ASSOCIATION 68 Churchway, London, NW1 1LT. Tel: 071 387 9592.
SCOTTISH PRE-SCHOOL PLAY ASSOCIATION 14 Elliott Place, Glasgow, G3 8EP. Tel: 041 221 4148.
WORKING MOTHERS ASSOCIATION 77 Holloway Road, London, N7 8JZ. Tel: 071 700 5771.

WORKPLACE NURSERIES LTD 77 Holloway Road, London, N7 8JZ. Tel: 071 700 0281.

Leaflets – Health and Social Security
Leaflets from any TAX OFFICE or TAX ENQUIRY CENTRE are free. Look under INLAND REVENUE in your phone book. Offices open between 10a.m. and 4p.m. SOCIAL SECURITY OFFICE leaflets are available (up to five) free from your local SOCIAL SECURITY OFFICE listed under SOCIAL SECURITY or HEALTH AND SOCIAL SECURITY in your phone book. Leaflet No:
NI 261 *Family Credit – A Guide*
FB 27 *Bringing Up Children?*
FC 10 *Family Credit.*
NP 27 *Looking After Someone At Home. How to Protect Your Pension.*
CH 11 *One Parent Benefit.*

Children's adventure holidays
CAMP BEAUMONT 9 West Street, Godmanchester, Cambridge, PE18 8HG. Tel: 0480 456123. One of the largest multi-activity holiday organisations with ten centres at leading independent schools. Ages 7–17.

PGL YOUNG ADVENTURE Alton Court, Penyard Lane, Ross-on-Wye, Herefordshire, HR9 5NR. Tel: 0989 764211. Offers range of activities. Ages 11–14.

Study
MUSIC: AVRIL DANKWORTH NATIONAL CHILDREN'S MUSIC CAMPS c/o Mrs Y. Speller, Ye Barn, Spinney Lane, Aspley Guise, Milton Keynes, MK17 8JT. Tel: 0908 583025. Children of all musical abilities camp and are taught folk, pop, vocal and instrumental music.

DRAMA: EAST 15 ACTING SCHOOL AND GALTRES THEATRE COMPANY Sheriff Hutton Park, Sheriff Hutton, York, YO6 1RH. Tel: 034 77442. Shakespeare summer school for teenagers.

Working
COUNCIL FOR BRITISH ARCHAEOLOGY 112 Kennington Road, London SE11 6RE. Tel: 071 582 0494. Work for teenagers on digs. Age 15+.

CATHEDRAL CAMPS Manor House, High Birstwith, Harrogate, North Yorkshire, HG3 2LG. Tel: 0423 770385. Preservation of cathedrals. Ages 16+.

YOUNG ORNITHOLOGISTS CLUB The Lodge, Sandy, Bedfordshire, SG19 2DL. Tel: 0767 680551. Young bird-lovers work with other young people in northern Italy. Ages 13+.

Many organisations belong to the BRITISH ACTIVITY HOLIDAY ASSOCIATION which inspects its members' safety standards, plus insurance scheme. Tel: 0597 823902.

LONDON MONTESSORI CENTRE holiday playschemes. LMC College and School, 18 Balderton Street, London, W1Y 1TG. Tel: 071 493 0165.

Books
Teenagers Vocation Guide to Work, Study and Adventure, Britain and Abroad (Vocation Work £6.95) by Victoria Pybus.

Pets
ANIMAL BEHAVIOURISTS and PSYCHIATRISTS.
Dr Roger Mugford (dogs and cats). Tel: 0932 566696.
Peter Neville (cats). Tel: 0747 870970.
John Fisher (dogs) Tel: 081 788 8224.

Chapter information sources
Working from Home – The Dream That's Becoming a Trend by Lindsey O'Connor, Harvest House; My Family!

INDEX

Note: page numbers *in italics* refer to the sections listing organisations, addresses and publications.

accident insurance 157–8
accountants 29, *53*, 109–12, *136*, 141–2
accounts, keeping 43, 71, 120
admail 214–15
advantages of working from home 3–4, 12, 13
advertisements, job 171–2
advertising one's business 193–6, *203*
 mail order 199–201
Advisory Conciliation and Arbitration Service *63–4, 188*
agents 76
animals in the home 294–6, *300*
answer phone machines 227, 272, 285
appointments 216, 217
architecture *54*
assets 117–18

bad debts 88–93, *100*, 126–8
bank statements 122–2
bankruptcy 92–3, *100, 136*
banks 40, 44, 112–16, *136, 137*
 Loan Guarantee Scheme 134
book-keeping 29, 110, 120–22
borrowing money 34, 35, 38, 115–16
 Loan Guarantee Scheme 134
breakfast 252
breaks 245–6, 272
briefcases 235–6
budgeting 132–5

building societies 112–14
Business Expansion Scheme 134–5
business knowledge 13–16, *19–20, 51–67*
business plans 39–44

calculators 216
capital costs 120
capital equipment 32, 34, 35
car telephones 229, *241–2*
careers, types 9–11, *52, 53–7*
carers 294, *198*
cash, petty 124
cash flow 25, 36–9, 42
catering 9, 10, *55*
 law 93–9, *104–5*
Chambers of Commerce *19–20*, 31
chasing up 88–93, *100*, 127–9
childcare 292–4, *298–9*
children 286–93, *298–300*
Citizens Advice Bureaux 81–2, *100*
City Action teams 57–8
City of London Polytechnic 50, *58*
cleaners, house 277–8
clothes 232–5
comfort 236–7, *240–41*, 245–7
communications 213–14, 225–30, *241*
 mobile 229, *241–2*
commuting 3, 12
companies 27–8, 71–4, *101*
 limited 72–4, 194

301

INDEX

computers *54*, 122
　using 224, 228–9
　　health precautions 246–7, *258*
conciliation service *63–4*, *188*
consumer credit *63*, *136*
contingency plans 118
contracts 74–9, 129
　outworkers' agreements 175–6
Co-operative Development
　Agencies *58*
copyright *43*, 76, 82–3, 87–8, *101*, *102*
costs, business 33–4, 35–8, 43, 121–3
　regular 129, 133
　running 33–4, 36–7, 38, 121
courses, training 9–10, 11, 13, 50, *51–2*, *137*
craft fairs 10, 198–9, *203–4*
craftsmen, professional *58*
credit
　consumer *63*, *136*
　control 88–9, *100*, 127–9
credit cards 218
crises, domestic 218
cycling 249

deadlines 268, 270, 272
death 72, 119
　life assurance 158–60, 163–4
debts
　collecting 88–93, *100*, 126–8
　paying off 116
Department of Trade and Industry
　Europe, sales to 201–2
　Regional Offices *58–9*
description of product or
　service 41–2
design team 223
designs *20*, *54*, *55*, *101–2*
　copyright 88
　registered 83–4
　unregistered 86–7
diary 217–18
disabled people 294, *298*

discipline 270, 271–2
divorce 119
domestic crises 218
domestic routine 220–21, 269–72, 277–80, 296–7
dress 232–5

eating, healthy 251–5, *257–8*
education *52–3 see also* training
efficiency 212–21
electric circuit 229–30
employees
　National Insurance
　　contributions 150–1, 153
employing staff 30
　legal requirements 74
employment protection and
　rights 25, 184–5, *187–8*
Enterprise agencies 48, *51*, *60*
Enterprise Allowance
　Scheme 44–7, *59–60*
Enterprise Initiative *59*
equal pay *136*
equipment 32–3, 34, 35, 223–5
　children and 286, 287–8
ethnic business
　development 49–50, *60*
European Market 201–2, *204–5*
exercise 247–51, *256–7*, 267–8
expenses
　business, allowable 121–2, 143–5
　outworkers 177–8
　regular 129, 132–3
exports 201–2, *204–5*
eyestrain 247

factoring 89
failure 50
family 267, 277–81, 284–6
　children 286–93, *298–300*
fax 228
fertiliser business 10–11, 17–18, 113, 193
filing 213

INDEX

finances 5, 6, 28, 32–5, 109–35, *136–8*
financial advice 114–15, 112, *137*
financial analysis 117–20
Financial Services Act 114
fitness 245–55
food
  fast 253–4
  healthy eating 251–5, *257–8*
  labelling 99
  law 93–9, *104–5*
  preparation, own 220
  temperature control 96–8
  see also catering
Food Safety Act 1990 95–9, *105*
friends 281–4
funding 28, 34, 35, *57–8*
  venture capital *65–6*
furniture 223–5, *238*
further education *52–3 see also* training

Government business shops 50
grants 38, 47
  Enterprise Allowance Scheme 44–7, *59–60*
graphics *55*, 195–6

health *188*, 245–51, *258*
  education *242*
  food 251–5, *257–8*
  law 93–9, *104–6*
  relaxation and stress *240–41*, 245–6, *258–9*, 272, *273*
health insurance 157–8
help from friends 282
HMSO (Her Majesty's Stationery Office) *66*
holidays 25
  children's *299–300*
home as workplace 35, 209–37, *238–42*
  kitchen 93–6
homeworkers
  addresses and organisations *187*

definition 171
numbers 12
sharing home 279–81
hourly rates of pay 124, 181–2
hours of work 218–19, 267, 269–70, 271–2, 286–7
housework 220–21, 269–72, 277–80, 296–7
hygiene 93–9, *104–5*

ice-cream making 9, 10, 13, 35, 224
  marketing 192, 194, 197, 198
ideas 16–17
incapacitation 118
Industrial Revolution 12
Industrial Tribunals *63–5*, 185–6
Inner-City Task Force *60*
inspiration 271
Instant Muscle 49, *60*
insurance *55–6*, 155–60, *163–5*, *166–7 see also* National Insurance
inventors *19–20*, *57*
invoices 130, 132
  ensuring payment 124–32
isolation 209, 263–8

'jam-jar budgeting' 132–4
job advertisements 171–2
jobs, types 9–11, *52*, *53–7*
jogging 250

Kinsman, Francis 6–7, *188*
kitchen 93–6

Law Centres 81, *100–1*
Lawyers for Enterprise Scheme 80, *104*
legal advice centres 81, *100–1*, 103
legal aid 80–81, *100*, *101*, 186
liabilities 118
libraries *102*
licences 27
life assurance 158–60, *163–4*

303

INDEX

light 230, 247
limited companies 72–4, 194
LiveWire 49, *61*
loans 34, 35, 38, 114–15
  Loan Guarantee Scheme 135
Local Authorities 31, 47
Local Authorities Economic Units 48–9, *61*
local enterprise development agencies *51*, *60*, *61*
logos 194, 195–6
loneliness 209, 263–8
losses 26, 43
  tax 143
lunch 252–3

machinery 209, 224
magicians, performing 45, 192–3, 195
mail order 199–201
market analysis and research 26, 41, *56*, 85
marketing 191–6, *205*
married women
  National Insurance Contributions 150, 153
meals 251–5, *257–8*
messages 213–14
mortgage agreements 210
motives for home working 9–10, 12–13

names, trading 71, 72, 73, *103*
nappy delivery service 11, 38
National Insurance *166–7*
  contributions 149–53
    (Class 1) 150–51, 177
    (Class 2) 151, 177
    (Class 3) 151–2
    (Class 4) 152
  married women 150, 153
  outworkers 176–7
  self-employed 24, 151, 152, 153, 176–7
  widows 153

neighbourhood Law Centres 81
neighbours 212
noise 209, 224

office furniture 223–5, *238*
offices, working in 3–4
organisation system 212–21
outlay, initial 32–3
outside work, conditions 3–4
outworkers 171–86, *187–8*
  rights 184–5
Ownbase *61*

partners (personal) 278–81
partnership, business 15, 27, 71–2, 79–80
patents 17, 82, 84–6, *101*, *102*
payment
  delays 125–6
  equal *136*
  methods 124–6
  rates 124, 181–2
pensions 24, 29, *138*, 151, 160–62, *164–6*
  Retirement 151–2, 153–4
personality 6–9, 17–18, 263–72, *273*
pets 294–6, *300*
petty cash 124
piracy 84
planning permission 210–12, *238–9*
plans, business 39–44
Portobello Business Development Agency *61*, *63*
postal services 214, *239–40*
posture 236–7, *240–41*, 245–7
pottery 10, 75–6
premises 35, 209–37, *238–42*
  kitchen 93–9
preparation, for working from home 13–16
pricing 39
Prince's Youth Business Trust *61–2*

INDEX

problem areas 30–31
procrastination 269–71
product description 41–2
professional organisations *53–7*
professionalism 3
profits 30, 34, 39, 43
    taxable 142, 152
promotional material 194–6
protective clothing 233
psychology 264, *273*

rates of pay 181–2
reasons for home working 9–10, 12–13
receipts 121–2
records, financial 121–3
redundancy 13
registered designs 83–4
regulations, business 31–2
relaxation *240–41*, 245–6, *258–9*, 272
rented accommodation 209–10
repetitive strain injury *188*, 224, *241*, 246, *258*
research 26, 43–4, 85, 193–4
    market 41, *56*
resources management 220–2
retail trade, pay rates 182
retirement 119–20
Retirement Pension 151–2, 153–4
rights
    contractual 76–8, 125–6
    employment 25, 184–5, *187–8*
    see also copyright
routine 267, 270–2, 277–80, 296–7
royalties 75–8, 125–6
RSI *see* repetitive strain injury
rules, business 31–2
running costs 33–4, 36–7, 38, 121
Rural Development Commission *58*, 134–5

safety *103*, *108*
    food 93–9, *104*, *105*
    see also insurance

sales
    forecast 37
    marketing 191, 193–4, *205*
sandwiches 254
sandwich-making, trade 39, 44, 93–9
Scotland *59*, *60*, *62*, *65*, 98, *100*, *101*, *104*
seating posture 236–7, *240–41*, 245–7
second-hand equipment 224–5
self-discipline 270, 271–2
self-employed 24–30
    classification 9, 23, 171
    National Insurance contributions 24, 151, 152, 153, 176–7
    pressure group 49
    tax 24, 142, 176
selling 197–202, *203–5*
    European Market 201–2, *204–5*
service description 41–2
service marks 82–4, *101–2*
shares 73, *163–4*
sharing home for working 279–81
Shell 49, *61*, *62*
shopping 221
sick pay
    outworkers 178–9
Single European Market 201–2, *204–5*
skills 42
small businesses *49*, *137*
    tax 142
small claims 89–93, *102–3*
Small Firms centres and services 47–8, *59*, *62–3*
snacks 254–5
Social Security
    Benefits 24–5, 153–5, *167*
        Unemployment 45, 149–50, 152
    DSS leaflets 154–5, *166–7*, *299*
sole trading 27, 72
solicitors 79–80, *103*, 128, 129

INDEX

staff
  employing 30, 74
  skills 42
starting your own business 23–50, *51–67*
state benefits 24–5, 153–5, *167*
  Unemployment 45, 149–50, 152
State Earnings Related Pensions 154, 160–61
statements 129, 131
stationery 215–16
stress *240*, 245–6, 248, *273*
suppliers, payment 38
supportive organisations 6, *19–20, 57–63*
swimming 250

taxation 29, 32, 43, 122, 141–9
  assessments 142–5
  leaflets *67, 137–8, 166–7, 299*
  Local Office 23, 24
  outworkers 176–8
teamwork 277–9
technical assistance *19–20, 57, 59*
telecommuting 173–5, *188*
telephones 226–7, *241*, 283
  answer machines 227, 272, 285
  calls 123
  children's use 288–9
  mobile 229, *241–2*
teleworking 173–5, *188*
time-keeping 218–19, 267, 269–70, 271–2
time management 216
tourism *57*
Trade Unions 81, 183
trademarks 82–3, *101–2*
trading names 71, 72, 73

training 9–10, 11, 27, 42, *51–3*
Training Agency *63*
travel to work 12

Unemployment Benefit 45, 149–50, 152
unit trusts 161–2, *163–4*

VAT (Value Added Tax) 145–9, *168*
  invoice 149
  reclaiming 122–3
  registering 29, 146–8
venture capital *65–6*
visitors
  business 230–32
  friends 281–4

wages, paying 35
  hourly rates of pay 125, 181–2
Wages Councils 179–82
Wages Inspectorate *187*
Wales *62, 63, 64, 104*
widows
  National Insurance contributions 153
will 119
women, married
  National Insurance contributions 150, 153
work, types of 9–11, *53–7*
work furniture 223–5, *238*
work records 176
work space 222–3
workaholics 271–2
workplace, away from home conditions 3–4, 12
worrying 221–2

Youth Business Initiative *63*

More Cookery Non-Fiction from Headline:

BARBARA KAFKA
MICROWAVE GOURMET
THE DEFINITIVE MICROWAVE COOKBOOK

'An extraordinary, comprehensive book'
Jane Grigson, *Observer*

What do you use *your* microwave for?

To warm up coffee? Defrost bread from the freezer? Heat up ready-prepared supermarket meals? Bake a potato or two?

Yes, but what else can it do?

In this definitive guide to microwave cooking, Barbara Kafka shows, with a dazzling combination of culinary flair and scientific exactitude, how, by using a little care and imagination, you can make delicious meals out of fresh ingredients quickly and efficiently.

With over 600 recipes, a comprehensive dictionary of foods and techniques and advice on what the microwave can and cannot do, *Microwave Gourmet* covers everything from such basics as vegetable stock through classic dishes like Moules Marinières to rich dinner-party fare. Using precise easy-to-follow instructions, Barbara Kafka explains how to cook Paupiettes of Sole Stuffed with Salmon in three minutes, plum jam in thirteen minutes and artichokes in seven. As she herself says, 'It may not be a mystic experience, but it sure is quick and efficient.' Whether you are a beginner or an experienced microwave cook, *Microwave Gourmet* will prove to be as indispensable as your microwave itself.

'I feel fairly certain that it will make all other books on microwave cookery redundant' Paul Levy, *Observer*

'This intelligent person's guide to the microwave ... is long overdue' *Sunday Times*

'The book I've turned to again and again has been Barbara Kafka's *Microwave Gourmet*' Sophie Grigson, *Evening Standard*

'This stupendously good book' *Cosmopolitan*

NON-FICTION/COOKERY   0 7472 3380 2

More Cookery from Headline:

GOOD HOUSEKEEPING
EATING FOR A HEALTHY *Heart*

WITH THE CORONARY PREVENTION GROUP

GOOD HOUSEKEEPING
– the recipe for healthy living

**Low in fat, sugar and salt, high in fibre –
and absolutely delicious!**

From breakfasts and brunches to dinner parties, picnics and barbecues – the 250 recipes in this mouthwatering collection show you how to cook healthily for every occasion. And with low-fat variations on such family favourites as moussaka and Cornish pasties – plus delicious new dishes like lamb fillet with leek sauce and chilled vanilla soufflé – it contains all you need to entice even the most unhealthy of palates to abandon the (bad) habits of a lifetime.

Each recipe is accompanied by an analysis of its nutritional value; the introduction provides reams of invaluable information on the prevention of coronary heart disease based on years of medical research. Eat the dishes and follow the guidelines – and you and your family can reduce the risk of heart disease and look forward to a longer and healthier life.

'A very practical book' *Woman's Realm*

'Gives all the recipes, nutritional information and advice that one would practically need' *Taste*

NON-FICTION/COOKERY   0 7472 3278 4

More Cookery Non-Fiction from Headline:

ELISABETH LAMBERT ORTIZ
THE FOOD OF SPAIN AND PORTUGAL

'Wondrous' Glynn Christian

Proving once and for all that there is more to Spanish and Portuguese food than paella and sardines, Elisabeth Lambert Ortiz, world-renowned expert on Latin-American cooking, shows in this inspiring but wholly practical book the glorious range and diversity of the cuisine of the Iberian peninsula.

Having over the ages been both conquered and conquerors, the Spanish and Portuguese have absorbed into their cultures – and therefore their cuisines – a wide variety of influences, from Latin and South America, and, in earlier times, from Rome, Northern Africa and the Middle East. The style of cooking that has evolved can be rivalled only by the great cuisines of France and Italy for subtlety and imagination.

The Food of Spain and Portugal lays its emphasis on what is essentially family cooking, using imaginative combinations of fresh, complementary flavours in easy-to-make recipes. Covering such regional specialities as fish soup with sweet peppers from Andalucia, chicken breasts with pine nuts from Seville, veal stuffed with cinnamon from Extremedura and figs in red wine from Oporto, this book provides the chance for enthusiastic cooks to explore Spanish and Portuguese cooking at its best in their own kitchens.

'The unquestionable queen of Latin-American cooking'
Jeremy Round, *Independent*

'A substantial, serious and expansive work which makes any more on the subject unnecessary' *Time Out*

'An interesting idea' *Taste*

'A volume to love and cherish' *Birmingham Post*

NON-FICTION/COOKERY   0 7472 3447 7

A selection of bestsellers from Headline

FICTION		
GASLIGHT IN PAGE STREET	Harry Bowling	£4.99 ☐
LOVE SONG	Katherine Stone	£4.99 ☐
WULF	Steve Harris	£4.99 ☐
COLD FIRE	Dean R Koontz	£4.99 ☐
ROSE'S GIRLS	Merle Jones	£4.99 ☐
LIVES OF VALUE	Sharleen Cooper Cohen	£4.99 ☐
THE STEEL ALBATROSS	Scott Carpenter	£4.99 ☐
THE OLD FOX DECEIV'D	Martha Grimes	£4.50 ☐

NON-FICTION		
THE SUNDAY TIMES SLIM PLAN	Prue Leith	£5.99 ☐
MICHAEL JACKSON The Magic and the Madness	J Randy Taraborrelli	£5.99 ☐

SCIENCE FICTION AND FANTASY		
SORCERY IN SHAD	Brian Lumley	£4.50 ☐
THE EDGE OF VENGEANCE	Jenny Jones	£5.99 ☐
ENCHANTMENTS END Wells of Ythan 4	Marc Alexander	£4.99 ☐

All Headline books are available at your local bookshop or newsagent, or can be ordered direct from the publisher. Just tick the titles you want and fill in the form below. Prices and availability subject to change without notice.

Headline Book Publishing PLC, Cash Sales Department, PO Box 11, Falmouth, Cornwall, TR10 9EN, England.

Please enclose a cheque or postal order to the value of the cover price and allow the following for postage and packing:
UK & BFPO: £1.00 for the first book, 50p for the second book and 30p for each additional book ordered up to a maximum charge of £3.00.
OVERSEAS & EIRE: £2.00 for the first book, £1.00 for the second book and 50p for each additional book.

Name ....

Address ....

....

....